MW00527923

Praise for Disproven

"I did not know it at the time, but the day after the 2020 election the Trump campaign hired a serious expert, Ken Block, to assess whether the outcome was the result of voting fraud. *Disproven*—Block's thorough, fact-based account of his work and conclusions—is a must-read and a great service to the country."

—**William Barr,** 77th and 85th US Attorney General

"Mr. Block has dissected the data and found the facts that show an election system across America that isn't perfect in all areas, that would certainly benefit from systemic improvements, but nonetheless accurately reflected the will of the majority of the people in 2020."

—**Brad Raffensperger,** Georgia Secretary of State

"In *Disproven*, Ken Block, an expert in data analytics, shares a compelling account of his careful examination of voter data in the days immediately following the 2020 presidential election. Block's clear and detailed assessment of the current state of our election infrastructure offers thought-provoking recommendations to improve the U.S. election system that will be of great interest to American politics scholars and students, election administrators and other public officials, as well as any reader who cares about the future of democracy in the United States."

—**Emily Lynch,** Associate Teaching Professor,
Political Science, The University of Rhode Island

DISPROVEN

DISPROVEN

MY UNBIASED SEARCH FOR

VOTER FRAUD FOR THE TRUMP CAMPAIGN, THE DATA THAT SHOWS WHY HE LOST, AND HOW WE CAN IMPROVE OUR ELECTIONS

KEN BLOCK

Disproven: My Unbiased Search for Voter Fraud for the Trump Campaign, the Data that Shows Why He Lost, and How We Can Improve Our Elections

Published by Forefront Books, Nashville, Tennessee.
Distributed by Simon & Schuster.

Library of Congress Control Number: 2023921838

Print ISBN: 978-1-63763-285-7
E-book ISBN: 978-1-63763-286-4

Cover Design by George Stevens, G Sharp Design LLC
Interior Design by Bill Kersey, KerseyGraphics

Printed in the United States of America

Dedication

This book is dedicated to facts

—empirical and irrefutable—

hoping they help to inform impassioned debate.

CONTENTS

Part III
How We Can Improve Our Election Infrastructure

Part IV
Better Elections

Part V
Consequences

FOREWORD

by Brad Raffensperger, Georgia Secretary of State

Ken Block faced a daunting challenge writing this book, one that anyone telling the story of the 2020 election would face: disproving the false allegations, conspiracy theories, and blatant lies that the 2020 election had been stolen through fraud. The reason that challenge is so great is that the human brain has been structured to use stories to understand complex issues, and the election-denying stories were exciting and far more interesting than dry data and hard facts.

Given a choice between hearing how the Chinese Communist Party forged millions of ballots and smuggled them into the country to steal an election or a serious and sober analysis of the voting data now available from the 2020 election, most people would opt for the story of the China plot. It sounds much more exciting! Who wouldn't prefer a good heist movie over a thorough analysis of voter registration records across the country?

I heard most of those stories in 2020 and after, not because I wanted to, but because they often involved me—or were aimed at me. I was accused in many ways of being "in on" some of the many false and fantastical plots to steal the election because of my role as secretary of state for the State of Georgia. I and my family received threats—some violent and some far worse. People believed the false stories, no matter how outlandish they were, because the human brain prefers stories to data.

But to counter *false* stories, we have no tool more powerful than facts. During my reelection campaign in 2022, I traveled across Georgia, meeting with local chambers of commerce, Rotary clubs, garden clubs—with anyone who wanted to hear me speak. My stump speech was laden with facts and figures, and it was probably not the rousing oratory that most politicians deliver. But it was not meant to be rousing, as Georgia and much of the nation had heard plenty of rousing speeches during that time. My speech was meant to be reassuring.

I would take questions from the audiences once I had finished speaking, questions that were very specific, and demonstrated the power of the false narrative about the 2020 election. People who believed the lies about the election were scared. They were angry about "their side" losing the election, but they were also scared that the system that makes America unique among nations, our system of voting, could not be trusted. They wanted reassurances about the process because our elections are what make us America and they are what makes America great.

Slowly over the course of my campaign, the people I spoke to came around to believing the facts that could be verified over the wild stories that could not, and were, in fact, falling apart. The most frequent question I heard was simple: "How could Trump lose Georgia?" I didn't do the kind of data analysis that Ken does in this book; my methodology and explanation were far less involved.

Publicly available data (published at the time of the elections and still available at my offices website) revealed that 33,527 voters who requested a ballot in Georgia's 2020 primaries but didn't participate—at all—in the 2020 general election. Also, there were 27,559 *more* votes for Georgia's fourteen Republican congressional candidates than President Trump received in the general election. (In other words, across Georgia, 27,559 voters were willing to vote for a Republican for Congress . . . but not for President Trump.) Additionally, there were another 27,967 ballots cast in Georgia with no vote at all for president; voters simply left that contest blank.

President Trump lost Georgia by 11,779 votes.

President Trump asked me, after the election results had been audited and certified, to ". . . find him, 11,780 votes, which is one more than we have . . ." Well, there they are. I found them—but they'd never been cast. Those votes were in the 33,527 Republican primary voters who didn't vote in the general election. They were in the 27,559 voters who marked a ballot for a Republican congressional candidate, but not for President Trump. And they were in the 27,967 who did not vote in the presidential contest at all. Ken Block calls this evidence of "bleeding support" among Republicans for President Trump, but these numbers are publicly available to anyone who wants to verify them. They don't require any skills in data analysis. If you can understand subtraction, you can see exactly "how Trump could lose Georgia."

I took no joy from Trump's loss of Georgia in 2020. I have been a conservative all my life and a Republican for my entire political career. Election year 2020 was the second time I had voted for him, and I didn't want to believe he had lost. But as we are reminded in James, 1:19, we should "be quick to hear, slow to speak and slow to anger." As a contractor for the Trump campaign, no one could have been more motivated than Ken Block to avoid that wisdom. He was hired to find evidence of massive voter fraud, and he didn't merely fail to find it—he found the *opposite*. Mr. Block has dissected the data and found the facts show an election system across America that isn't perfect in all areas, and that would certainly benefit from systemic improvements, but nonetheless accurately reflected the will of the majority of the people in 2020.

As of this writing, despite the ongoing debunking of those entertaining and compelling and fantastical and phony stories about the 2020 election, many Americans remain dubious about our election system. This book will provide both relevant criticism of the system, and hopefully, reassurance to the disillusioned.

INTRODUCTION

There may be no better-qualified person to discuss whether voter fraud impacted the 2020 presidential election than the person hired by the Trump campaign to find it.

I am that person.

I am an expert in database technologies and data analytics. My specialty is digging into a large data set, figuring out what questions can be answered by that data, and then letting it take me wherever it leads.

Admittedly, I was an odd choice for a campaign looking for voter fraud. I am not a hard partisan. While I am currently a registered Republican, I founded a centrist political party in Rhode Island—the Moderate Party—in 2009 because I could not stand what partisan politics was doing to our country. Today I look back at the political dysfunction of 2009 as the good old days. My motivation for writing this book is to attempt to inject hard data into the national conversation regarding voter fraud and how we conduct our elections.

I earned a bachelor of arts in computer science from Dartmouth College, where I also enjoyed government and political science classes, but my expertise in voting data has been acquired over the last decade. In that time, I have processed and analyzed data from every state that allows the public to view it. My analysis has been used in multiple lawsuits regarding the conduct of elections, but never to contest the results of an election. I have helped defend states from lawsuits and have supported organizations suing states over the conduct of their elections. In addition, my analysis has helped willing states address data issues within their election infrastructure.

It is also worth mentioning that I am a two-time candidate for governor in Rhode Island. I achieved my goal in my first-ever political race, winning 6.5 percent of the vote representing my newly formed, centrist political party. This was a high-stakes race for me, the party's founder; Rhode Island would not have recognized the party if I had received less than 5 percent of the vote. My second run for governor was as a Republican. I lost my statewide primary by about three thousand votes. Voter fraud was not to blame.

Being a candidate takes loads of time and enormous effort. My second campaign lasted a year and a half. It was costly financially, and it was grueling for myself, my family, my employees, and my businesses. I often got home after 9:00 p.m., and weekends provided no break. Between the two campaigns combined, I participated in more than fifty debates and forums.

For some candidates, the experience inevitably becomes emotional. It was tough to lose a statewide election by just a few thousand votes—easily one of the worst experiences in my life—but on election night, I conceded the race to someone I would rather have punched in the nose. I lost with as much grace as possible. I knew that life would go on.

Former President Trump has turned losing with grace into losing with disgrace. He has spawned a group of losing candidates who would rather howl about voter fraud—without justification— than display the leadership qualities demanded by the positions for which they ran. Some of these failed candidates who make meritless accusations of voter fraud don't seem to understand their own claims. Others spurn factual accuracy. For these folks, the end goal has nothing to do with winning an election. It is about raising money or profile—or worse, about undermining our republic.

Claiming voter fraud has become a big business. Lawyers make millions of dollars filing lawsuits claiming voter fraud. Likewise, pseudo-technologists make huge amounts of money by providing false "analysis" that yields the results requested by those who paid for the work.

Analysis conducted to reach a predetermined outcome cannot be trusted. The bonkers claims of voter fraud made in the aftermath of the 2020 general election were wrong across the board. When those claims had data at their foundation, it was easy to identify where the analysis was faulty. True fraud is detectable, quantifiable, and verifiable—especially fraud sufficient to alter the outcome of an election in which thousands of votes measure the margin of victory.

Voter fraud has not swung any election outcome I am familiar with on a national level. A primary for a congressional seat in North Carolina was nullified in 2018 and ordered by the courts to be redone due to the uncovering of a ballot-harvesting operation (which was illegal in North Carolina but is not in some other states). The same operation also apparently created false ballots.[1]

Millions of dollars have been spent looking for massive voter fraud, and dozens of court cases have been filed claiming massive voter fraud—all to no avail. As of the writing of this book, no evidence of organized, massive voter fraud has been discovered or documented anywhere in the United States.

That said, the infrastructure with which we conduct our elections can be described, at best, as disjointed and, at worst, as seriously lacking. I say this with the certainty of a technologist with over thirty years of experience designing and building complex computer systems with mission-critical purposes. One of these systems delivered billions of dollars of SNAP (Supplemental Food Nutrition Program, or food stamp) benefits. Another was a lottery system in which a winning

1 Michael Graff and Nick Ochsner, "'This Smacks of Something Gone Awry': A True Tale of Absentee Vote Fraud," *Politico*, November 29, 2021, https://www.politico.com/news/magazine/2021/11/29/true-tale-absentee-voter-fraud-north-carolina-523238.

billion-dollar ticket could not be lost as it traveled electronically from the point-of-sale device to the main computer.

It is hard to imagine anyone claiming that the voting infrastructure that implements our elections is not mission-critical.

Many of you will assume that our country has fifty different election jurisdictions and systems, one for each state. That assumption, while logical, would be very wrong. Just a few states have a single statewide system. Many states push the responsibility of conducting elections to county governments, including the technical infrastructure with which to do it. I have seen estimates that number our country's election jurisdictions at over five thousand. Some estimates claim ten thousand.

When you dig into the data, you begin to see that these jurisdictions do things differently from one another. County-to-county differences exist within the same state, and differences in how election issues are handled between states constantly crop up.

It is difficult to find any aspect of voting that does not yield politically polarized disagreements, which is not surprising. What *hasn't* become politically polarized? Vaccinations have left the scientific realm and become ideological fodder. Education. Voting. Activities fundamental to our personal and national well-being are now fought about through a prism of ideology rather than pragmatism. But ideology has never fixed anything.

The red and blue sides spend enormous sums of money duking it out in court about removing dead voters from the rolls, whether mail ballots should exist, and on and on. These fights are fought in every state.

An uneven hash of laws mandate that most (but not all) states follow specific rules regarding how elections are conducted. Our federal elections rely upon these laws. The only way to ensure that everyone's vote is treated the same no matter where they live is to apply all our election laws evenly to every state and, by extension, to every voting jurisdiction in the United States. For our national elections to have the highest possible integrity, ensuring that all states administer those elections the same way cannot be aspirational—it must be foundational. Inconsistency is the enemy of integrity.

I will describe data in many of the pages that follow with a good dose of law on the side because, unfortunately, this is the only way to discuss the intersection of our current election laws and what is happening within our election infrastructure.

The first part of the book discusses the work I did for the Trump campaign, the results found and not found, the personalities I encountered who pushed different claims of voter fraud, and what was done with the results of my findings. (Spoiler alert: I found no fraud sufficient to impact the election in any state whose data I was asked to analyze.) I document how hard the Trump administration and individuals from around the country tried to find analysis to support the claim of massive voter fraud. Most importantly, I discuss an analysis I performed in March 2023 that disproves former president Trump's claim that the 2020 election was stolen.

If you have ever wondered what it is like to receive a subpoena as part of a federal lawsuit, I'll tell you about that too.

The book's second part discusses how our fifty states manage to bring chaos to our federal elections. The mess is brought about by different states performing the same job differently—some well and some poorly. The uneven performance of our state-based election infrastructure means that our federal elections rely upon data that is outstanding in some cases but is, in too many others, terrible. States implement their elections differently, which means that voters in our national elections can have vastly different voting experiences depending on where they live, which is unfair.

The book's third section offers my suggestions for legislation that Congress can enact to address technical and integrity issues embedded in our current election infrastructure. I know that many of you have no confidence that Congress can agree on what to order for lunch, but I am an optimist.

I hope that you find the discussions interesting and compelling—but, of equal importance, I hope that state legislatures, members of Congress, and election officials throughout the country give some thought to the picture I paint of what we are doing and how we can improve things.

It was challenging to keep up with current events as I wrote this book, and ultimately futile as I had to stop writing so the pages you are reading could be printed. Significant events that shed light on issues I discuss will undoubtedly have occurred once I stopped writing and before you started reading.

I was paid by the Trump campaign to look for evidence of massive voter fraud. I did so to the best of my ability. I left no stone unturned. No evidence—at all—of massive voter fraud was discovered. My findings were communicated to the highest levels of our federal government. And yet, to this day, former president Trump, failed politicians such as Kari Lake, and hangers-on such as Mike Lindell (CEO of My Pillow) talk about massive voter fraud as if it has been proven many times over.

It is critical to set the record straight regarding voter fraud and the results of the 2020 election: it has never been proven, and most certainly had no role in impacting the results of the 2020 presidential election.

The claim that voter fraud was the cause of former president Trump's 2020 election loss has been disproven. Enough already.

PART I

WORKING FOR THE TRUMP CAMPAIGN

Chapter 1

RECRUITED

The call came late in the afternoon the day after the 2020 election. I did not recognize the number. The caller introduced himself as Alex Cannon, a lawyer for the Trump campaign. After some brief introductions, he asked if I would look for voter fraud.

There was a wide range of reactions as I discussed the phone call with my family.

"Why would you do it?" my daughter asked.

I told her that somebody was going to do this work. That person should do the work honestly, thoroughly, and most importantly, impartially. I knew I could do this job that way, but I did not know how many others could. Also, if there was indeed massive voter fraud, I felt it was critical to find it, publicize it, and get it addressed. Our country would be at dire risk if our elections were fraudulently decided. It would be a matter of pride to be the person who found the fraud.

This project represented a unique opportunity—the chance to perform a nationwide audit of election data with a large budget and the data-gathering resources of the Republican National Committee. The job, done well, would be about something more than the candidate. It would be about the process.

I knew that it would be contentious. Any work done on behalf of President Trump would immediately be seen as hugely positive by about half of the country and tremendously negative by the other half. Any results produced would similarly generate a harsh partisan response. Half of the country would be upset no matter what I found or did not find.

What made it possible for me to say yes was that the data, and the data alone, would drive my findings. I would have the data to back up a finding of massive fraud; and if the data indicated no fraud, I would have the proof.

The next day, after sleeping on it and having more conversations with my family and close friends, I called Cannon back and told him I would do the job.

One of my most significant concerns was getting paid. I was well aware of the stories of contractors who struggled to get paid after working for Trump, and I did not want to be one of them. The job I had to do would involve expensive work performed by other data vendors, and I did not want to be stuck paying those bills. When I broached the subject with Cannon, he assured me that money wouldn't be a problem and that all payments would be wired to me before any work commenced. Problem solved.

Another issue that concerned me was setting expectations. I did not want anybody to believe that I had promised a result that could overturn an election. In fact, I wanted to make sure it was known that in my seven years of experience researching voting data, I did not think it likely that I would find voter fraud sufficient to alter the outcome, but that I would do everything in my power to find it if it was there.

Cannon said he appreciated my candor and that my approach to the work was good. In addition, he said that my involvement in the project would be closely guarded to keep political pressures away from me. The importance of that decision can only be fully appreciated in hindsight.

I communicated to Cannon that I assumed I would have to sign a nondisclosure agreement and that I had no problem with that. Surprisingly, he responded that a nondisclosure agreement would not be necessary. Hence, this book.

The signed contract retained me to look for voter fraud in the swing states whose names were continuously in the news: Georgia, Pennsylvania, Arizona, Nevada, Michigan, and Wisconsin. I would data mine for voter fraud, looking for deceased voters and people who voted in multiple states. I stated that my results would be of sufficient quality to stand up in a court of law.

I was perfectly happy to keep this endeavor strictly confidential. Not even my in-laws knew of the work I did. The illusion of secrecy would be pretty much shot to hell when my company was identified to the January 6 Committee in April of 2022.

To this day, I do not for sure know how my previous work in election data analysis found its way to the Trump campaign. I did not seek out this gig. I did not apply for it. I even told the campaign that I would be surprised if we found what they were looking for.

The contract was signed on November 5, 2020. I had no idea then how finding so little would lead to so much.

Chapter 2

SEEKING VALIDATION

Within days of beginning my work, I started getting requests from Cannon to validate some wild voter fraud claims. The number of claims snowballed, and I was frequently given very short time frames, on the order of twenty-four hours, to verify or disprove them. The intention was to use the claims I was asked to validate as the basis of lawsuits challenging election results. At first, the requests were worded "Please try to verify this claim." By the end, the requests were phrased "Tell me why this claim is wrong."

States have different time frames for making legal challenges to election results. In the case of the states I was working on, less than three weeks were allotted from Election Day to the deadlines for filing lawsuits. As a result, I had little time to access the election data (if it was even available), process it, analyze it, and produce a report. Wisconsin had a deadline of November 17. Georgia provides a two-day window after vote certification to contest the result; they certified their vote on November 20.

The job was much larger and more difficult than I had expected, mainly because the data available in the days immediately after an election are sometimes deficient and incomplete compared to the data states release to the public months afterward. I was not told whence these individual fraud claims originated, although I was told that some of them had found their way to the White House, then to Cannon, then to me. Otherwise, I was walled off from everything else that was swirling around the campaign. I did not need to know sources, where my findings went, or what was done with them.

COVID-19 had shut Rhode Island down. My car was one of the few on the road when I went to the office. In fact, I had been going to the office daily since the beginning of the pandemic—I was not equipped at that time to work from home at 100 percent capacity.

The depositions taken by the Select Committee to Investigate the January 6th Attack on the United States Capitol (the January 6 Committee) have helped me understand how my work made its way to the highest reaches of our government. Those depositions also provide a road map for where some of the fraud claims I disproved originated and how different participants in former president Trump's orbit reacted to my findings.

The January 6 Committee deposition taken from Timothy Murtaugh on May 19, 2022,[2] provides the names of those who initiated my project. Murtaugh was employed by the Trump campaign from 2019 through January 2021, working on the communications team. On page 27, the questioner states that Alex Cannon sent an email to Murtaugh that said: "Good morning, Tim. I'm running a post-election fraud detection program as directed by Eric and Jared. Can we sit down at some point this morning to connect on the comms side?"

The same email is discussed in Alex Cannon's April 3, 2022,[3] deposition. The committee questioner asks Cannon on page 20 to

2 Select Committee to Investigate the January 6th Attack on the US Capitol, US House of Representatives, Interview of Timothy Murtaugh, May 19, 2022, Washington, DC, https://www.govinfo.gov/content/pkg/GPO-J6-TRANSCRIPT-CTRL0000083780/pdf/GPO-J6-TRANSCRIPT-CTRL0000083780.pdf.

3 Select Committee to Investigate the January 6th Attack on the US Capitol, US House of Representatives, Interview of Alex Cannon, April 13, 2022, Washington, DC, https://www.govinfo.gov/content/pkg/GPO-J6-TRANSCRIPT-CTRL0000062449/pdf/GPO-J6-TRANSCRIPT-CTRL0000062449.pdf.

clarify that the Eric and Jared referred to in the email are Eric Trump and Jared Kushner, which Cannon confirms. Neither Kushner nor Eric Trump knew I was doing the fraud investigation work while the project was ongoing—Cannon had assured me that no one up the chain of command would know that I was doing the work.

Alex Cannon's deposition sums up the final results of my work: no evidence of voter fraud sufficient to overturn the election in any state. Cannon's recorded testimony that the campaign found no evidence of massive voter fraud is one of the only pieces of his deposition that made it to the televised hearings. Cannon is shown quoting former president Trump's chief of staff, Mark Meadows, who stated, in the context of Cannon telling him massive voter fraud was not found, "There is no there, there."[4] Cannon and Meadows had been discussing the results of my work.

Cannon's testimony identifies my company as doing the fraud analytics work, although he does not quite get my company name correct. On page 28,[5] he says that "Simpatico System" was doing his fraud detection work. My company's name is "Simpatico Software Systems" . . . close enough, I guess.

On page 63,[6] Cannon states: "I trusted Simpatico to be very diligent, and that's why I wanted to work with them." Cannon does not mention me by name, for which I am thankful. While I appreciate the work the January 6 Committee performed, I had zero interest in receiving a subpoena from the committee and incurring the costs of appearing before them. More importantly, I did not want someone else framing my work and story.

On February 3, 2022, while questioning Jason Miller, a senior adviser to the Trump 2020 campaign, the committee appeared to be probing to determine who had performed the fraud work for the

4 Ibid., 34.
5 Ibid., 28.
6 Ibid., 63.

campaign. On page 115 of Miller's deposition,[7] he is asked if someone named Matt Braynard is "the expert"—a reference to me. Miller responds, "[No]. I thought that the person who actually did the database work was more of a database professional as opposed to a, say, political consultant." Yup.

Matt Braynard, on the other hand, was responsible for some terrible data analytics. He was also, for a time, a Trump campaign employee. We will meet him again later.

7 Select Committee to Investigate the January 6th Attack on the US Capitol, US House of Representatives, Interview of Jason Miller, February 3, 2022, Washington, DC, https://www.govinfo.gov/content/pkg/GPO-J6-TRANSCRIPT-CTRL0000041286/pdf/GPO-J6-TRANSCRIPT-CTRL0000041286.pdf.

Chapter 3

BAD BLOOD, BAD ANALYTICS, AND BIG MONEY

If it seems odd to you that the Trump campaign contracted me to look for voter fraud when I told them it was unlikely to be found, you are probably unaware that there were (at least) two legal camps when it came to litigating the election. One camp consisted of the lawyers employed by the Trump campaign in early November. Those I interacted with were young professionals who had most of their careers ahead of them. As a result, they were unwilling to risk their reputations and careers on false claims and lawsuits. The other group consisted of more reckless lawyers, including Rudy Giuliani, John Eastman, and Sidney Powell, who legally pursued wildly false and unsubstantiated claims of voter fraud. I should add that Giuliani's legal team took over all aspects of election litigation on November 19, 2020, a fact that I was unaware of as my project wound down.

The chasm between these lawyers and other individuals involved with the campaign was vast. Some January 6 Committee depositions expose outright hostility between the groups.

In Cannon's deposition, he is asked about Cleta Mitchell. In November of 2020, Mitchell was infamously on the phone with President Trump when Trump insisted that Georgia election officials find him enough votes to overturn the election results in that state.[8]

"I just want to find 11,780 votes, which is one more than we have," Trump said.

On page 40 of Cannon's deposition,[9] he says this about Mitchell in response to a question regarding his communications with her: "My email exchanges with—my contact and email exchanges with Cleta Mitchell were not directly about any claims of election fraud. So, you know, I don't believe that—Cleta was—Cleta—it was my understanding Cleta was going in and trashing a lot of my colleagues and people that I respected, and I wanted to keep my distance from her."

Many people made, and are still making, piles of money off the voter-fraud/election-denial industry. Although the money that drives that industry is not the main focus of this book, I need to discuss it here because money must be motivating some who push election lies.

Attorney Sidney Powell, whose overhyped "Kraken" lawsuits were tossed out of court for having no merit, raised over $16 million in the year immediately after the 2020 election.[10] Why donors have thrown so much money at her preposterous, doomed-to-failure legal gambits is puzzling. Powell's nonprofit, Defending the Republic, saw mass resignations in the spring of 2021 due to a lack of financial transparency,

8 Jaclyn Diaz, "Attorney on Call with Trump and Georgia Officials Resigns from Law Firm," NPR.org, January 6, 2021, https://www.npr.org/2021/01/06/953823383/attorney-on-call-with-trump-and-georgia-officials-resigns-from-law-firm.

9 Select Committee to Investigate the January 6th Attack on the US Capitol, US House of Representatives, Interview of Alex Cannon, April 13, 2022, Washington, DC, https://www.govinfo.gov/content/pkg/GPO-J6-TRANSCRIPT-CTRL0000062449/pdf/GPO-J6-TRANSCRIPT-CTRL0000062449.pdf.

10 Jared Gans, "Sidney Powell Nonprofit Raised More Than $16M Following 2020 Election," *The Hill*, October 14, 2022, https://thehill.com/business/3688693-sidney-powell-nonprofit-raised-more-than-16m-following-2020-election.

according to the *Washington Post*. Among those who resigned was the group's chief financial officer.[11]

Was Powell taking advantage of donors whose desperation to see Trump in office for another four years blinded them to the emptiness of her claims? It is hard not to come to this conclusion considering the financial chaos that occurred within her nonprofit corporation.

Former Trump campaign staffer, data analyst, and January 6 apologist Matt Braynard claimed to have found evidence of more voter fraud in Georgia than the 2020 margin of victory. He then had his findings destroyed by former Georgia state legislator Bee Nguyen.[12] Nonetheless, Braynard is reported to have raised close to half a million dollars to support his hunt for voter fraud.[13]

As the Texas saying goes, Mike Lindell is all hat and no cattle. As far as I can determine, he has yet to be right about any of the voter fraud he yells about or his wild predictions of when the 2020 election will be overturned and former president Trump "reinstated" to the presidency. Lindell is raising money into a "legal offense fund,"[14] but purports to have spent tens of millions of dollars of his own money pushing election claims he cannot prove are true.[15] I find it hard to believe that Lindell has liquidated colossal sums of money in a charitable effort to somehow put Trump back into office by any means possible.

11 Emma Brown, Rosalind S. Helderman, Isaac Stanley-Becker, and Josh Dawsey, "Sidney Powell Group Raised More Than $14 Million Spreading Election Falsehoods," *Washington Post*, December 6, 2021, https://www.washingtonpost.com/investigations/sidney-powell-defending-republic-donations/2021/12/06/61bdb004-53ef-11ec-8769-2f4ecdf7a2ad_story.html.

12 Georgia State House Governmental Affairs Committee, "Georgia State Reps Question Matt Braynard," @11Alive, https://www.youtube.com/watch?v=LXvybaYCSIM.

13 Lachlan Markay, "A Trumper Raised $650K to Prove the Dead Voted, but You Have to Take His Word on How He's Spending It," *Daily Beast*, November 16, 2020, https://www.thedailybeast.com/matt-braynard-raised-dollar650000-to-prove-the-dead-voted-but-you-have-to-take-his-word-on-how-hes-spending-it.

14 https://lindelloffensefund.org.

15 Peter Stone, "MyPillow Chief Spends Tens of Millions in Fresh Crusade to Push Trump's Big Lie," *Guardian*, August 4, 2022, https://www.theguardian.com/us-news/2022/aug/04/mypillow-mike-lindell-trump-big-lie-election-fraud.

One of the primary motivations for me to break my silence and discuss my work for the Trump campaign is the parade of failed candidates who join the likes of Lindell and Powell in echoing Trump's false claims of voter fraud. While working for the campaign in November of 2020, I watched as Rhode Island candidates I knew began repeating the false claim that voter fraud had caused their own losses in the 2020 election cycle.

One of these candidates was a retired military chaplain who held a seat in the Rhode Island legislature and ran for Congress in 2020 as a Republican. Bob Lancia's race was an extreme long shot in a state such as Rhode Island, which is among the bluest states. It had been decades since Rhode Island sent a Republican to Congress, and Lancia's efforts were likely doomed to failure due to his party affiliation and low name recognition. On election night, the counting of votes cast in person on Election Day showed Lancia with an improbable lead over the multiterm incumbent, Jim Langevin. Mail ballot totals were not released until well after midnight. Once counted, the mail ballots yielded a decisive win for Langevin, which was the anticipated outcome for most political observers.

Lancia claimed that the mail ballot counting amounted to a theft of his race, a dastardly deed conducted in the dark of night—never mind that voting by mail is legal in Rhode Island, that local election rules mandated that mail ballots be tallied only after the polls closed, or that the odds of an upset in this race were minuscule.

There are meaningful discussions to be had about mail ballots. But of the likely issues to come up in those discussions (among them security and ballot harvesting), none are direct or even oblique proof that voter fraud occurred. More on this later.

The 2022 election did not provide a break from baseless claims of voter fraud. Failed candidate Kari Lake cried fraud after losing the

Arizona governor's race.[16] Mike Lindell went so far as to claim that incumbent Florida governor Ron DeSantis's landslide victory in 2022 was only possible due to massive, unsubstantiated voter fraud.[17] Lindell vowed to go to Florida and prove his claim. I have seen nothing to indicate that Lindell went to Florida or delivered a shred of evidence to back up his claims.

As of this writing, I have not had a chance to look at Arizona's election data to attempt to validate Lake's fraud claims. But I don't have to see how individuals voted to determine that Lake's claims ring hollow. The top statewide vote-getter in Arizona in 2022, from any party, out of every candidate for US Senate, governor, secretary of state, attorney general, and treasurer, was a Republican. Kimberly Yee—a Republican—garnered 1,390,135 votes in her winning race for treasurer. Lake lost her race for governor by more than 17,000 after netting 1,270,774 votes.[18] Lake is trying to claim that a bizarre fraud that cost her the governor's race somehow spared Yee in her race for treasurer, which can only be classified as nonsense. Yee earned over 119,000 more votes than Lake in 2022. Notably, every statewide Republican candidate in Arizona but Yee embraced election conspiracy theories—and lost. Not all candidates are capable of introspection, but, come on! Republicans can clearly win statewide elections in Arizona, but not by embracing far-out conspiracy theories.

Of course, neither Lake, Lindell, nor any of those who shouted about voter fraud before them has provided a shred of verifiable proof to back up those fraud claims. And when their claims of voter fraud were disproved, they only screamed more loudly.

16 Devan Markham, "Gubernatorial Candidate Lake Claims Arizona Election Fraud," *News Nation*, November 17, 2022, https://www.newsnationnow.com/politics/elections-2022/lake-evidence-arizona-election.

17 OK Dodo, "My Pillow Guy Believes Ron DeSantis Won Because of Voter Fraud," *Daily Kos*, December 22, 2022, https://www.dailykos.com/stories/2022/12/22/2143402/-My-Pillow-Guy-believes-Ron-DeSantis-won-because-of-voter-fraud.

18 Fox 10 Phoenix, "2022 Arizona General Election Results," November 8, 2022, https://www.fox10phoenix.com/election-results.

Chapter 4

THE BIRTHDAY PROBLEM

I received an urgent request from Alex Cannon on November 11. A lawsuit was soon to be filed claiming that 16,097 voters had cast ballots in Nevada as well as in some other state.

John Eastman was one of the key legal players on Trump's team of attorneys who pushed boundaries. Before he became infamous for proposing that Vice President Pence had the constitutional authority to ignore the certified results of our election and name Donald Trump as the winner, Eastman participated in the barrage of lawsuits contesting election results. He was keenly interested in the doozy that was handed to me. Someone had performed a data analysis looking for people who voted twice in the 2020 general election. I'll refer to this as a *double vote*. The analysis looked for ballots cast by voters in two states who shared the same last and first names, along with a middle initial "when available," and who shared the same birth year and birth month. The text describing the analysis included this critical caveat: "Please note that this file is a prospect file, so will contain false positives. All these records should be independently verified."

Even with this warning, a lawsuit was being prepared using the data to support a claim of massive voter fraud in Nevada. This was outrageous. How could a lawyer be so reckless as to go to court with a set of data that is admittedly only a partial step toward definitively identifying voter fraud?

People sometimes take two bites of the electoral apple by double voting in two states. Some people occasionally double vote in the same state. There is no national infrastructure to identify instances of double voting, but voting twice in a federal election is a felony under federal law, with severe consequences; a conviction can lead to up to five years of jail time and a fine of up to $10,000.[19] Beyond that, there is little desire on anyone's part to do anything about it.

Until the last few years, no one was trying to identify double voters. Before 2008, there was no way to perform this kind of analysis because many states did not have modern voter registration systems and could not provide the data needed to do the work.

Whoever did this analysis made a critical mistake in their assumptions about how to confidently match two people based on names and dates of birth—an error that meant that most of the findings were wrong. I knew this analysis was off the rails when I read one line in the email containing the claim: "not all Nevada registered voters have a day of birth, just month and year." It meant the analysis was not being performed against an official Nevada voter registration file, which in 2020 provided full dates of birth.

In all likelihood, the analysis was performed against a marketing database sold as a reliable voter data resource. Few states provide only birth year and birth month in their voter data. Most either provide a full date of birth or a birth year only. A few do not give any birth date information, an issue to which we will return.

Remember that this analysis was to be used as the foundation of a lawsuit asking the court to declare the Nevada election result . . . well, I guess I don't know what the campaign was going to ask. Even if 16,000 duplicate votes could have been confirmed with a high degree

19 52 USC 10307: Prohibited Acts, https://uscode.house.gov/view.xhtml?req=(title:52%20section:10307%20edition:prelim).

of confidence, no one has any way of knowing for which candidate those duplicate votes were cast. There would have been no way to claim harm had been delivered to a specific candidate!

When we vote, the candidate we vote for is kept private—for a good reason. The last thing we need is an election worker, government official, or someone from the political world hassling us because we voted for someone they don't like. We vote anonymously after we check in.

Without a way to know for whom a duplicate voter cast their ballots, this lawsuit, if it had correctly identified duplicate votes, would be pointing out a flaw with our election systems (which does exist), but it would likely fail to prove that those duplicate votes put the wrong candidate into a position of power.

As an aside, when I find duplicate votes, roughly 60 percent of the duplicate ballots are cast by voters registered as Republicans. This ratio, which reduces to about 50/50 in solidly blue states, throws much doubt on the oft-repeated message that voter fraud is a partisan activity on the part of just one party. Double voting appears to be a crime of privilege—those who can afford to own two homes are usually the ones who double vote.

I doubt the data source used in this analysis would have survived legal scrutiny if the case had been filed. A court case based on voting data that did not come directly from state election officials is dubious—especially when the data had clearly been modified in a meaningful way. In Nevada's case, full dates of birth are available in the state's voter data, but the voter fraud analysis was performed against data that only provided a year and month of birth.

The problem this analysis ran into, aside from being performed against data that likely did not come directly from Nevada election officials, is what I call "the birthday problem." If you match two people with the same last and first names and the exact full birth dates, can you confidently state that the match is valid? For example, is John Smith, born on July 4, 1983, who lives in New York, the same person as John Smith, born on July 4, 1983, who lives in Connecticut? The answer in most cases, surprisingly to many fraud hunters, is no.

Performing a match on full first and last names and full dates of birth is wrong over 90 percent of the time. I know this empirically, having run hundreds of thousands of potential matches based on name and birth date through an expensive process involving third-party vendors, credit bureau data, and a specialized database used for fraud detection purposes. This process can confirm, with a high degree of certainty, that two individuals are the same person by looking at the same data used when they apply for a loan, among other data points. The process I follow is conservative—I err on the side of not identifying matches if there is a question about the result.

When the campaign sent me the spreadsheet with the 16,097 claimed duplicate votes, I told them my processing would yield maybe 160 confirmed duplicates.

The number of confirmed exact matches with the same voter in two different states came in at 299. I was still uncertain if this data involved actual votes cast or not. However, there was no time to explore that at the time, and it was unnecessary to go further; the number of possible fraudulent votes needed to be much larger to matter to the campaign and the prospective lawsuit.

In what amounted to the knockout punch for this analysis, only the final result was provided to me in the form of names and birth date information. I had no way of knowing what data was relied upon and no way of confirming that whoever did the analysis had correctly identified valid votes. I was concerned that this analysis was not based on actual votes cast but was instead looking at duplicate registered voters, which is not illegal. A voter can have active voter registrations in two states—a bad thing from an election integrity standpoint, but legal. A crime has been committed only if that voter casts a vote in each state.

As part of preparing this book, I made time to dive more deeply into some of those 299 confirmed matches. I wanted to look at data I knew was valid to see if those matches were actually duplicate votes cast.

I looked only at matches where I could identify two people (likely a couple) who were registered together at an address in one state and also at an address in another state. According to the original analysis I was given, six matched sets of voters might have voted together in two states, committing a shared felonious experience.

Did these couples commit voter fraud? Yes and no. I could confirm two of the six sets of votes. For the others, votes were not cast at one of the addresses, confirming the worst of what I suspected about the analysis handed to me back in 2020—the person who did the work did not understand how to identify an actual vote that was cast, only potential duplicate registrations.

Couples committing voter fraud together have always fascinated me. I have documented a couple of hundred sets of couples who cast votes together in two states over the years. Dozens of families of three and four members have also crossed my desk after voting together in multiple states.

From the Nevada analysis, the following sets of duplicate votes were confirmed by me:

> A couple born in the mid-1950s voted together in Las Vegas, Nevada, and Chula Vista, California. Both are registered Republicans in both states.
>
> A couple born around 1940 voted together in Reno, Nevada, and South Lake Tahoe, California. Both are registered Republicans in both states.

The Many Ken Blocks

There were a couple of hundred confirmed duplicate registrations and, perhaps, duplicate votes. So why was the original analysis so off? The original claim was over 16,000. The answer: we are a country of over 330 million people, and many of us share the same name.

You would think that my name is relatively unique. Ken Block. How many of us can there be? For starters, some of you might have purchased this book because you thought I was the far more famous race car driver Ken Block. For that, I am very sorry. Ken Block, the race car driver and founder of DC Shoes, tragically died in January 2023 in a snowmobile accident. My Twitter account (I guess I should call it X now), which usually gets a few new followers every week who think that I race cars, got a bunch of new followers in January 2023, eager, apparently, to follow the account of someone who had recently died—and who inexplicably talked a lot about Rhode Island and good government. Worse, people tagged me as having died, which caused some concern for those who know me.

The lead singer of the band Sister Hazel is also named Ken Block.

Tragically, another Ken Block lives in my home state of Rhode Island, about a dozen miles from me. During my campaigns for governor, he sometimes got my hate mail, and I received some bills meant for him. We are not related, but I have some high school friends on Facebook who seem to prefer him over me. The other Rhode Island Ken Block used to live in Florida in the same city as Sister Hazel's Ken Block and received attention from Sister Hazel fans, which would undoubtedly be preferable to receiving attention from fans of Rhode Island politics.

In the forty or so states I have in my voter registration database, there are seventy-two Ken, Kenny, or Kenneth Blocks. While I am the only one in my birth year, four Ken Blocks were born in 1966.

Imagine running this same exercise for "John Smith." Well, I did. There are 14,656 John, Johnny, Jonathan, or Johnathan Smiths in my system's combined voter registration databases. Seven Mr. Smiths were born on May 22, 1985, six on January 22, 1986, and five on February 19, 1948. When we only look at the year of birth, 298 Mr. Smiths were born in 1963, 298 in 1947, and 295 in 1962.

I omit a discussion of middle names here because it is complicated and gets into a technical conversation that uses terms such as "fuzzy matching." The issue with middle names is that sometimes people fill out forms and include their full middle names, or use a middle initial, or leave the middle name blank. Middle name matching does not add the information needed to ensure that an individual has been uniquely identified.

Matching on name and any piece of the date of birth cannot be relied upon to claim voter fraud. The best use for this kind of matching, where the analysis stops at names and birth dates, is to prepare a list of *potential* duplicates requiring far deeper research—not to go to court.

Any match based on name and birth date needs additional confirming data to prove the match. I have used online property records to connect a person to two addresses in different states. One of the earliest attempts I made at matching votes cast in two states involved two voters who appeared to vote in both Rhode Island and Florida. The voters (a couple) were matched as having voted in Newport, RI, and Palm Beach, FL. I found Palm Beach property records that reference the Newport, RI, address. In addition, both voters' names were on the Florida property record. I brought these voters to the attention of law enforcement. Interestingly, there was never any action taken to enforce federal election law, although the voter registrations in Newport disappeared.

Based on my work over the years, the most likely explanation when two people with the same name and birth date cast a vote is that those are two different people, not one person committing a felony—more than 90 percent of the time.

Tricky Data and Shortcuts

My communication back to the campaign with my findings was: "DO NOT ALLOW THIS [analysis] TO GO OUT." A lawsuit was about to be filed with false information.

The campaign contacted the lawyer who was going to file the challenge and told him that the data on which he intended to base the lawsuit was terrible. I did not know who the lawyer was. The lawyer initially told the campaign that they would proceed with the lawsuit anyway. Later, after some back and forth, the lawyer was convinced not to file.

In the spring of 2021, I learned that Eastman was very interested in my Nevada findings. He pulled me aside in a hallway after I had met him for the first time and demanded that I tell him why the data in the Nevada lawsuit was bad.

I explained the birthday problem to him, but I do not think he really heard or understood me. He handed me his business card, and I told him I would email a more straightforward explanation to his Claremont College email address, which I did.

Perhaps the worst example of the birthday problem yielding a flawed analysis happened publicly in Georgia on December 10, 2020. On that day, Matt Braynard testified to the Georgia legislature's House Governmental Affairs Committee about an analysis he publicly released of all manner of claimed instances of voter fraud in Georgia.[20]

Former state representative Bee Nguyen questioned many of Braynard's findings. Nguyen researched some of Braynard's claims of fraudulent voting activities, going so far as to contact voters Braynard claimed committed crimes to provide evidence that he was wrong. Nguyen interviewed voters accused of casting duplicate votes (one in Georgia and one in Arizona). She found that while two voters with the

20 Georgia State House Governmental Affairs Committee, "Georgia State Reps Question Matt Braynard," @11Alive, https://www.youtube.com/watch?v=LXvybaYCSIM.

same name who were born in the same year cast votes in the two states, the full dates of birth for those voters were different.

Nguyen effectively disproved many of Braynard's claims of voter fraud by simply reaching out to some of the voters Braynard claimed had committed voter fraud. Braynard's analysis stopped far short of what was needed to make a credible fraud claim. He fell into the birthday problem trap.

When confronted with this, Braynard's deer-in-the-headlights response was to thank Nguyen for her questions; he then asked her to send him her findings so that he could do some deeper digging.

Was Braynard engaged in an unbiased investigation of voter fraud in Georgia? Almost certainly not. He was a Trump campaign staff member at one point and is listed as the leader of a group named Look Ahead America, which, among other things, organized rallies to support "J6 prisoners" (people accused of crimes associated with the mayhem at the US Capitol on January 6, 2021).[21]

It is important to note that Georgia and Arizona only supply birth years in their voter data. In his testimony, Braynard stated that Georgia and Arizona gave full birth dates, which was flatly wrong. My best guess and personal opinion are that Braynard was not working off voter data provided directly by Arizona and Georgia—or he was lying about the nature of his data because he had been so publicly called out.

I can understand why Braynard may have taken a shortcut when looking at the data; processing Arizona's available election data just days after the election would be no simple task. The only Arizona voter data with election results available immediately after the election came from each Arizona county.

There are fifteen Arizona counties. Thirteen report their early election results using the same file format. However, Maricopa County

21 https://lookaheadamerica.org.

and Pima County each have different file formats. This leads me to believe that Arizona has at least three different sets of voting infrastructure across the state, which includes voter registration systems.

Braynard's probable use of data that did not come directly from election officials dramatically reduced the likelihood that his analysis would be accurate. But it did allow him latitude to reach the conclusions he wanted.

Chapter 5

DID 740,070 VOTERS IN WISCONSIN CAST DUPLICATE VOTES?

Umm . . . no. After the legal window to contest most state elections had closed, fraud claims continued to roll in.

This claim was by far the wildest of all the claims I looked at. It was also the silliest, in that the whole thing was built on a basic lack of understanding about the election data on which it was based.

On December 6, 2020, I was asked to examine a claim that 740,070 voters cast votes twice in Wisconsin. If true, this would have represented an astonishing problem with elections in Wisconsin.

As Cannon and I discussed this claim by phone, I remember his clear skepticism. For this claim, he told me to tell him why it was wrong.

While the path this false claim took to reach my desk is telling and unique, the reason the claim was wrong is not. Whoever performed the analysis was unfamiliar with how Wisconsin reported its election data.

The claim originated with "a group of volunteers" who "analyzed" Wisconsin's voter data file. Their analysis found that 740,070 voters cast ballots by mail and also "by machine." The volunteers were ready to present the "double voters" list to the Department of Justice.

This finding became a hot topic on a web forum dedicated to everything Donald Trump: thedonald.win. I know this because the fraud claim directed me to this website for background information. Trump supporters on the forum were convinced that this Wisconsin finding was the smoking gun to prove the corruption of elections nationwide.

When Cannon mentioned to me that I should visit the website for more information, I could not help but blurt out, "Are you kidding me?" He made a noise that I think was a chuckle and said, "Nope."

From the email chain forwarded to me, it looks like one of the volunteers informed a manager at one of the Trump golf clubs of the budding Wisconsin scandal. That manager then notified Eric Trump, who sent it along to Alex Cannon, who then brought me in.

I had not spent much effort working with Wisconsin's voter data because Wisconsin is one of the states that does not provide any part of the date of birth in a voter's registration file. With no piece of the date of birth, it is impossible to uniquely identify a person with any level of certainty. That lack of confidence would have been a real problem in any court case filed using data provided from Wisconsin.

The fraud claim came down to this, which was taken directly from the analysis: "There were 2,560,102 voter reg[istration] numbers (VRN) used to cast a total of 3,179,274 in-person and returned active mail-in ballot. . . ."

Every time I subtracted 2,560,102 from 3,179,274, I got 619,102 as the difference, not 740,070. I addressed the claim assuming that a math error had been made in claiming the total number of duplicated votes, but I already knew that did not matter.

The data file the volunteers had to use for their analysis was the absentee ballot file provided by the state. On December 5, Wisconsin had not yet released a voter history file that included votes cast in person on Election Day. Rhode Island is the only state I know of that releases in-person vote details so soon after an election. Many states do not make final election data available until February of the year after an election, or later. Some states do not make data available until May.

The Wisconsin absentee voter file contains a list of every voter who cast a ballot by mail and every voter who cast a "mail ballot" in person. In Wisconsin, a mail ballot cast in person is applied for at town hall, filled out at town hall, and turned in, all at the same visit. Perhaps the volunteers did not appreciate the difference between an in-person mail ballot and a vote cast in person on Election Day.

The Wisconsin absentee voter file did not contain information about votes cast in person on Election Day, which is where the fraud claim falls apart. The fraud claim was based on the reported Wisconsin vote count of nearly 3,200,000 votes, but the data file they used lacked the information for over 600,000 votes that were cast in person on the day of the election.

The volunteers concluded that monumental voter fraud was the best possible explanation for the discrepancy.

How and why did a group of people make such a severe blunder? How is it possible that no one involved in making this claim stopped to ponder whether a reason other than fraud could explain this wild finding?

Confirmation bias. There is no better explanation.

The United States suffers from a national case of confirmation bias. Rational and intelligent people have abandoned their ability to process information logically. Instead, they exclusively search for information that confirms their existing beliefs, reject information that undermines their views, and interpret (and even misinterpret) information in ways that validate what they already think.

Confirmation bias drives how and where folks get their news. Any news source that delivers narratives contrary to one's beliefs must be fake and avoided in the minds of those swept up in confirmation bias.

Social media plays a huge role in deepening confirmation bias's hold on us. Participating in groups where your beliefs are confirmed rather than challenged is easier and more pleasant.

And there may be no more remarkable example of how confirmation bias has gripped our country than how people responded to Trump's claim that massive voter fraud was responsible for his 2020 election loss. Benign activities such as storing ballots in boxes have been dubiously misinterpreted to claim fraud. Reasonable explanations for these innocent activities are discounted or ignored, while wild conspiracy theories are embraced.

A substantial portion of the population of the United States has been deftly manipulated regarding the topic of voter fraud. Confirmation bias is the tool used for that manipulation, powered by former president Trump's continuous repetition of the false claims of massive voter fraud.

I passed my analysis of the Wisconsin volunteers' claim back up the line. I never heard anything more about it.

Chapter 6

WERE DEAD PENNSYLVANIANS CASTING BALLOTS BY MAIL?

The very first claim of voter fraud I had been asked to evaluate, the day after my contract with the Trump campaign was signed, was a claim that voters appeared to have cast mail ballots in Pennsylvania after they had passed away. Some providers of services to the deceased and their families had concerns.

Reviewing claims of voter fraud made by others was something that Cannon and I had not discussed prior to executing our contract. I'm pretty sure he was as surprised that these claims were landing in his inbox as I was. We were already up against impossible deadlines for the work we *had* signed up for. Now I was being asked to spend time diving into new claims arriving daily. To Alex's credit, he never once sent me a claim to evaluate that did not rely on data. I had no ability to research claims such as fraud committed while counting ballots.

A spreadsheet was given to me with the names, dates of birth, dates of death, and counties of death of individuals who had passed away within a month or so of Election Day. Also included in the spreadsheet was mail ballot information that someone had dug out of the state's file by matching the names and birth dates of the deceased individuals with entries in the mail ballot file.

Mail ballot data files are often complicated because the mail ballot process is complicated. The steps in the mail ballot process in many states go something like this:

1. A registered voter requests a mail ballot.
2. Election officials receive that request.
3. A mail ballot is sent to the voter at the address provided in the request—which might not be the same as the residential address in the voter registration.
4. The mail ballot is mailed back to election workers if the voter votes. The ballot itself has no markings that indicate who the voter was who cast the vote. Instead, the ballot is enclosed in an envelope that contains the voter's biographical information, signature, and possibly, depending on the state, a witness signature or even a required notary stamp. That envelope is enclosed in an outer envelope used for mailing purposes.
5. Election officials receive the envelope in the mail.
6. The inner envelope is removed from the mailing envelope, and election workers try to confirm the information on the inner envelope. The confirmation process can include verifying the signature, ensuring that witness signatures or notary stamps are provided, and confirming that requested information on the envelope has been provided and is accurate, such as date of birth, full name, and the correct address corresponding to the voter registration.
7. Once the inner envelope has passed all of the checks, the envelope can be opened and the ballot removed. This happens at different times in the process, depending on the state. When the ballot is separated from the envelope, the vote is considered officially cast.

8. If the information on the inner envelope fails the checks, election workers might begin trying to contact the voter to remedy whatever is wrong.

The mail ballot files provided by many states include information that documents the date that steps in the process were completed. Some states' mail ballot files have no information about each specific step. Some states include multiple statuses for the mail ballot, which can be very confusing to those who do not take the time to understand what each status means. In states whose counties are responsible for the operation of the election, each county can have different mail ballot information in its file than other counties in the same state. To properly analyze each state's and county's mail ballot file requires properly understanding what is in the file.

The mail ballot process and the information in the data files pertaining to mail ballot voting is the most complex election process (and corresponding data) I have encountered in elections.

In the spreadsheet of nearly one hundred voters of concern provided to me, only one vote could have represented a vote cast after the voter passed away. And that one situation was iffy because the voter passed away (based on whatever source the creator of the spreadsheet used for death information) one day after the state mailed the ballot out to that voter.

A couple of problems cropped up in this spreadsheet.

Sometimes, mistakes were made when matching by name and birth date—the birthday problem. The people doing the research assumed that matching on the same name and date of birth ensured a correct match when pairing up the data they collected on deceased individuals and the information in the mail ballot file.

Some of the voters identified as casting a dead vote did not vote. The analyst misinterpreted the absentee voter file.

Most of the claimed instances of a dead voter casting a mail ballot fell into the same category: voters who cast a valid mail ballot and then died before Election Day. In some circumstances, those voters died a day or two before the mail ballot was noted as received by election workers. Those voters passed away while their vote was in transit.

There was no smoking gun in this analysis. But there were a bunch of dud bullets.

That did not stop this false claim from percolating into the media. Some supporters of President Trump latched onto this false claim as evidence that the Pennsylvania election was rigged. All because some folks got excited that they had found voter fraud, when all they proved was that they did not understand how Pennsylvania's mail ballot file worked.

The zombie voters were back in the ground, but I was about to spend a lot more time thinking about Pennsylvania.

Chapter 7

BENFORD'S LAW

On November 11, 2020, I was tasked with looking at a claim of statewide voter fraud in Pennsylvania. I was given twenty-four hours to assess whether it was valid to apply a mathematical theory known as Benford's Law to county vote totals to determine if voter fraud had occurred.

Benford's Law observes that in wide sets of numerical data, the first digit in those numbers is likely to be closer to 1 than to 9. This theory works with numbers that represent the cost of many, but not all, things. It also works when a numbering scheme starts with the number 1, such as the street number part of street addresses. This is because street numbers are often assigned beginning with the number 1 at one end of the street.

I had heard of Benford's Law but had never used it in my work. I needed to understand how the theory should be applied and in what situations. This nonintuitive theory states that in a set of a million random financial transactions, for example, the number 1 will be the first digit 30.01 percent of the time, while the number 2 will be the first digit 17.6 percent of the time. The number 9 will be first just about 5 percent of the time.

Here is the Benford's Law expected distribution of first digits in chart form:

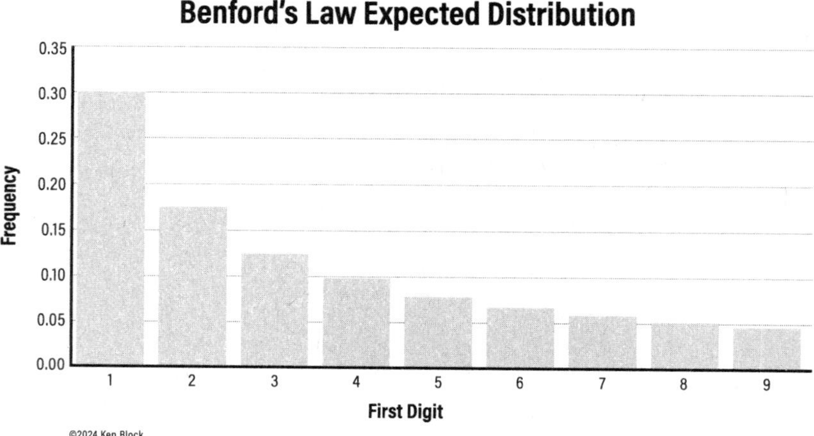

The American court system accepts Benford's Law as a tool to highlight fraudulent transactions. In a set of financial transactions, if the distributions of the first digits of those transactions do not conform to the theory, a fraud challenge may be raised.

The claim of widespread voter fraud in Pennsylvania was solely based upon applying Benford's Law to the first digit of the vote totals for each Pennsylvania county in the 2020 general election.

Cannon had far more interest in this claim than in any of the others he sent my way. A conference call was scheduled the next day for me to present my whirlwind analysis of the claim. Participants included those who had brought the claim forward.

There was much urgency attached to this request, and thanks to the January 6 Committee, I now understand why. In her May 7, 2022, deposition,[22] Sidney Powell was asked about information she supplied to the White House during the election challenge window. She offered up as an example of this type of information a fraud claim based on Benford's Law.

Powell had tremendous White House access and was even considered (maybe not seriously, but she *was* considered) for a role as a special prosecutor to investigate voter fraud issues. The voter issues she presented to the Oval Office would have been assigned a high priority in my inbox.

Powell is infamously attached to a set of election lawsuits she named the Kraken. She hyped these lawsuits as the ultimate proof of election fraud and promised that they would keep President Trump in power. The Kraken lawsuits were filed with great fanfare in several states, including Michigan and Georgia. Unsurprisingly, they were filled with errors, typos, and raw red meat for followers of QAnon and others who believed that President Trump's electoral loss could only be explained via voter fraud.

In Michigan, Powell's Kraken lawsuit flopped spectacularly. Federal court judge Linda Parker sanctioned Powell and her team for basing the case on unsubstantiated claims not backed by law or evidence and making allegations without performing necessary due diligence.[23]

Powell quietly withdrew her Kraken lawsuit in Georgia, which drew this comment from Georgia Secretary of State Brad Raffensperger:

22 Select Committee to Investigate the January 6th Attack on the US Capitol, US House of Representatives, Interview of Sidney Powell, May 7, 2022, Washington, DC, https://www.govinfo.gov/content/pkg/GPO-J6-TRANSCRIPT-CTRL0000082296/pdf/GPO-J6-TRANSCRIPT-CTRL0000082296.pdf.

23 Clara Hendrickson, "Judge Imposes Sanctions on Sidney Powell, Lawyers Involved in Election Conspiracy Lawsuit," *Detroit Free Press*, December 2, 2021, https://www.freep.com/story/news/local/michigan/2021/12/02/sidney-powell-michigan-election-conspiracy-lawsuit/8843626002.

"[The] claims in the Kraken lawsuit prove to be as mythological as the creature for which they're named."[24]

But for sure, Powell made a fortune while angering the federal judiciary with empty lawsuits. The *Washington Post* reported on October 14, 2022, that Powell's nonprofit legal group had raised more than $16 million in the year after the election.[25]

According to Powell's January 6 Committee testimony,[26] most of which is contained on pages 26 and 27, up to ten different groups of "math geniuses" brought forward analyses such as the Benford's Law claim in an attempt to prove allegations of voter fraud.

No Place for Benford

Benford's Law must be applied against sets of "appropriate" data. The data against which the theory is used should be random, and the data set should be "large."

There were claims of voter fraud based on a Benford's Law analysis made in several states after the 2020 election. Academic papers showing why the theory was inappropriate to voting data were produced in response to those claims. Unfortunately, these papers were authored too late for my purposes, or their language was hedged enough that they could not be used as "proof" that this Pennsylvania claim was false.

Pennsylvania has sixty-seven counties. The vote totals for each county make for a small set of data—not a large one. Unfortunately, I did not find a consistent description of what constitutes a "large" set

24 Office of Georgia Secretary of State Brad Raffensperger, "Secretary of State Certifies Election, Kraken Case Dismissed," December 7, 2020, https://sos.ga.gov/news/secretary-state-certifies-election-kraken-case-dismissed.

25 Jared Gans, "Sidney Powell Nonprofit Raised More Than $16M following 2020 Election," *The Hill*, October 14, 2022, https://thehill.com/business/3688693-sidney-powell-nonprofit-raised-more-than-16m-following-2020-election.

26 Select Committee to Investigate the January 6th Attack on the US Capitol, US House of Representatives, Interview of Sidney Powell, May 7, 2022, Washington, DC, https://www.govinfo.gov/content/pkg/GPO-J6-TRANSCRIPT-CTRL0000082296/pdf/GPO-J6-TRANSCRIPT-CTRL0000082296.pdf.

of data in the context of Benford's Law. One of the papers I read said a set of fifty numbers is large enough to use the theory; most papers I read set the threshold for data set size at five hundred or more.

A real challenge lay ahead of me. Could I disprove a claim based on a mathematical theorem without relying heavily on a mathematical proof using mathematical notations I last saw and used in college? I had to convince a lot of people who lacked a strong mathematical background that something they desperately wanted to believe was not true.

Here are the first digits of the vote totals for each Pennsylvania county graphed against the Benford's Law expected distribution.

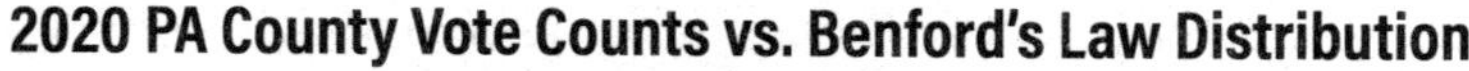

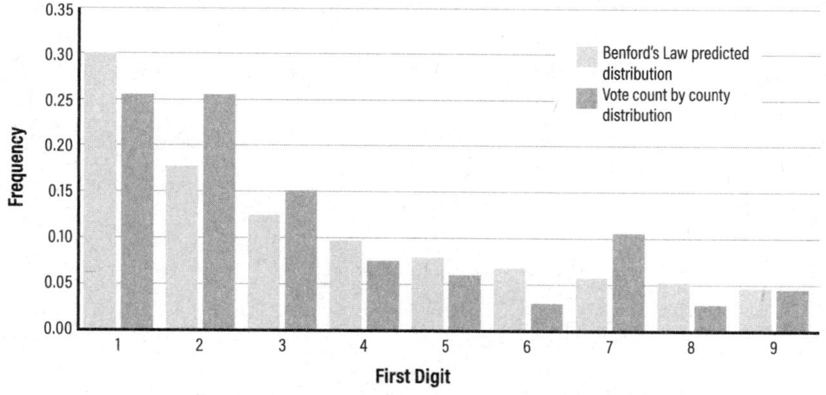

Vote counts by county came from PA elections website: https:llwww.electionreturns.pa.gov/ReportCenterlReports

The distribution of the first digits for each county's vote totals does not conform to the expected distribution according to Benford's Law. Fraud! Right?

As I thought about it, I realized that the first digit of each county's vote totals must be a function of the overall population size of the county. Therefore, you can't (or should I say, *shouldn't*) have more votes cast than registered voters, and you shouldn't have more registered voters than citizens eighteen years of age or older.

Unfortunately, in some states and counties, there *are* more registered voters than citizens eighteen years of age or older. Until just a few years ago, my town had registered voters equal to 120 percent of the town's population including children. I will discuss bloated voter rolls a little later.

Even with the complication of bloated rolls, I believed it was still valid to assert that for Benford's Law to be applied to county-level vote totals appropriately, the theory also had to hold true for the population counts for each county.

Here are the first digits of the populations for each Pennsylvania county graphed against the Benford's Law expected distribution.

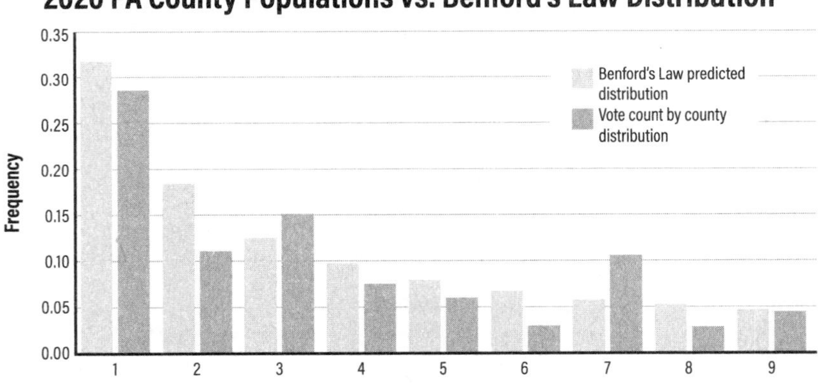

Population data from 2020 Redistricting Census. https://pasdc.hbg.psu.edu/

As you can see, the population counts do not conform to Benford's Law expected distribution. Therefore, unless one was prepared to declare that the population sizes of all Pennsylvania counties were fraudulent, Benford's Law cannot be applied to county population counts in Pennsylvania.

It makes sense that Benford's Law cannot be applied to the populations of counties. While a county with a population of 1.5 million people adds up its population starting from the number 1, the total population count has no other dependency on that number. The size of the population is a function of the number of large, densely populated areas and the percentage of lightly populated rural areas. A county small in landmass and rural in nature will have a population far lower than a large county with multiple, densely populated urban areas.

Benford's Law also cannot be applied to the selling price of homes. For example, imagine a higher-end community where the median home price is $400,000. Graphing the sales prices of homes in that community will show that the number of homes sold with the first digit of the sales price as 1 or 2 is lower than what Benford's Law predicts.

To be thorough, I also graphed the counts of active, registered voters in each county against the Benford's Law expected distribution and got this result:

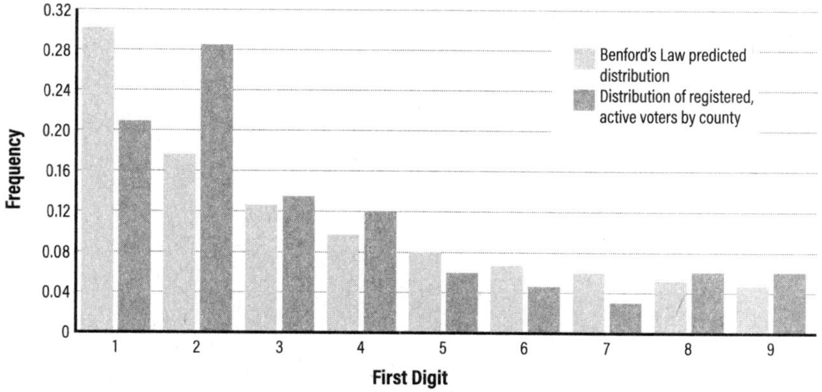

Registered voter counts per county calculated from the Feb. 2021 PA voter registration file

Lastly, because I just had to see if Benford's Law works against a valid, real-life situation, I tested the theory against the first digit of every street number for every address in the Pennsylvania voter registration file. Specifically, I applied the theory against 8,788,475 addresses from the voter file; 22,802 voter records in the file had street numbers that did not start with a digit, so I excluded them from this analysis.

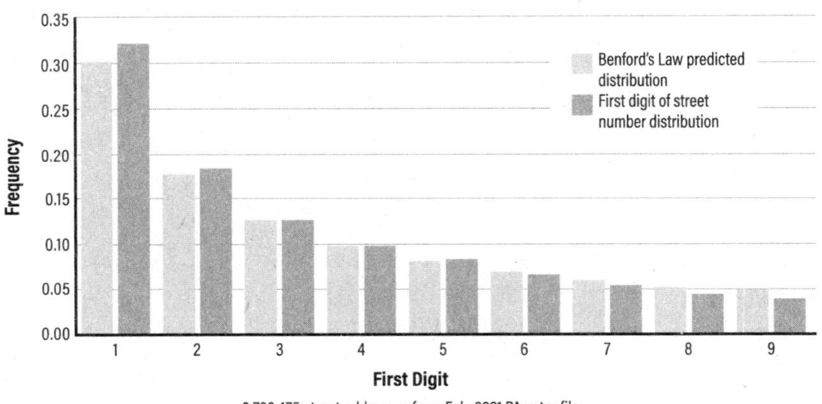

The theory does work when the set of numbers being tested is appropriate. The variances from the expected distribution are likely because multiple voters can reside at the same address. I played around a bit trying to get this analysis to land perfectly on the Benford's Law predicted outcomes, but I could not get that to happen.

In the conference call on November 12, I presented this simple fact: since the population sizes by Pennsylvania county don't conform to Benford's Law, no one can credibly expect the county vote totals to conform.

There was an extended silence when I finished, broken by someone (I wish I knew who it was) who said, "We are done here."

I had given Cannon a verbal preview of my findings before we held the conference call. He did not have an audible reaction to my bad news that the claim was false, but there were several moments of silence as he digested what I had told him.

Highly technical claims such as this Benford's Law analysis were directed straight to the White House or the top of the campaign staff, where no one was equipped to evaluate their validity. But few of the people and organizations involved with protesting the election results for Trump were carefully vetting fraud claims. Folks such as Sidney Powell were willing to stake their professional reputations on pretty much anything that could impugn the election and create a narrative that massive fraud had occurred.

So much for the "math geniuses."

That said, many people will be surprised to learn that the Trump campaign itself—at least the less reckless side of the campaign—was performing due diligence. Another day, another voter fraud claim disproven.

Chapter 8

MORE MATH AND MORE MAIL

I received two claims of fraud that had higher-level mathematics as part of the claim—the Benford's Law false claim and this one: that nearly 100,000 mail ballots in Pennsylvania were fraudulently requested. This wild claim was based on mathematical extrapolation based on faulty data.

There were three parts to this claim, which had analysis provided by Williams College mathematics professor Steven J. Miller and others, including our old friend Matt Braynard, whose research in Georgia was torn apart during a state legislative hearing. The first claim used National Change of Address (NCOA) data from the US Postal Service to claim that many voters were voting where they did not live. The second claim was that 742 Pennsylvania voters had cast votes in Pennsylvania and also in some other state. The third was the 100,000 fraudulently requested ballots.

In researching Miller for this book, I discovered that the professor once edited a book about Benford's Law.

The three subclaims were rolled into a circus of a lawsuit that was filed against Pennsylvania election authorities: *Donald J. Trump for*

President, Inc. v. Kathy Boockvar.[27] Boockvar was Pennsylvania's secretary of state at the time of the 2020 election.

Circus might be a kind word to describe this lawsuit. In the span of two weeks, the lawsuit was filed, the attorneys representing Trump changed at least twice, and the case was dismissed with prejudice. Most of the original attorneys resigned,[28] except for one who wanted to withdraw but was not allowed to by the court. What would a circus lawsuit be without a guest appearance by Rudy Giuliani, who was added to the case just days before it was tossed out?[29]

The judge handled the plaintiffs roughly in his memo supporting the dismissal.[30] The Trump campaign's claims, including Miller's analysis, never got their day in court because the judge ruled that the Trump campaign did not have standing to sue, nor did the campaign provide the evidence of harm necessary to allow the case to proceed.

It is just as well that Miller's analysis never saw the courtroom. First, he did not bring forward direct evidence of voter fraud. Worse, he was working off data from a source, Matt Braynard, who had badly botched data and analytics in Georgia.

Miller tried to make the case, based on statistical analysis, that he could extrapolate massive issues with Pennsylvania's 2020 election. His research had many shortcomings, but one of the key ones was that there was no earthly way he could prove that votes were swung from Trump to Biden because of his claims of fraud. The filed lawsuit was meant to nullify the results of Pennsylvania's 2020 election or even

27 United States District Court, Middle District of Pennsylvania Filing November 21, 2020, https://www.pamd.uscourts.gov/donald-j-trump-president-v-boockvar-et-al-420-cv-0207.8.

28 Rachel Abrams, David Enrich, and Jessica Silver-Greenberg, "Once Loyal to Trump, Law Firms Pull Back from His Election Fight," *New York Times*, November 13, 2020, https://www.nytimes.com/2020/11/13/business/porter-wright-trump-pennsylvania.html.

29 Marc Levy and Mark Scolforo, "A Rusty Giuliani Returns to the Courtroom on Trump's Behalf," AP News, November 18, 2020, https://apnews.com/article/rudy-giuliani-returns-courtroom-trump-b81328c5a74ab348d8b7e21f93eed3f9.

30 Mark Scolforo and Colleen Long, "In Blistering Ruling, Judge Throws Out Trump Suit in PA," AP News, November 21, 2020, https://apnews.com/article/judge-throws-out-trump-suit-pennsylvania-87eaf4df86d5f6ccc343c3385c9ba86c.

possibly to change the winner. With such a dramatic ask, the bar for demonstrating harm was set pretty high—a bar neither the lawsuit nor Miller's analysis could possibly meet.

The wheels were entirely off in this claim from go. A valid finding of fraud could not emerge from inaccurate data. And yet this Pennsylvania lawsuit commanded national attention and provided a rallying point for election conspiracy theorists.

Missing Mail

The NCOA (National Change of Address) database is a tool the Postal Service provides that allows individuals and businesses to have their mail forwarded when they move. This service is optional—not everyone who moves files a change of address form. The data available in the NCOA database is complex. For example, some people file temporary instead of permanent address changes. If a person utilizing the NCOA database for analytic purposes does not fully understand the data in the file and how to use it, they will likely end up with erroneous results.

The primary thrust of the NCOA analysis pertaining to the 2020 election came down to this: people sometimes cast ballots at addresses that did not match what the analyst identified as that person's current address as found in the NCOA.

In my research applying the NCOA to voting data, I found that any results from an analysis that includes the NCOA need to be taken with a large grain of salt. This is because members of the military and students are allowed to vote by mail from wherever they are currently living—and they very well might have a valid entry in the NCOA database stating that their mailing address is in a different state than their voter registration. There is also no guarantee that the NCOA is up-to-date for any given individual. An entry in the NCOA is not a slam-dunk indicator of a person's current primary residence.

The analysis I was given included top-level data showing that Georgia had more voters who, based on their NCOA data, voted in states that did not match the NCOA than the other states in the analysis, which looked like this:

State	NCOA Count
AZ	5,084
GA	15,700
NV	5,145
MI	1,688
PA	7,426
WI	6,207

Georgia is the home of Fort Benning, where more than 100,000 people live and work at any point in time. None of the other states in this analysis has the same military presence. So the 15,700 voters who appear to be voting where they do not live is explainable and, more important, legal.

More importantly, the primary point in my response to Alex Cannon about this NCOA issue was that conflicts with the NCOA address don't matter—only if duplicate votes were cast would there be a legal issue substantial enough to raise a red flag.

The claim of 742 duplicate votes cast in Pennsylvania was part of an analysis of the six contested states. Note in the following chart that the Pennsylvania data was reported twice in the original report; that is not a typo on my part. The missing Michigan count was also part of the original report.

State	Duplicate Count
GA	395
PA	742

State	Duplicate Count
MI	
NV	987
PA	742
WI	234

I know that this duplicate vote analysis was done by Matt Braynard, whose Georgia duplicate vote analysis failed so spectacularly. In his summary, Miller credits Braynard for his work and data. Pay no attention to the duplicate vote numbers in the preceding table—they are bunk, as was proven in Georgia, and for the same reasons. Braynard fell into the birthday problem trap, just like the Nevada lawsuit attempt.

In my email to Cannon, I told him the duplicate voting numbers reported in the preceding table would likely be both high and wrong due to the birthday problem.

The most surprising and irresponsible claim was the "scandal" of unreturned absentee ballots.

Someone came up with the idea to phone Republicans with a mail ballot request in Pennsylvania's mail ballot file to ask if the voter had requested the mail ballot and had cast a mail ballot in the election. Just over one thousand out of roughly twenty thousand attempted contacts were successful and yielded responses.

Imagine being a Republican voter in Pennsylvania and receiving a phone call about whether or not you did anything with mail ballots. Meanwhile, your president is publicly railing against mail ballots, and the state is afire in controversy surrounding the election in general. Any answers received were suspect already.

On top of that, mail ballots are complicated. One has to request a mail ballot application, fill it out, mail it back, receive the mail ballot in the mail, and then fill it in and mail it to complete your vote. I can guarantee that many of the recipients of these phone calls did not understand some of the questions they were asked.

Miller claims that 452 of those surveyed said they mailed their ballots back to election authorities. How can he be sure that the respondent to this question understood the difference between applying to obtain a mail ballot and actually casting a vote by mail?

Plowing ahead, Miller then extrapolates the estimated number of "fraudulent" votes cast in Pennsylvania to be roughly fifty thousand—based on a couple of hundred survey responses with dubious questions and unreliable answers. Miller threw in some statistical probability calculations and some pretty dense language describing how he arrived at his result.

I sent Cannon several emails as I digested these claims. The one that I felt hit the hardest said this: "If the question is: is this stuff a game changer . . . it is not. The premise of essentially convicting via extrapolated data will not hold water."

I did not bother double-checking his math because his conclusion was—how do I say this artfully—*immaterial.* As I told Cannon, "Unreturned mail ballots are not voted—who cares? The vote was not cast. This is not admissible evidence that fraud has occurred. The vote has to have been cast."

A far better approach to this specific issue would have been to identify people who claimed not to have voted by mail but whom the data identified as having cast a mail ballot. Examining the ballot envelopes would help determine if the voter cast the ballot in question based on the signature. But, of course, since the mail ballot file shows the vote was cast, it means the ballot was removed from the envelope and the vote was counted. But that's all it shows. There is absolutely no way to demonstrate that the vote cast benefitted Biden instead of Trump.

To this day, I am mystified about how this analysis would have been used in court. It proves no fraud. It would have failed to survive legal scrutiny for various reasons, including shaky or completely wrong data.

One finding in this report that deserves a deeper look is this: some people who applied for a mail ballot cast votes in person. That is not supposed to happen. If a voter applied for a mail ballot, an in-person vote is not allowed unless the mail ballot is turned in unfilled. It is very possible that unused mail ballots were turned in so that these voters could cast votes in person. Unfortunately, the analysis does not get into that piece of the process.

The basic issue is valid—I have seen inklings of this problem in other states. There appear to be six votes in Rhode Island in 2022 where early votes were cast in person when an outstanding mail ballot was requested. In two cases, it appears votes were cast using each mechanism. I provided my analysis to the secretary of state's office, which confirmed that they were aware of those votes and that they had already made Rhode Island's Board of Elections aware of the issue.

Rhode Island has two different state agencies responsible for operating the state's elections. Addressing issues in this environment can be maddening, as each agency can and does point at the other when things go wrong. There is no single entity to hold accountable for Rhode Island elections. The Rhode Island Board of Elections, in my experience, has not been a proactive or accommodating place to get issues addressed.

Miller's overblown report failed to prove that voter fraud had occurred in Pennsylvania in sufficient quantities to impact the election. But let's imagine that large-scale voter fraud *had* been proven. Suppose Miller's analysis had proved, beyond a shadow of a doubt, that ninety thousand fraudulent votes had been cast in Pennsylvania in the 2020 general election, way more votes than the margin of victory for Biden. What impact might this finding have produced?

Proving that massive voter fraud occurred is only the first hurdle. To win a court challenge to the election result, it is also necessary to show that the fraudulently cast ballots benefited one candidate at the expense of another. That is nearly impossible to do due to the anonymous nature of how we cast our ballots.

Imagine that ninety thousand fraudulent votes had been proven, and the request was made to toss the election results and rerun it in Pennsylvania. Without proof that those fraudulent ballots had changed the election's outcome (which is impossible), it is hard to imagine any judge granting that request. It is impossible to imagine a scenario where a judge would overturn an election and grant the losing candidate a legally determined victory.

Chapter 9

DID NONCITIZENS VOTE IN ARIZONA?

A few—almost certainly. A lot? Impossible to know.

Some mornings in November 2020, I spoke with Alex before speaking with anyone in my family. A text message would come in early, and I would either handle it or call him from a place such as my basement or outdoors if the weather was nice enough. He had a lot on his plate, and I was willing to speak with him whenever he had a moment. As I remember, the issue of noncitizens voting in Arizona was brought to my attention via an early morning text message.

The question of whether or not noncitizens are voting in our elections has percolated for many years. Do some noncitizens vote in our elections? Yes. I know this for a fact. Someone I know held a green card and voted in some of our elections until I set him straight. A green card holder is not a US citizen. I don't understand how he was issued a voter registration.

Like many forms of voter fraud, noncitizen voting does happen, at least in small quantities. There are news stories from all over the country regarding noncitizens getting into trouble for voting in our elections.[31] But the big question is: Do enough noncitizens vote to impact the results?

Former president Trump has made various claims over the years, at times claiming anywhere from one million to as many as five million "illegals" cast ballots in the 2016 general election.[32] He claimed these fraudulent votes caused him to lose the popular vote that year. As with every other claim Trump has made about voter fraud, he provides no data to back this one up.

I explored this topic with my data vendors after the 2016 general election. My thought was that most US citizens have Social Security numbers. Why not match voter registration data with Social Security numbers to see who might not be a US citizen?[33]

These attempts at finding Social Security numbers were only somewhat successful. Many registered voters returned as not having Social Security numbers that matched the address information in their voter registration file. Our processing today is much better than in 2017, so we would undoubtedly encounter fewer missed matches if I tried this again. However, I won't bother trying again because there are good reasons why Social Security numbers do not show up for some people at specific addresses in my vendors' data.

31 United States Attorney's Office, Middle District of North Carolina, "Federal Authorities Charge Nineteen with Voter Fraud," September 2, 2020, https://www.justice.gov/usao-mdnc/pr/federal-authorities-charge-nineteen-voter-fraud; WTOL News Room, "13 Non-Citizens in Ohio Illegally Voted in the 2020 Election; LaRose Refers 117 People for Investigation, Possible Charges," WTOL.com, July 12, 2021, https://www.wtol.com/article/news/politics/state-politics/13-people-in-ohio-illegally-voted-2020-election/512-1b7fd295-55a3-4b78-871c-9d42c06135fb; Mark Maxwell, "State Board of Elections Admits Non-US citizens May Have Voted Illegally in 2018," WCIA.com, January 20, 2020, https://www.wcia.com/illinois-capitol-news/state-board-of-elections-admits-non-u-s-citizens-may-have-voted-illegally-in-2018.

32 Samuel Chamberlain, "Trump Tells Congressional Leaders 3-5 Million 'Illegals' Cost Him Popular Vote," Fox News, January 24, 2017, https://www.foxnews.com/politics/trump-tells-congressional-leaders-3-5-million-illegals-cost-him-popular-vote.

33 Whenever I ask my vendors to look for Social Security numbers for registered voters, those numbers always stay in the computer systems of my vendors. I never see those numbers. I only want to be told whether or not a number was found.

When my data vendors identify a specific voter as not having a Social Security number, that voter might not be a citizen, or that voter might simply be invisible to the credit bureaus. The credit bureaus can overlook people who lack a credit history, credit cards, utility payments, bank accounts, and mortgages. One type of voter this technique might incorrectly identify as not having a Social Security number would be a student, who likely has no credit history. With that much uncertainty, this approach is of little use.

In 2017, I was invited to Vice President Pence's office in the OEOB (Old Executive Office Building) to meet with his staff to discuss voter integrity issues. The issue of noncitizen voting arose during the meeting, and I was asked to try to confirm the claim of millions of fraudulent votes cast by noncitizens. I described what I had tried and told them that I knew of only one data resource that might be useful—the Department of Homeland Security's immigrant database. I also said that it was my understanding that this database could not be used for this purpose, per federal law. But I figured if anyone could check into that, it was the folks with me in the room. I did not hear again about this issue.

(As an aside, if you can wrangle your way into the OEOB, I strongly recommend it! I was able to (and was urged to) roam the halls while I was there. The Secretary of War Suite is extraordinary. Views of the White House and the Washington Monument are available from many windows if you can get to them. The desk tray of the vice president's ceremonial desk was the icing on the cake for me. Protected under Plexiglas, the bottom of the tray contains graffiti and signatures from vice presidents going back to Rockefeller.)

PII (Personally Identifying Information)

The 2020 Trump campaign asked me to attempt to verify whether anyone on a spreadsheet of more than 2,600 registered voters in

Arizona was not a citizen. I made sure the shortcomings of the only method I knew were understood, but I was told to try anyway.

I had no idea who had compiled this catalog of voters or what caused some of these names to appear on the list. There was no pattern, and there were as many Smiths as there were Rodríguezes.

More than 1,600 of the names on the list matched a Social Security number based on name, address, and, in the case of Arizona, birth year. We could find nearly thirty people in the database but could not confidently find a Social Security number—meaning that my vendor's databases had information regarding the person, but did not have a Social Security number on file. For everyone else, just over one thousand people, we could not find a person with the same name, year of birth, and address in my vendor's databases.

Of the thirty voters whom we found at their registration address but for whom we could not confidently find a Social Security number, most had names such as "Rogers," "Glover," or "McGuire."

The roughly one thousand names and addresses we could not find in my vendor's database included a wide variety of names with no discernible pattern. More than half of them were born after 1990, meaning they were no older than thirty years old at the time of the election. About three hundred of these registered voters were twenty years old or younger at the time of the election, making it very likely that these voters were students and lacked credit histories.

No conclusions could be made from the results of this analysis other than that young voters showed up disproportionately in the results—as was expected.

I do not believe that anyone can determine, through data, whether or not noncitizens are voting in droves. While I cannot say that data disproves Trump's claims of massive noncitizen voting fraud, I feel strongly that Trump must provide supporting data for his claim that the fraud is occurring in gigantic quantities.

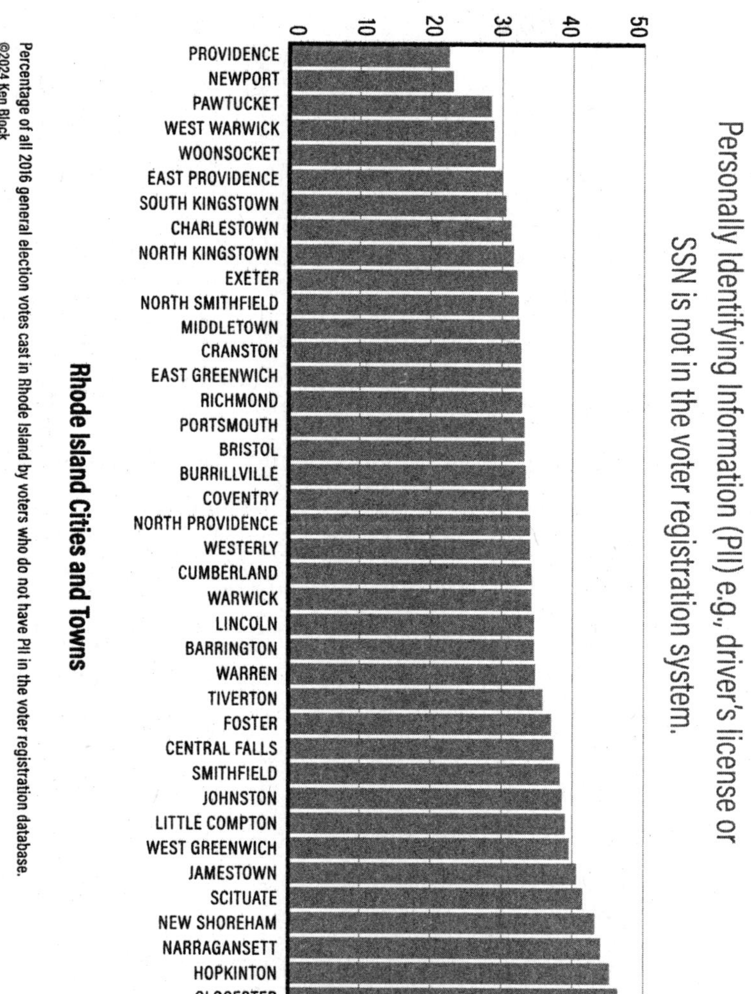

Is it worth it for someone in this country illegally to stick their neck out and commit a crime by casting a fraudulent vote? In most cases, I think that the answer would be no, which is not to say that it does not happen.

I have an analysis that hints at a broader problem but cannot take it beyond a hint. When Rhode Island reported to me that over a third of the votes cast in the state's 2016 general election were cast by voters without Personally Identifying Information (PII—which is either a driver's license or Social Security number) in the voter registration database, I decided to take a look at who was voting without PII on a town-by-town basis. Rhode Island has a grand total of thirty-nine cities and towns, making this analysis easy to handle.

State election officials provided me with a spreadsheet of every registered voter who did not have PII in the voter registration database.

The town with the highest percentage of votes cast in the 2016 general election by voters without PII was Glocester—a small, rural community. Glocester is not, for the most part, a community of immigrants. This was clear evidence that Rhode Island had not done a good job backfilling PII for voters who had been registered to vote for a long time. Of the votes cast in Glocester in 2016, 45 percent were by voters who did not have PII in the voter registration database. The community with the lowest percentage of voters who cast votes without PII was the city of Providence, which came in at around 20 percent. To repeat but to be clear, the preceding graphic does not identify fraud of any kind. Instead, it identifies sloppy data maintenance. After I publicized this finding, state election officials provided voters with a way to update PII for their voter registration records.

However, a surprising finding emerged when I ran the same analysis but only looked at voters who were registered to vote after 2004 (when, in theory, the Help America Vote Act mandated that newly registered voters must provide PII to complete their registrations). (See the following graph.)

The RI community with the highest percentage of 2016 general election votes cast by voters who registered after 2004 but who did not

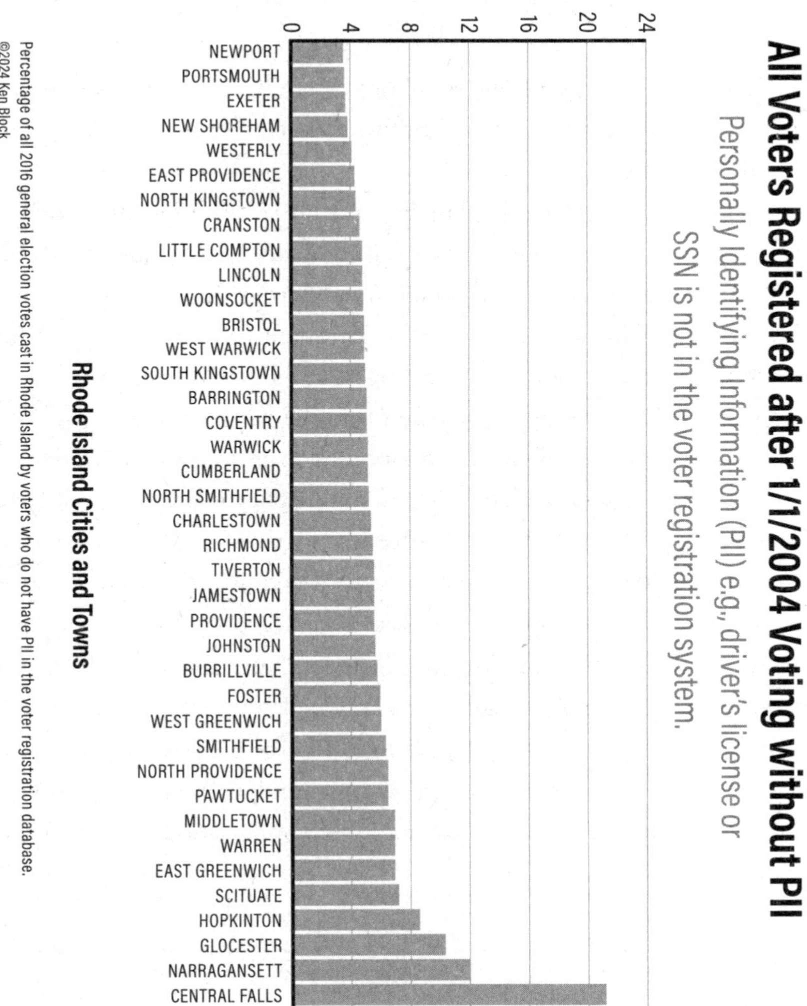

have PII in their voter registration was Central Falls, a small, densely populated city. Central Falls is known as a vibrant immigrant community. More than 20 percent of the votes cast by the city's voters in 2016 were registered after 2004 and did not have PII.

The next closest community was Narragansett, at 12 percent. Narragansett is home to many students attending the University of Rhode Island.

The community with the smallest percentage was Newport, at not quite 4 percent. Providence was in the middle, at somewhere between 5 and 6 percent.

Whenever a comparative analysis results in a significant outlier—as was the case with Central Falls—it indicates that things should be looked into more deeply. Although I publicized this finding, no one did anything with it, which is not surprising given how controversial anything to do with enforcing existing voting rules has become.

Can anyone other than the federal government determine whether an individual is a noncitizen? No, not based on my experience. Is it a valid concern that noncitizens vote in our elections? Sure. Our federal laws clearly state that only US citizens may vote in federal elections. With some election jurisdictions testing allowing noncitizens to vote in local elections, the opportunity for mishandled election procedures could allow noncitizens to vote in our federal elections. We see plenty of evidence that some election jurisdictions make mistakes that allow prohibited votes to be cast. Speaking for myself, I would like to see evidence that our current election laws are implemented evenly across the country before making our complex voting system much more complicated.

Chapter 10

FRAUD FOUND FOR THE CAMPAIGN

The contract I signed with the Trump campaign required me to data mine for voter fraud in Arizona, Nevada, Wisconsin, Pennsylvania, and Georgia. My job entailed looking at mail ballot, early, and in-person voting data. I was initially asked only to look for deceased voters. After the contract was signed, the scope of the work was expanded to include looking for interstate duplicate votes cast in one of the five states of interest, and any other state whose data I could include in the search. Although no mention was made in my contract of evaluating claims of voter fraud made by others, I spent a significant amount of time doing just that.

I knew that the campaign was hugely invested in my being able to find fraud sufficient to credibly challenge an election result. It was an uphill fight from the very beginning.

While I did not appreciate this when we kicked the project off, this was the first time anyone had tried to perform a national look at election data as due diligence to contest an election result. What I found were shocking and significant obstacles that stand in the way of successfully interrogating not only national but also statewide results immediately after an election:

- The roughly three-week window to contest election results is not nearly enough time to acquire and process election data from all over the country. Our state-based election infrastructure does not consider the data needs of our federal elections.
- Too many states do not provide the documentation (such as full dates of birth) that is necessary to evaluate voter data for deceased and duplicate voters.
- Reports for in-person votes cast are unavailable from any state in the crucial three-week window in which one can contest an election result.

This last point is one of the most critical pieces of information I provide in this book: no state makes official in-person voting data available within the small window in which election results can be contested. In normal election years (2020 was not normal due to COVID-19), many more voters cast ballots in person than vote by mail. Without in-person voter data, critical information for evaluating election results is not available. This represents a huge problem when considering the totality of a state's election results. The details for more than half of the votes cast cannot be seen.

How can a campaign evaluate the results of an election when more than half of the votes cast in that election cannot be reviewed? Why is in-person voting data only available well after an election has been completed? We are told how many people cast in-person ballots soon after an election, but we are only told who cast those ballots once it is way too late to use that data to contest the election result.

There are two main ways election systems track who casts votes in person on Election Day: 1) electronic systems that check in voters via computer (often using technology called e-poll books), and 2) paper-based systems. Yes . . . many of the election systems in our country still track who voted in person with paper-based systems.

If you check in to vote electronically, you might interact with a tablet where you sign your name and possibly provide identification. Once checked in, you are provided with a ballot to cast your vote. The fact that you checked in is how it is determined that you cast a vote in the election data. Your ballot is tallied anonymously using different hardware located elsewhere than where you checked in.

If you check in to vote in a paper-based system, your name is looked up by a poll worker scanning through a thick stack of paper. In many paper-based election systems, stickers indicate that a person checked in to vote. Unfortunately, poll workers can easily make mistakes and apply stickers to the wrong voters in those unwieldy stacks of paper. Once you are checked in, you are provided with a ballot. After the polls are closed, election workers often must go through the piles of paper, identify who voted, and then electronically compile that data into one place. It's hard to imagine this is happening now, but it is.

Election jurisdictions that check in voters with paper-based systems conduct their elections as they did a century ago. It is ridiculous that after spending billions of dollars on our election infrastructure, we still have elections being tracked on stacks of paper.

Even election jurisdictions that use electronic check-in do not provide in-person data in a timely way. I don't fully understand why. In Rhode Island, it was explained to me that the e-poll books must all be collected after the election and brought back to the Board of Elections before the vote details are extracted from the devices.

Whatever the explanation, the unavailability of in-person voting data immediately after an election creates a massive gap in our election transparency.

The unavailability of in-person voting data meant analyses such as looking for people who cast duplicate votes in person and by mail could only be partially performed. I could not see if any deceased voters had in-person ballots cast in their names. In short, I had no visibility on a considerable chunk of the votes cast in the 2020 election.

Does the fact that in-person voter detail was missing from the data I looked at change my finding that massive voter fraud did not happen in 2020? No. In-person voting is the most difficult type of vote with which to commit fraud. Would deceased voter counts be higher if in-person voting detail was available? Maybe. Substantially higher? Very unlikely. Also, when states release in-person voting data months after the election, an analysis can be run to look at the issues previously mentioned. I am confident of my assertion that no evidence of massive voter fraud exists in the 2020 voting data.

To return to my first point above, to properly contest an election, a vast amount of preparatory work should happen well before the first vote is cast by mail. The three-week window after an election is too brief to perform all the necessary data analytics and legal legwork. The voter rolls should be evaluated for deceased voters and other bloated voter roll issues well before the election. The data team should get the previous election's mail ballot and early voting files to deal with whatever technical problems are buried there before seeing the mail ballot and early voting files for the current election. Understanding how each mail ballot file is put together is critical. When mail ballot voting and early voting begin, daily mail ballot and early voting files should be obtained and evaluated in real time.

Why daily? When I analyzed Rhode Island's daily mail ballot and early voting files after the 2022 election, I discovered that some of the mail ballots cast early disappeared from the later mail ballot files. It turns out that those votes were removed because the voter had died during the mail ballot window. This could be very problematic for someone trying to track every vote cast in the election, because once a voter has passed away, Rhode Island no longer reports that voter or their voting history in the publicly available data. In this circumstance, I identified ghost votes—valid votes that are part of the vote totals for the election, but with no public record of who cast them. After I raised this situation to Rhode Island election officials, I was given a list of all mail ballots cast, including voters who had died after casting their vote.

Raising questions about deceased voters or making other challenges to a voter's qualifications are much more effective if made before an election than after. Once a vote is cast, there is no realistic way of uncasting it.

States that do not provide full dates of birth in their voter files should be sued in advance of the election in order to secure the data necessary to properly evaluate results. States where the margins of victory are expected to be close should be identified well in advance of the election, and their voter registration data should be carefully examined; problems with that data can be corrected and potentially have a meaningful impact—before votes are cast.

Of course, no preparatory work occurred before Election Day to help the Trump campaign evaluate the election results in the search for voter fraud. The entire effort, from my vantage point, was reactive and unplanned.

Chapter 11

DECEASED VOTER HUNT

Whenever I hear people discuss voter fraud, dead voting is always high on the list of perceived problems. Isolated incidents of the deceased casting ballots do happen, and some made the news after the 2020 election (such as the Judy Presto case).

Actual votes cast in the names of the deceased—and the perception of the dead voting—lead to mistrust of our election systems. Based on prosecutions and convictions, we know that some people easily committed voter fraud in 2020 by registering someone deceased to vote and then casting a mail ballot for that dead person. In both successfully prosecuted deceased voter cases in Pennsylvania, the registration for the deceased voter was submitted within two months of the election.

Is the problem widespread? Did a legion of zombie voters result in the wrong guy being elected president of the United States? I was given the opportunity and the budget to find out.

Who's Dead

It is more difficult than you would think to determine who among a list of people has been bureaucratically declared deceased. Two primary sources can be accessed to determine this: the Social Security

Administration's "Death Master File" (DMF) and state-managed lists maintained by each state's department of health. To look up an individual in the DMF and avoid the birthday problem, you need that person's Social Security number. The problem with a state's department of health list is that it only documents deaths for people who died in the state. Plenty of voters pass away in states other than the ones where they are registered to vote. Also, looking up voters in department of health lists involves the birthday problem.

My process to determine which voters from a state's voter registration file are deceased works like this:

1. Load the voter registration file into our computer system. This step includes figuring out how the voter file is laid out (every state, and sometimes county, has a unique layout), dealing with any issues that make the data unreadable (this happens much more often than it should), loading the data, and then ensuring that the voter file was loaded correctly.
2. Export a file for our data vendor, which includes name, address, and birth date information. This file is securely transmitted.
3. The vendor attempts to identify a Social Security number for each person in the file using name, address, and birth date information. If no Social Security number is found, nothing further can be done for that person. This process is complex and has been years in the making.
4. For people whose Social Security number is found, that number is used to look for the person in the DMF. If found, the vendor notifies us that the person has been found in the DMF.
5. A list of all confirmed hits in the DMF is returned securely to us. We are given information about when and where that person died. We take that list and then see if any registered voters confirmed as deceased cast a vote.

My process is better than what many states can do when looking for deceased registered voters because I do not rely on a Social Security number provided by a voter. I know many states do not have Social Security numbers for many voters. Also, I can find voters who passed away in a different state than where they were registered to vote.

Data entry errors are a problem with voter registration data. Voters can make errors when entering their Social Security number into the voter registration system. Election workers can make transcription errors when copying numbers off a piece of paper. I have seen thousands of errors in birth date information where the birth date for a voter differs by one character from the birth date found by my vendor. Older voter registration records have more transcription errors than records more recently added. This is because newer records are more likely to be entered by the voter directly into the computer, eliminating the possibility for election worker transcription errors.

Inevitably, there were data challenges for some of the states I was supposed to evaluate for deceased voters in 2020.

Wisconsin

Wisconsin provides no piece of a voter's date of birth in their publicly available voter registration file. Without even a year of birth, there is no way to identify someone with certainty using only name and address. Given more time and with the benefit of hindsight, the Trump campaign should have sued Wisconsin election officials before the election to get the full dates of birth necessary to perform meaningful data analytics. I could not evaluate Wisconsin's voter file to determine how many deceased ballots were cast because Wisconsin withholds all birth date information. As an aside, Wisconsin is not obligated to remove dead voters from its voter rolls. The state is exempt from the law that mandates that activity (the National Voter Registration Act of 1993). Wisconsin is exempt because, when the NVRA was passed, Wisconsin did not have voter registration enacted as law. Eliminating exemptions such as this is crucial to strengthening national election integrity.

Nevada

Several unpleasant surprises were waiting for me in Nevada's mail ballot and early voting data files. Nevada did not supply a statewide mail ballot file. The state's seventeen counties do not appear to share the same computer system, so I had to deal with more than ten different file formats representing the same thing: mail ballots applied for and cast in Nevada. Some of those data files lacked important information that other files included. Some of the files had embedded gibberish (I know, not a technical term) that had to be cleaned up before the file could be processed. Precious time was spent dealing with Nevada's messy mail ballot data infrastructure.

Of particular note in Nevada, the voter identification numbers provided by each county for that county's mail ballot file were identification numbers specific to the county—not to the state. But it turns out that county identification numbers in Nevada are not unique to each county. That means a county identification number of 11223343 in Clark County identifies a different voter than a Washoe County voter with the identification number of 11223343. I figured this out after seeing many dead voters appear in Nevada's data—too many from what I knew about the general quality of Nevada's election data. This could have led to a disastrous analysis if I had started jumping up and down, yelling that we had discovered massive voter fraud, without asking why the result was so unexpected.

I use the word *disastrous* because the worst threat that confronts someone performing data analysis like I do is to be horrifically wrong. The general challenge in uniquely identifying someone using data provides some latitude for individual cases of error. Making a process-related error such as not understanding that Nevada counties can use the same number to identify two different voters will shred the credibility of the analysis and the analyst.

Arizona

Arizona also had multiple mail ballot file formats to deal with and electronic gibberish to clean up before I could work with the data.

Arizona and Nevada's county-based mail ballot files did not include statewide voter identifiers, but instead only provided the county identifiers. This wreaked havoc on my analytics because I used statewide voter registration files, not the county-based mail ballot files, to determine who was deceased. With more time I could have worked around this problem, but time was not on my side, and there was not enough evidence of dead voters in other states to warrant spending the time on it in Arizona.

Georgia

In Georgia's mail ballot file, the "county code" data element was not a county code but a different identifier altogether.

Ideally, all these issues should have been worked out before the election. Instead, valuable time was lost figuring all this out while deadlines loomed.

Results

On November 7, two days after my contract was signed, I provided the first analysis of deceased votes cast in Pennsylvania. I provided the campaign with a spreadsheet of fifteen votes cast by individuals that I could determine were dead. The spreadsheet was color coded: individuals identified in red had been registered to vote *after* the date we had determined that the voter had died. (Keep in mind that Pennsylvania provided full dates of birth in their voter data, which enabled us to identify those deceased with high certainty.)

Of these fifteen, two were successfully prosecuted cases of voter fraud: the Presto and Bartman cases. It does not appear that any of the other identified deceased votes cast were prosecuted. Were they investigated? Many of the dead voters we identified still have active voter registrations in Pennsylvania—even the four whose online obituaries can easily be found. Pennsylvania does a terrible job at identifying and removing deceased registered voters.

This spreadsheet of fifteen deceased voters was a topic of conversation in Alex Cannon's January 6 Committee deposition,[34] where Cannon had to remember what the red-colored names meant.

We also delivered a separate, color-coded spreadsheet on twelve deceased votes cast in Georgia. Unfortunately, Georgia only provides a year of birth in its voter registration file, which makes our matching less certain. I was uneasy about looking for deceased voters with just a birth year. The chance of a mismatch increases significantly due to the birthday problem. I took care to explain this to Alex at every opportunity I had. He clearly heard and took my caution to heart, as his testimony to the January 6 Committee makes clear.[35]

These Georgia results made the news, but for all the wrong reasons. A critical line in the spreadsheet I sent Alex read:

> Note: Georgia only supplies a year of birth with their voter data. This makes for a more uncertain match. We removed 90 percent of the potential matches from this list, as [we] could not with certainty determine that the voter was properly matched with a death record. Some number of those removed matches are sure to be good matches, but the time frames on this project preclude the ability to spend the time to go deeper.

34 Select Committee to Investigate the January 6th Attack on the US Capitol, US House of Representatives, Interview of Alex Cannon, April 13, 2022, Washington, DC, https://www.govinfo.gov/content/pkg/GPO-J6-TRANSCRIPT-CTRL0000062449/pdf/GPO-J6-TRANSCRIPT-CTRL0000062449.pdf.

35 Ibid.

Part of this short list was provided to the media, and two of the identified deceased voters were determined to be alive and well. In one case, a widow cast a vote registered not with her name but instead as Mrs. Name of Her Husband. Both were born in the same year, which is all that Georgia provides for the birth date information for a voter. I matched based on first names, last names, and years of birth—and got it wrong. Had Georgia provided full dates of birth—or had the widow registered with her given first name—I would not have had this issue.

The other match I got wrong was a situation in which two women had the same name and were born in the same month and year, with the living woman being identified in my matching as the deceased woman. Again, with the full date of birth information, this situation would not have arisen. This is a prime example of why states should supply full birth dates—especially for checking on integrity issues.

I also attempted to process Arizona, although we could not work through data issues with the data file from Maricopa County, Arizona's most populous county. I found just three matches on deceased voters in Arizona, with the same caveat as Georgia's: with only a year of birth provided, my matching was less certain.

Lastly, I also processed Michigan data, which only provides year of birth. I found just nine strong matches.

What I did not see was a legion of votes cast by the dead. I tried to err on the side of caution. My original processing returned, in some cases, hundreds of possible matches, not dozens. But even if I had gone with the higher numbers, there were nowhere near enough dead votes to impact the 2020 election outcome in any state.

The prosecuted cases of voter fraud where a vote was cast in the name of a deceased person are sad. The cases I know of were not part of some industrialized voter fraud operation; they were family members choosing to commit a voting crime using their deceased family member's identity. I find this crime despicable, and for all its sadness, I don't think the punishment meted out was enough. I say this because these deceased votes provide a road map for others to take advantage of a significant weakness in our election infrastructure—the inability to identify and remove dead voters. In the two Pennsylvania cases, the punishment was probation, while the federal crime of voter fraud can carry a sentence of up to five years in prison and a fine of $10,000.

While some states do a reasonably good job finding and removing dead voters, many more do not.

Chapter 12

DUPLICATE VOTE HUNT

Looking for duplicate votes cast between one of the five states of interest (Wisconsin was excluded due to the lack of birth date information) and every other state brought its own impossible challenge. Looking for duplicate votes across mail ballot and early voting files from every state in the country would have involved processing 576 data files—nearly all formatted differently.

The challenge was not just figuring out where things such as the name and voter identification number were located in each file. The much more difficult challenge was figuring out how to correctly identify a vote cast in each of these files. You will have to take my word for it that this was difficult enough to end any hopes that we could do a nationwide search for duplicate mail ballot votes in the narrow time window we had to contest the election.

A straightforward file can be confidently assessed, processed, and triple-checked in an hour or so. A complicated file can take many hours to process its data correctly. Processing 576 files at one hour per file would take twenty-four days for one technician who worked nonstop. The entire project had a duration of fewer than twenty-four days. If I had put three people on just this piece of the project, it could not have been done in the allotted time.

We had to pick and choose which states to look at. Accordingly, we selected states where people would likely own vacation homes—Florida, South Carolina, North Carolina, and so forth. Unfortunately, we had issues with South Carolina's data that we did not have the time to resolve. In addition, of course, Arizona and Georgia are states where people are likely to own a second home. The only way to fully assess duplicate voting involving those states would have been to look at every other state's data.

We also did not have data from votes cast in person from any state. This means we did not have data for probably half of the votes cast in the election.

So we did not perform a comprehensive national look at duplicate voting. It is not going out on a limb to state that no one has ever performed a comprehensive, national assessment of duplicate voting in the United States in which the voting data from each state is compared to the voting data from every other state. It is impossible to obtain voting data from all fifty states, and the data provided by some states lack key information like date of birth, which is necessary to perform this analysis. As a result, no one empirically knows how many duplicate votes have been cast in any election. Sure, mathematical extrapolations can be used to take an educated guess at the number of these illegal votes. But identifying states where this problem is more prevalent due to issues with data maintenance requires much more than extrapolation.

Does this mean that I am wrong to claim that there was no voter fraud sufficient to change the results of an election in 2020? No. I know this because of the quantity of fraud we found in the 2020 election and what I have found in previous elections.

The process we use to identify duplicate votes cast between states in the three weeks after an election is as follows:

- Load up as many early voting and mail ballot files as possible, taking care to determine votes cast in each file correctly.

- Compare every vote cast in each state with every vote cast in every other state, matching name and birth date information. The results of this step are the list of potential duplicate votes. In my experience, 90 percent of the potential matches will be proven wrong if full birth dates are available. If only the birth year is available, over 99 percent of the potential matches will be wrong.
- Send the potential matches, including address information, to my vendor via secure file transfer.
- The vendor attempts to find a Social Security number for the person on each side of the potential match. That lookup uses the person's name, address, and date of birth. Only if a Social Security number can be found for both voters in the potential match, and only if those Social Security numbers are the same, will the match be declared good.
- The vendor returns to me a list of the confirmed matches.

To help you understand how much more difficult states that only supply a year of birth make things, in 2018, with about forty states' worth of data, we had about 100,000 potential duplicate vote matches based on full dates of birth—and 13 million potential duplicate vote matches based on just the year of birth. We ended up with about 9,000 confirmed duplicate votes cast from the 100,000 full date-of-birth matches and fewer than 5,000 confirmed from the 13 million year-of-birth matches.

Results

The results of this analysis were beyond underwhelming. Unfortunately, we did not have sufficient time to load up enough states' data to produce much impact. And we did not have data for any votes cast in person. We tried and failed to stuff a multimonth project into about a week and a half.

We sent out just 1,284 potential duplicate vote matches based on full dates of birth and received back confirmations on just 11. We sent out 1,519,998 potential duplicate vote matches based on birth year and received back confirmations for just 57. That's 68 confirmed duplicate votes. I know Alex was unhappy with this result—as was I.

I provided one other type of duplicate vote to Alex that did not require my vendor to perform expensive data matching to confirm. Most states allow voters to provide out-of-state mailing addresses in their voter registrations. We looked to match voters with the same first and last names where the out-of-state mailing address in one registration matches the residential address in the other state. This analysis uses voter data provided by the voter to confirm that fraud had been committed. I provided Alex with a list of 14 of these duplicate votes. Again, this is a measly result. Eight months later, in 2021, with forty states loaded up with every vote cast, we identified 167 duplicate out-of-state mailing address votes involving votes cast in Florida and some other states.

If enough time had been allowed by the election timelines to load all available data, I expected 2020 to have more than the 10,000 confirmed duplicate votes I identified in the 2018 election. I am very comfortable saying this because, on September 3, 2020, President Trump told his supporters to try to vote twice, once by mail and then in person.[36] Anyone trying this would be committing voter fraud, no matter how it is framed. Trump suggested attempting to vote twice as a way to stress-test voting systems, but what he was encouraging people to do was try to cast illegal votes. I have no doubt that many of his supporters tried to commit felonious voter fraud due to this request. I also have no doubt that our election infrastructure is porous enough to allow some of those fraudulent votes to have been cast and counted.

36 Zach Montellaro, "Trump Seemingly Encourages North Carolina Residents to Try to Vote Twice," *Politico*, September 2, 2020, https://www.politico.com/news/2020/09/02/trump-vote-twice-voter-fraud-408007.

I tried a couple of times to get Alex to submit the duplicate votes we had identified to law enforcement. He told me the campaign did not want to bring attention to such a small amount of fraud.

In every way, the duplicate vote piece of my work for the Trump campaign was disappointing. We did not directly prove or disprove anything. Nevertheless, I am hopeful that some of the lessons learned can lead to changes in how we conduct our elections.

Chapter 13

DEAD PEOPLE DO SOMETIMES VOTE

As a society, we have developed remarkable technology. We can reliably chart a course for a rocket to reach Mars and even objects billions of miles farther away from our sun. Social media companies know as much about you as any real person you know. You can talk to your car, it can drive itself (sort of), and now artificial intelligence programs can write passably good papers for you.

How is it possible, then, that so many of our government technology systems fall down when it comes to the seemingly simple task of identifying and removing dead people from the rolls?

Some of you are likely experiencing a reflexive aversion to this topic. That's OK; I'm used to it. I talked about deceased people on the rolls of social services programs during my campaign for governor in 2010. As a result, a local journalist tweeted, "Ken Block sees dead people."[37] A few years afterward, Rhode Island's auditor general found that dead people had indeed been receiving benefits from state systems.[38]

37 Ted Nesi (@TedNesi), "Ken Block sees dead people," Twitter, October 26, 2010, 7:13 p.m., https://twitter.com/TedNesi/status/28840230648.

38 NBC 10 News, "Auditor General: RI Paid $11.6M in Medicaid to Dead People," turnto10.com, April 5, 2019, https://turnto10.com/news/local/auditor-general-ri-paid-116m-in-medicaid-to-dead-people.

Recent incidents that involved dead people receiving benefits include: the Treasury Department sending one million COVID-19 relief checks to dead people,[39] FEMA sending Hurricane Sandy disaster benefits to forty-five dead people, and the Department of Veteran's Affairs sending $677,000 to those no longer with us.[40] Even the Social Security Administration, a federal bureaucracy tasked with maintaining an accurate file of everyone who has died in our country, has struggled with paying benefits to those who are dead.[41] That is the tip of a massive iceberg, as my list does not include state, county, and municipal systems.

Some of the benefits paid above were being properly made while the beneficiary was alive, but when that person died the benefit payments continued. In other cases, someone fraudulently applied for benefits in a dead person's name.

Some dead people voted in the 2020 election. I predicted some of these fraudulent votes well before they occurred. In one case, Pennsylvania election officials were notified of a new, fraudulent voter registration in the name of a dead person made weeks before a fraudulent vote was cast and counted. However, they only did something about it after the election was over.

I must state up front that the voter fraud I am about to discuss is not evidence that the Pennsylvania election was rigged, stolen, or otherwise sufficiently compromised to impact the results of the 2020 presidential election.

39 Erica Werner, "Treasury Sent More Than 1 Million Coronavirus Stimulus Payments to Dead People, Congressional Watchdog Finds," *Washington Post*, June 25, 2020, https://www.washingtonpost.com/us-policy/2020/06/25/irs-stimulus-checks-dead-people-gao.

40 Courtney Rozen, "Why the US Government Still Sends Millions of Dollars to the Dead," *Bloomberg*, August 10, 2021, https://www.bloomberg.com/news/articles/2021-08-10/dead-americans-get-millions-in-checks-as-feud-over-data-drags-on?embedded-checkout=true.

41 Office of the Inspector General, Social Security Administration, "Examining Federal Improper Payments and Errors in the Death Master File," March 16, 2015, https://oig.ssa.gov/congressional-testimony/2015-03-17-newsroom-congressional-testimony-march16-hsgac.

The work I describe here looked for deceased voters for every mail ballot vote cast in the election—more than three million votes. Unfortunately, the data to look for dead votes cast in person was not available to me (or anyone) during the period I was performing this work. I found fifteen votes cast by what appeared to be dead voters; two of these cases were prosecuted. I don't know the status of the others. I suspect they were never brought forward for investigation.

Nearly 80,000 votes separated Joe Biden and Donald Trump in Pennsylvania in 2020. The fifteen claimed deceased votes I found are in no way proof that massive voter fraud occurred—or that the election should have been overturned. The 79,380 votes earned in Pennsylvania by the Libertarian candidate Jo Jorgensen more likely explain Trump's loss than does massive voter fraud.

Judy Presto

In January 2021, a Pennsylvania man was charged with voter fraud for voting on behalf of his deceased wife in the 2020 election. In September 2020, I had predicted this particular case of fraud would occur. Had I not found it, this instance of voter fraud would likely not have come to light.

That a deceased person can be registered to vote just months before an election, apply for a mail ballot, and then vote is not good from an election integrity perspective. This episode highlights some awful holes in how Allegheny County's election system works. I name Allegheny County here because, in Pennsylvania, the conduct of elections falls to each county in the state.

The Public Interest Legal Foundation (PILF), ahead of the 2020 election, asked me to process all eight-plus million registered Pennsylvania voters to determine if any were deceased. This work is quite tricky because of the difficulty in confirming an individual's identity solely based on (say it with me) name, address, and date of birth.

We have covered the process already, but it is essential that you understand it, so I will give another quick primer. The process I use involves a specially licensed data vendor identifying the individual based on name, birth date information, and street address and then finding that person's Social Security number. Once the Social Security number is obtained, it is used to look up that individual in the Social Security Administration's Death Master File (DMF). The DMF is a compilation of every death reported to the Social Security Administration.

There are two ways to identify voters in the DMF: by name and date of birth or by Social Security number. Using Social Security numbers is the only way to know with maximum certainty that the person identified as deceased in the DMF is the same as the one registered to vote. Without using the Social Security number to look up someone in the DMF, the birthday problem ensures that any matches made will be wrong more than 90 percent of the time unless other data is used to help confirm the match.

My vendors are licensed to access extremely sensitive information, like Social Security numbers, for uses including fraud detection. Social Security numbers are never disclosed to me—I don't want them, and my vendor would not disclose them to me even if I did. I need to know how the process works and the final results; sensitive information is kept private unless we are asked to disclose it to law enforcement or election officials. I do not publicly disclose information about specific individuals identified in my matching. Even though I have high confidence in the matches, an individual's privacy takes priority over any public need to know. Also, while my matching is as good as can be had, no one should be subjected to an outing in public without first being accorded a proper (and private) investigation by election officials or law enforcement.

In this circumstance, I am comfortable discussing the specifics because a proper investigation was performed, charges were brought, and a verdict was rendered.

During my research, a curious datapoint emerged. A woman named Judy C. Presto was registered to vote on September 3, 2020. Mrs. Presto was born in August 1943. What I discovered about Mrs. Presto was that she passed away on June 23, 2013.

I thought this "registered voter" would likely participate in voter fraud because of how close in time to the election a voter registration was applied for in the name of this deceased individual.

After submitting my declaration[42] to PILF, I did not consider it further. PILF had filed a lawsuit against the State of Pennsylvania, *Public Interest Legal Foundation v. Boockvar*.[43] This lawsuit concerned state election officials failing to remove nearly 20,000 deceased voters from the rolls.

On October 15, 2020, the court denied PILF's request for emergency relief before the 2020 general election. The case was ultimately settled, with the state agreeing to review PILF's findings and take appropriate action.

Ironically, although no one working on the Boockvar case—including me—knew, on October 12, 2020, the fraudulent mail ballot vote cast in Mrs. Presto's name arrived in front of county election officials, three days before the judge in *PILF v. Boockvar* questioned the findings about voter registration dates after the date of death in court.

After the election, as I worked for the Trump campaign, I saw Judy Presto's name come up as having cast a vote by mail in the election, fulfilling my prediction. Her ballot was one of fifteen deceased votes cast in the 2020 election in Pennsylvania that I identified. Unfortunately, I doubt the campaign did anything with this information because the numbers of fraudulent, deceased votes cast in Pennsylvania were far

42 Declaration of Kenneth J. Block, *Public Interest Legal Foundation v. Boockvar*, Doc. 6-9, No. 1:20-cv-01905 (filed Oct. 15, 2020)

43 Public Interest Legal Foundation, "*PILF v. Boockvar*," https://publicinterestlegal.org/cases/pilf-v-boockvar.

too small to matter when the campaign's goal was to prove that massive voter fraud had occurred.

In December 2020, a public records request made in Allegheny County revealed Mrs. Presto's voter registration history. The following activity regarding her Pennsylvania voter registration came from the public records request, Mrs. Presto's obituary, my data vendors, and Pennsylvania's file of mail ballot information for the 2020 general election.

- 06/23/2013 Judy Presto passed away
- 09/03/2020 Presto registered to vote online
- 09/03/2020 Election officials noted that Presto's ID must be confirmed
- 09/23/2020 Election officials made Presto's registration a "permanent absentee" registration (Reread that. Pennsylvania made a dead person a "permanent absentee" voter.)
- 09/23/2020 Application for a mail ballot was received by election officials
- 09/28/2020 Mail ballot was sent out to voter
- 10/12/2020 Completed mail ballot was received and approved by election officials
- 10/12/2020 Election officials noted that ID no longer needs to be confirmed
- 10/15/2020 Election officials mailed out a voter ID card for Mrs. Presto
- 11/10/2020 Vote counted for 2020 general election
- 12/04/2020 Mrs. Presto identified as deceased and removed from the voter rolls

Law enforcement investigated, prosecuted, and convicted Francis Presto of committing voter fraud when he voted in his dead wife's name. Presto was sentenced to a diversion program for two years and ordered to complete 250 hours of community service.[44]

Francis Presto is a registered Republican and registered his deceased wife as a Republican.

This incident raises some serious questions in terms of how any election official performs their job:

- At what point in the voter registration process do election workers confirm the identity of a voter who requests a voter registration?
- At what point in the process do election officials look to see if newly registered voters are deceased? How do they determine if a voter is dead or not?
- In this case, two months transpired from the time when the fraudulent voter registration was made to when the fraudulent vote was counted on Election Day. How is it possible that this type of fraud was not discovered? I discovered the problem with a process that took just three days (and a lot of effort). Election officials theoretically have data (Social Security numbers) that should make identifying deceased voters simple and affordable. They should be able to check their voter rolls for dead voters quickly.
- What documentation do election officials accept as proof that a voter is a real, living person? In the Presto case, what documentation was used? A fraudulent driver's license? A photoshopped utility bill?
- Do voter registrations made within a month or two of an election receive less scrutiny by election officials than those made nine months before an election?

44 Court of Common Pleas of Allegheny County, Docket Number: CP-02-CR-0000303-2021, *Commonwealth of Pennsylvania v. Francis Fiore Presto*, https://the2020election.org/wp-content/uploads/2023/01/PA-Presto-Court-Records.pdf.

These questions are essential because, without any doubt, the process as executed by Allegheny County failed to prevent a fraudulent vote from being cast on behalf of a deceased individual. It would be cheap and easy to state that the problem must reside within this one specific Pennsylvania county. And it would be wrong.

Another deceased 2020 voter I identified to the Trump campaign was a woman named Elisabeth Bartman, who passed away in 2008. Her son, Bruce Bartman, was convicted of applying for a mail ballot in her name in early September 2020 and casting a vote on her behalf. Once again, the voter registration process failed to identify, in a timely way, that a newly registered voter was deceased. The Bartman voter fraud happened in Delaware County.

Bartman is a registered Republican and admitted that the fraudulent vote he cast in his mother's name was for Trump. Bartman received five years of probation as punishment for his crime.[45]

The Presto fraud would not have been visible to me had I not been able to broadly look at Pennsylvania's voter data immediately before the election. This is because election officials removed Mrs. Presto from the voter rolls soon after the election but before the state finalized its voter data with the 2020 results that the public can purchase. Most states make final election data available a few months after the election, with many states making the data available in February the year after.

Many folks who examine voter data do so using this late-coming data. Because of the Presto fraud, I realized that it was very likely that I did not see a lot of the most questionable data because the voter registrations involved were likely removed and cleaned up before the state released its "complete" trove.

45 Associated Press, "Man Admits to Voter Fraud in Casting Dead Mother's Ballot," AP News, April 30, 2021, https://apnews.com/article/election-2020-government-and-politics-d34effeea6c341d-6c44146931127caff.

The Judy Presto issue in Pennsylvania came up several times in the January 6 Committee deposition transcripts.

In Timothy Murtaugh's (a Trump campaign communications employee) deposition,[46] he is asked about my finding that Judy Presto had a vote cast in her name in 2020 though she died in 2013. The questioner was probing him to see if he was aware that the campaign had withheld the finding that the Presto vote was cast because her husband, a Republican, had committed the voter fraud. Murtaugh claimed he was not aware of the Presto issue.

Bernard Kerik, a reportedly close friend of Rudy Giuliani and former commissioner of the New York Police Department, was asked in his interview[47] about his work in researching deceased voters. Kerik was a vocal proponent of the theory that specific instances of voter fraud caused votes to be fraudulently cast for Biden. He was shown the Presto and Bartman dead voter issues from Pennsylvania and informed that the people charged with voter fraud in these two cases were Republicans. When asked if this fact caused him to reconsider his position that voter fraud caused the wrong result in the election, he acknowledged that "it would be taken into consideration, I guess," and then went on to claim without evidence that thousands of fraudulent votes had been cast in the election.

46 Select Committee to Investigate the January 6th Attack on the US Capitol, US House of Representatives, Interview of Timothy Murtaugh, May 19, 2022, Washington, DC, https://www.govinfo.gov/content/pkg/GPO-J6-TRANSCRIPT-CTRL0000083780/pdf/GPO-J6-TRANSCRIPT-CTRL0000083780.pdf.

47 Select Committee to Investigate the January 6th Attack on the US Capitol, US House of Representatives, Interview of Bernard Kerik, January 13, 2022, Washington, DC, https://www.govinfo.gov/content/pkg/GPO-J6-TRANSCRIPT-CTRL0000036628/pdf/GPO-J6-TRANSCRIPT-CTRL0000036628.pdf.

Chapter 14

CAMPAIGN WRAP-UP

There wasn't a formal conclusion to my work for the Trump campaign. We didn't have a summary meeting or conversation stating that the work was done. The multiple daily phone calls and text messages trickled down to just a few and then none.

Knowing firsthand the whirlwind that defines campaigns, I fully understood that other fires were now Alex's priority. I was asked for a summary of costs at the request of "Eric." The last campaign-related email from Alex said "Thanks" in response to my summary of campaign costs.

Cannon knew we did not find any evidence of substantial voter fraud during my work for the campaign. He said so many times to the January 6 Committee. He said so to Mark Meadows, Trump's chief of staff. I assume he has said so in response to any subpoenas he might have received in response to either Jack Smith's investigation of Trump or the Fulton County, Georgia, investigation of Trump.

The unavoidable truth is that I looked for and failed to find fraud sufficient to overturn any election result. The Berkeley Research Group also looked for and could not find evidence of substantial fraud in their work for the Trump campaign. Using thorough and recreatable data analytics, I disproved multiple claims of voter fraud made by others as well. This was well understood up the chain of command within the Trump campaign.

Some of you will viscerally and negatively react to the preceding paragraph. You will question my credentials, my credibility, my "agenda" (which was to deliver findings as required in my contract that would stand up in court), or my conclusions due to the unavailability of large amounts of data. There are important things to remember about what was happening in November 2020, my task, and the cold realities of our legal system's requirements for meeting the burden of proof:

- My contract tasked me with providing data analytics of sufficient quality to survive legal scrutiny. None of my results could provide the basis for a legitimate challenge to any election result. The data simply did not support a credible claim of voter fraud large enough to matter.
- The data set that was available to me—and everyone else—in this time period was incomplete. Yet this was the environment in which a legitimate fraud claim had to be made. A fraud claim cannot be credibly made based on data that is not available. Well after Joe Biden was installed as president, most of the data was available to everyone to allow someone to produce the proof that the election was stolen. No one has done so, even though so many people were heavily vested in proving that voter fraud impacted the 2020 election. If the evidence of that fraud was in the 2020 data, it would have been prominently exposed. There is no evidence of massive fraud in the data.
- I was willing to go to court to defend my findings of voter fraud, had any been identified that could have supported a lawsuit.
- Every claim of voter fraud I evaluated that others brought forward was false, usually because the person doing the

analysis did not understand the data or made egregious errors in their analysis. Hearsay claims such as "I saw someone do something" do not generally meet the legal burden of proof, and some of those hearsay claims that were made were later acknowledged to be lies by those who made them.

This did not mark my last communication with Cannon. That occurred in early June 2021, as I pulled into the driveway of a vacation rental for a week on the shore near Cape Cod, Massachusetts. I hid the call from my wife because bringing politics back into our lives at the start of a badly needed vacation would have marked me as an idiot.

Alex was calling on behalf of a group of folks who had performed some data research and determined that there were serious mail ballot problems in one of the special elections in Georgia (I don't remember which one). He asked me if I would speak with them regarding their findings.

As the family unpacked, I sat in on the call from my car when the issue was described. The "smoking gun" was the fact that the mail ballots they were looking at were numbered sequentially—in alphabetical order. They thought this was impossible and indicative of fraud. I explained that it was entirely feasible that the ballots could be numbered sequentially for a couple of different practical reasons and that this was not a foundational fact on which they could prove fraud.

There was pushback from the group, composed of something like physics or math instructors or CPAs; I honestly don't remember and was pretty distracted while this was happening. At the end of the call, I was asked if I would be willing to have a follow-up conversation with someone associated with the group.

My very last communication with Alex Cannon was a June 11, 2021, introductory email titled "Connections" with the text "Ken/ Bob – Connecting you both. Thanks, Alex." The Bob referred to in the email was Robert Cheeley, an attorney in Georgia.

Cheeley is one of nineteen individuals indicted in the Fulton County election matter. He is charged with perjury, violating Georgia's RICO Act, and eight other charges.[48]

I had not included this email in my Jack Smith subpoena response because it was outside the window that the subpoena covered. I did not initially include it in my Fulton County, Georgia, subpoena response because I had supplied everything I had given to the federal prosecutors. Once I found the email, I did provide it to the county's lawyers.

I can find no communications with Cheeley, and I don't remember speaking with him. Unfortunately, I replaced my phone in September 2021 and have no earlier text message or phone email history. If I did talk to him, the conversation was not memorable.

Reliving all these experiences through writing this book has been sobering. I had a front-row seat to many attempts to overturn the 2020 election result and stopped some of them because they relied upon a false claim. It was impossible then to appreciate how massive these efforts were and the many different attempts that were made beyond those I saw.

Had I known then what I know now, would I still have performed this work? I would—an unbiased, straight-up analysis of voter fraud claims needed to be done. Every voter fraud claim presented to me by the Trump campaign was disproven. The stakes—the integrity of our elections and the leadership of our country—are too high to be decided on false claims and data.

48 WSB-TV News Staff, "Here's What Each Defendant Is Charged with in Georgia Election Interference Indictment," WSBTV.com, August 15, 2023, https://www.wsbtv.com/news/local/fulton-county/heres-what-each-defendant-is-charged-with-georgia-election-interference-indictment/CV64AGLPZJC3XG7ZJIPWYI2FOI.

PART II

THE NUMBERS: DID FRAUD CAUSE TRUMP'S LOSS?

Chapter 15

COMPARATIVE ANALYTICS

Did nationwide voter fraud throw the 2020 presidential race to Joe Biden? Is there any way to use data to prove or disprove this claim? Is it possible that after Trump won so many more votes in 2020 than his 2016 performance, the only possible explanation for his 2020 loss is massive voter fraud?

Comparative analytics is the best way to begin digging into these questions. Comparative analytics involves taking two similar sets of data and, well . . . comparing them. Comparative analytics is often used to look for outliers in data. For example, fraud involving SNAP (commonly still referred to as food stamp benefits) was identified in Texas by looking at the number of transactions made late at night. A few retailers that accepted food stamps stood out as having many more late-night transactions than most other retailers, and it turned out after investigations that those retailers were committing SNAP fraud.

Comparative analytics is also used to compare similar sets of data collected at different times. For example, since Trump claimed massive fraud impacted the 2020 election results, can we find evidence of that fraud when comparing 2020 election data to 2016? Do broad data patterns emerge between the 2016 and 2020 elections? When taken side-by-side, could the results of those two elections tell us anything about what might have happened?

Do they ever! With the benefit of time, hindsight, and clean data, I took another look at the results of the 2020 election in March 2023. I used a data set of county-level presidential election results covering elections from 2000 to 2020 from the Massachusetts Institute of Technology's Election Data and Science Laboratory (Election Lab).[49] I only focused on election data from the 2016 and 2020 presidential elections. All the following data and analysis that flows from that data came from this set of Election Lab data. This data was not available immediately or anytime soon after the 2020 election.

The hours I thought I would spend on this turned into ten days of effort as some of the results of this seemingly straightforward analysis came out very interesting—at least to me.

County-level election data is something I had not looked at before. There are fascinating facts to know about counties in our country. For example, there are 3,155 counties in the United States. The smallest county in the country by 2020 vote totals is Loving County in Texas, where 66 votes were cast. In 78 counties nationwide, fewer than 1,000 votes were cast in the 2020 election. The three largest counties in the country by votes cast are Los Angeles County, California, with 4,264,365; Cook County, Illinois, with 2,321,486; and Maricopa County, Arizona, with 2,068,144.

The average number of votes cast in our counties in 2020 was 50,230, but 2,568 out of 3,155 counties had fewer than 50,230 votes cast in 2020, while 587 counties had more.

In 2020, tiny Loving County, Texas, cast 60 out of 66 votes for Trump. Trump cleaned up in our smallest counties in 2020, winning 89 percent of the counties with less than the nationwide average of

49 MIT Election Data and Science Lab, "County Presidential Election Returns 2000–2020," https://doi.org/10.7910/DVN/VOQCHQ, Harvard Dataverse, V11, UNF:6:HaZ8GWG-8D2abLleXN3uEig.

50,230 voters per county. Conversely, Trump won 51 percent of the counties with more votes than the average.

Just 183 counties had more than 200,000 votes cast in 2020, and Trump only won 20 percent of them. This is the quantification of the urban/rural divide in our country. But this divide is *not* why Trump lost the 2020 election.

In short, Trump won far more counties than Biden in 2020, but most of those counties had small or even tiny populations. When you see a map of our country painted red and blue depending on which state or county voted for which party, red overwhelms blue. However, the populations in those red places are typically much smaller than those in the blue places.

Chapter 16

RESULTS AND REASONS: WAS FRAUD TO BLAME?

I want to discuss my final results before walking through the process I used because that process was very data-heavy.

Trump took a smaller percentage of the votes compared to his Democrat challenger almost everywhere in 2020 compared to 2016. Let's call this dynamic *bleeding support.* Trump bled support from the vast majority of states but improved on his 2016 results in some of the bluest. Trump performed more poorly in 2020 than in 2016 in all but three red states.

In some large, blue counties, Trump narrowed the size of his loss in 2020 compared to 2016. He did not win, mind you, or come close to winning in these counties. However, his loss was not as bad in 2020 compared to 2016. This result does not support the narrative of voter fraud in those places. There is no reasonable way Trump can claim voter fraud caused his loss in these large, blue counties when he gained ground there relative to 2016.

In some of the 2020 battleground states, Trump's bleeding of support in red counties that he won in 2016 and 2020 represented more votes than Biden's margin of victory in that state. Put another way, Trump's 2020 election loss in states such as Arizona and Georgia can be blamed on his smaller margin of victory in the reddest counties in those states compared to 2016.

Why would anyone commit massive voter fraud in a red state where Trump enjoyed his most significant margin of victory? That state was Wyoming, where he engaged in a nasty war with Liz Cheney. Trump took a staggering 69.5 percent of the vote in Wyoming in 2020, an improvement from his 2016 performance of 68.17 percent. However, Biden improved on the Democrats' 2016 performance in Wyoming, pulling in 26.39 percent of the 2020 vote versus Clinton's 21.88 percent in 2016. Is this evidence of some unspecified and unproven fraud, or did the war with Cheney cost Trump nearly 9,000 votes in Wyoming?

Voter fraud cannot explain what amounts to a nationwide decrease in support for Trump in 2020 compared to 2016. With nothing but hot air behind the claim of massive voter fraud, the more reasonable explanation is the correct answer. This sagging support must have been known to Trump's campaign team well before the 2020 election.

It is not hard to explain why Trump bled support in so many places. How many voters that abandoned Trump were Republicans whom Trump had labeled and maligned as RINOs? How many Republicans and conservative-leaning independent voters heard Trump's siren call to the Proud Boys in a nationally televised debate just weeks before the election and decided they could bear no more? Trump's messaging became much more extreme during the campaign. While that helps to fire up "the base," it can be costly in terms of support from those who might lean conservative but stop short of MAGA.

Trump's 2020 campaign messaging perplexes me. It was simply not inclusive enough to appeal to enough voters to win. A chunk of the GOP is not in Trump's base. They don't wear MAGA caps, demonize Democrats, or revel in chaos. Trump has made it increasingly difficult for those voters to vote for him. And everything I just said predates the events leading up to and on January 6, 2021. I would expect that for every GOP-leaning voter Trump lost before the 2020 election, he lost many more after January 6. It is tough to see how he has a path to victory in 2024 without a massive change in his messaging, which seems unlikely.

Our national elections have become incredibly close as the level of partisanship has ratcheted way up. Every vote matters when ten thousand or twenty thousand votes can decide some statewide elections. Yes, a fraudulent vote cast in an election that close is highly problematic. However, how can a candidate express so much concern about losing a fraudulent ballot but appear not to care in the least about keeping a substantial number of conservative voters on board?

It is clear that Trump experienced a rejection of his message. The rejection was not massive; it only swung a few red states and counties to blue. However, the two- to three-percentage-point loss he experienced almost everywhere was sufficient to doom his campaign in the swing states that mattered. While no one can truly know how much Trump's messaging harmed his campaign, no one can reasonably discount that harm in races that were whisker-close.

The loss of support that Trump experienced should have been identified by campaign polling, which typically spares no expense—especially in national elections. Did Trump know about this loss of support before the election, then lose, blame voter fraud for the loss, and use the false claim to prod his supporters to violence? The Trump campaign had the results of my work that disproved every claim of voter fraud they sent my way, and yet Trump claimed voter fraud without any evidence. Ignoring multiple, expensive indications that voter fraud was not the cause of his loss makes an outrageous situation even more so.

Chapter 17

DATA

County Data

In the US, there are 2,580 red counties, which I define as having voted for Trump in 2016 and 2020. In 1,151 red counties (44 percent), Trump bled support in 2020 relative to 2016.

Across all 3,155 counties in the country, Trump bled support in 1,553 (49 percent). In just under half of the country's counties (including many red ones), Trump did worse in 2020 than in 2016. This is not indicative of fraud—it is a catastrophic, nationwide abandonment by enough Trump voters to swing the election to Biden.

Trump's performance in 2020 improved in roughly half of the counties compared to 2016. His problem is that those counties are relatively or very small in terms of total votes cast compared to the areas where his performance declined. The average number of total votes cast in the counties where Trump's performance improved was 26,200. The average number of total votes cast in counties where his performance declined was 74,975.

Third-Party Candidate Impact

The impact of third-party candidates on the contested swing states in 2020 cannot be ignored. Libertarian presidential candidate Jo Jorgensen earned more votes than Biden's margin of victory in Arizona, Georgia, Pennsylvania, and Wisconsin. Does this mean that Jorgensen was a "spoiler"? Did she cost Trump the election?

My introduction to politics was as a third-party gubernatorial candidate. I worked extremely hard for the 6.5 percent of the vote I won in Rhode Island in 2010. The Republican candidate (John Robitaille) entered the race late and with as little name recognition as I had. He lost by a small margin to a wealthy and well-known independent candidate in a four-way race. (In this race, the Democratic candidate, Frank Caprio, told President Obama to "shove it" when Obama refused to endorse him.)[50] Some Republicans, more than a decade later, still blame me for the GOP loss in 2010, which is bunk. Robitaille told me privately that he knows I was not the cause of his loss in 2010, and he endorsed my candidacy for governor as a Republican in 2014.

No candidate is entitled to anyone's vote. Votes are earned or lost based on what a candidate says or does or doesn't say or do. Many voters are often faced with a choice of just two candidates, neither of whom is a terrific choice. When a voter casts a vote for a third-party candidate, that vote is lost by the major party candidates—not stolen by the third-party candidate.

The Trump campaign should have targeted Libertarian voters in the swing states, convincing those voters that Trump was a more compelling choice than Jorgensen. If that effort was made, it fell quite short.

In an example of how the major parties fear third-party impacts, the Green Party was perceived as enough of a threat by Pennsylvania

50 Stephanie Condon, "Frank Caprio: Obama Can Take His Endorsement and 'Shove It,'" cbsnews.com, October 25, 2010, https://www.cbsnews.com/news/frank-caprio-obama-can-take-his-endorsement-and-shove-it.

Democrats in 2020 that the Dems used a legal technicality to keep the Greens off the ballot.[51]

Confirmational Evidence

One of Trump's chief pollsters was someone named Tony Fabrizio. In the interest of transparency, I will mention that Fabrizio did my polling in 2014. I last spoke with him in 2015 or 2016. Fabrizio authored a postmortem examination of what happened in ten swing states in 2020. He published this study in December 2020. I found the document in a link from a *Politico* story.[52] What is notable about this analysis is that it is based on exit polling—conversations with voters as they leave the polling place. The data upon which this analysis was built was not theoretical but concrete. The voters in these exit polls were not fraudulent—they were real-life people who told those conducting the exit poll why they voted and for whom.

Fabrizio broke the ten states into two groups: those that voted for Trump in 2016 and 2020 ("held") and those that voted for Trump in 2016 but went for Biden in 2020 ("flipped").

Some of Fabrizio's findings included:

- "POTUS [Trump] lost ground in both groups [flipped and held states] largely due to a massive swing against POTUS among Indies [independent voters] in both state groups and more GOP 'leakage' in 'Flipped' states." [Fabrizio's term *leakage* has the same meaning as my *bleeding support*.]
- "Voters who did not vote in '16 but voted in '20 accounted for roughly 1-in-6 voters and they broke markedly for Biden, especially in the 'Flipped' states. 1-in-10 voters say they decided their vote in the final month of the campaign, and contrary

51 Marc Levy, "Green Party Candidate Is Ordered off Pennsylvania Ballot," AP News, September 17, 2020, https://apnews.com/cbd7947a020a1c5983a69e804ce3a5f8.

52 "Post Election Exit Poll Analysis: 10 Key Target States," Prepared by Fabrizio, Lee & Associates, December 2020, https://www.politico.com/f/?id=00000177-6046-de2d-a57f-7a6e8c950000.

to conventional wisdom, they broke in Biden's favor in both [flipped and held states]."

- "9-in-10 voters in both groups said that SCOTUS [the Supreme Court of the United States] was a factor in deciding their vote. Ironically, those who said it was a factor voted for Biden in both state groups while those who said it wasn't a factor voted for POTUS [Trump] by large margins."

Messaging matters. Fabrizio's analysis indicates that what Trump said and did in the lead-up to the 2020 election turned off more voters than it attracted.

Trump's underperformance in 2020 relative to 2016 was large and widespread enough to have shown up in polling data. I suspect that it did. The trick, however, was in *who* was polled. Polling that just considered "likely voters" would have missed the "1-in-6" voters that Fabrizio identified who did not vote in 2016 but came out to vote in 2020.

In general, pollsters took a beating for getting the call wrong in 2016 and 2020. Before 2016, polling "likely voters" was safe—those who vote consistently in elections. Trump's candidacies motivated new voters to vote GOP in 2016, just as his presidency and 2020 candidacy motivated even more new voters to come out against him in November 2020.

National Data

Let's get into it. All the vote totals discussed here came from the data set I took from the Election Lab. They may or may not match up with vote totals that you find elsewhere.

2016 National Vote Totals	2020 National Vote Totals
136,491,561	158,477,710

2016 DEM Votes	2016 GOP Votes	2020 DEM Votes	2020 GOP Votes
65,841,224	62,978,383	81,264,648	74,218,999

When I look at the votes expressed in the preceding table as a percentage of all votes cast in the election, I get this:

2016 DEM Percent of Vote	2016 GOP Percent of Vote	2020 DEM Percent of Vote	2020 GOP Percent of Vote
48.23 percent	46.14 percent	51.27 percent	46.83 percent

Some of you might have done the math and wondered why the above percentages do not add up to 100 percent. The reason is third-party and write-in candidates. In 2016, the Democrats and Republicans combined to win 94.37 percent of the votes cast, meaning that 5.63 percent of the 2016 vote (7,684,474 votes) went to alternative candidates. In 2020, the Democrats and Republicans took 98.1 percent of the votes cast, meaning that 1.9 percent of the 2020 vote (3,011,076 votes) went to alternative candidates.

This is a stunning decrease in alternative candidate votes (and also write-in votes). While 2020 voter participation broke records, and the Democrat and Republican candidates smashed vote total records, third-party candidates won fewer votes in 2020 than in 2016.

No one can say for sure why this happened, although I have a theory. The Libertarian and Green parties take more votes than most other alternatives. While it is always dangerous to generalize as I am about to do, Libertarian-leaning voters are probably more likely to vote Republican than Democrat, and Green-leaning voters are probably more likely to vote Democrat than Republican. Both alternative parties saw a sharp decrease in votes won in 2020 compared to 2016. I suspect those voters felt more strongly about the Trump/Biden matchup than supporting their alternative candidate.

To compare how the Democrats and Republicans did between the two elections, let's subtract the 2016 DEM percentage of the vote from the 2020 DEM percentage of the vote, and subtract the 2016 GOP percentage of the vote from the 2020 GOP percentage of the vote, which gives us this:

DEM Percent Increase from 2016 to 2020	GOP Percent Increase from 2016 to 2020
51.27 - 48.23 = 3.04 percent	46.83 - 46.14 = 0.69 percent

Nationwide figures don't mean too much in the context of presidential elections in the United States since the winner is not necessarily the candidate who wins the most votes nationwide. Nevertheless, I provide the preceding data to help frame what follows. Observe how Biden, on a national scale, enjoyed a much more significant increase in the percentage of the vote won between 2016 and 2020 than Trump did.

State Data

Now let's move things down to the state level. We will look separately at red, blue, and purple states. I am defining a red state as a state that voted for the Republican in 2016 and 2020, a blue state as one that voted for the Democrat in those two elections, and purple for states that split or were one of my six states of interest in the work done for the Trump campaign (Arizona, Georgia, Michigan, Nevada, Pennsylvania, and Wisconsin).

There are two calculated columns in the next chart. The first is labeled "GOP Margin Difference" and is calculated this way: take ("GOP 2020 % of Vote" – "DEM 2020 % of Vote") and subtract ("GOP 2016 % of Vote" – "DEM 2016 % of Vote"). This tells us whether Trump's performance in 2020 was better or worse than in 2016. The last column of data is labeled "Vote Difference," which is the "GOP Margin Difference" multiplied by the total votes cast in that state for 2020. Negative vote differences represent a state where Trump's overall performance declined in 2020 from 2016.

The following chart shows how Trump performed in 2020 relative to 2016 in red states.

State	DEM 2016 % of Vote	GOP 2016 % of Vote	DEM 2020 % of Vote	GOP 2020 % of Vote	GOP Margin Difference 2020 - 2016	Vote Difference
AK	36.57%	51.32%	43.01%	53.12%	-4.62%	-16,534
AL	34.36%	62.08%	36.57%	62.03%	-2.26%	-52,583
AR	33.68%	60.61%	34.78%	62.40%	0.68%	8,315
FL	47.82%	49.02%	47.86%	51.22%	2.16%	239,029
IA	41.74%	51.15%	44.89%	53.35%	-0.95%	-16,109
ID	27.48%	59.25%	33.09%	63.89%	-0.97%	-8,387
IN	37.77%	56.94%	40.96%	57.02%	-3.11%	-94,201
KS	36.05%	56.65%	41.56%	56.21%	-5.95%	-81,642
KY	32.68%	62.52%	36.17%	62.13%	-3.88%	-82,895
LA	38.45%	58.09%	39.85%	58.46%	-1.03%	-22,118
MO	38.15%	56.80%	41.41%	56.80%	-3.25%	-98,476
MS	40.11%	57.94%	41.06%	57.60%	-1.28%	-16,828
MT	35.75%	56.17%	40.55%	56.92%	-4.05%	-24,464
NC	46.17%	49.83%	48.59%	49.93%	-2.31%	-127,463
ND	27.23%	62.96%	31.76%	65.11%	-2.37%	-8,581
NE	33.70%	58.75%	39.36%	58.51%	-5.90%	-56,127
OH	43.56%	51.69%	45.24%	53.27%	-0.10%	-5,781
OK	28.93%	65.32%	32.29%	65.37%	-3.30%	-51,567
SC	40.67%	54.94%	43.43%	55.11%	-2.59%	-64,987
SD	31.74%	61.53%	35.61%	61.77%	-3.63%	-15,337
TN	34.72%	60.72%	37.45%	60.66%	-2.80%	-85,411
TX	43.24%	52.23%	46.48%	52.06%	-3.42%	-387,069
UT	27.46%	45.54%	37.47%	57.86%	2.31%	34,507
WV	26.48%	68.63%	29.70%	68.63%	-3.22%	-25,577
WY	21.88%	68.17%	26.39%	69.50%	-3.18%	-8,866
					Red State Lost Votes	-1,069,153

Here are Trump's vote percentages, graphed by state.

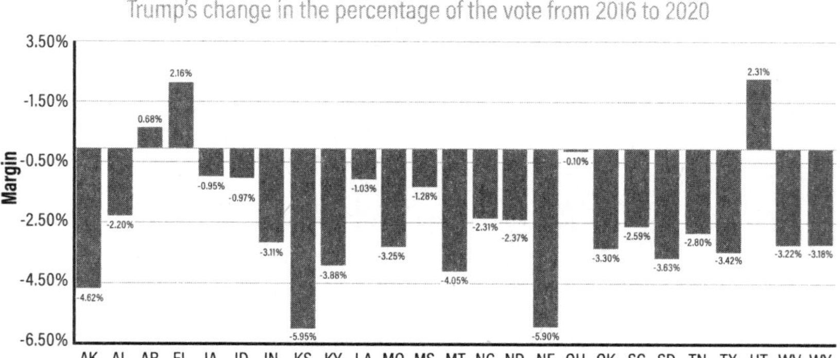

Raw data from MIT's Election Data and Science Laboratory. https://doi.org/10.7910/DVN/VOQCHQ
©2024 Ken Block

On average, Trump's 2020 margin of victory in the red states was 2.36 percent *lower* than his 2016 margin of victory. Arkansas, Florida, and Utah were the only red states where Trump did not lose ground relative to his performance in 2016.

Now let's look at the blue states. Nevada, by the definition I gave previously, is a blue state since it voted Democrat in both 2016 and 2020. However, since Nevada was one of the states into which I was asked to look by the Trump campaign, I put it in with the purple states.

State	DEM 2016 % of Vote	GOP 2016 % of Vote	DEM 2020 % of Vote	GOP 2020 % of Vote	GOP Margin Difference 2020 - 2016	Vote Difference
CA	61.73%	31.62%	63.48%	34.32%	0.95%	165,571
CO	48.16%	43.25%	55.40%	41.90%	-8.60%	-279,971
CT	54.57%	40.93%	59.26%	39.19%	-6.43%	-117,351
DC	90.86%	4.09%	92.15%	5.40%	0.02%	83
DE	53.18%	41.79%	58.78%	39.80%	-7.59%	-38,237
HI	62.22%	30.04%	63.73%	34.27%	2.72%	15,604

State	DEM 2016 % of Vote	GOP 2016 % of Vote	DEM 2020 % of Vote	GOP 2020 % of Vote	GOP Margin Difference 2020 - 2016	Vote Difference
IL	55.60%	38.61%	57.54%	40.55%	0.01%	424
MA	60.93%	33.31%	65.12%	31.91%	-5.60%	-204,803
MD	60.33%	33.91%	65.36%	32.15%	-6.79%	-206,334
ME	47.68%	45.02%	52.33%	43.75%	-5.92%	-48,712
MN	46.44%	44.92%	52.40%	45.28%	-5.59%	-183,195
NH	46.83%	46.46%	52.86%	45.49%	-7.01%	-56,322
NJ	55.45%	41.35%	57.33%	41.40%	-1.83%	-83,479
NM	48.26%	40.04%	54.29%	43.50%	-2.58%	-23,834
NY	59.00%	36.52%	60.39%	37.46%	-0.45%	-38,627
OR	50.07%	39.09%	56.45%	40.37%	-5.11%	-121,286
RI	54.41%	38.90%	59.39%	38.61%	-5.27%	-27,267
VA	49.73%	44.41%	54.08%	43.98%	-4.79%	-213,674
VT	56.68%	30.27%	65.48%	30.39%	-8.68%	-32,192
WA	54.30%	38.07%	57.97%	38.77%	-2.97%	-121,391
					Blue State Lost Votes	-1,614,995

On average, Trump's 2020 vote margin in the blue states was 4.08 percent *lower* than his 2016 vote margin. His performance was worse, on average, in 2020 relative to 2016. Surprisingly, Trump did better in 2020 than in 2016 in California, Washington, DC, Hawaii, and Illinois.

Blue State Margins

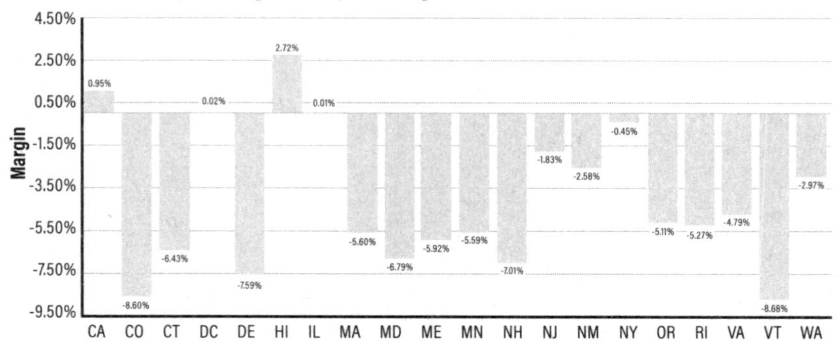

Raw data from MIT's Election Data and Science Laboratory. https://doi.org/10.7910/DVN/VOQCHQ
©2024 Ken Block

Finally, the purple states.

State	DEM 2016 % of Vote	GOP 2016 % of Vote	DEM 2020 % of Vote	GOP 2020 % of Vote	GOP Margin Difference 2020 - 2016	Vote Difference
AZ	44.59%	48.09%	49.39%	49.09%	-3.81%	-129,052
GA	45.64%	50.77%	49.51%	49.25%	-5.38%	-269,161
MI	47.27%	47.50%	50.62%	47.84%	-3.01%	-166,542
NV	47.92%	45.50%	50.06%	47.66%	0.02%	253
PA	47.85%	48.58%	50.01%	48.84%	-1.89%	-130,640
WI	46.44%	47.20%	49.45%	48.83%	-1.39%	-45,669
					Purple State Lost Votes	-740,812

On average, Trump's 2020 vote margin in the purple states was 2.58 percent *lower* than his 2016 vote margin. The purple states are, except Nevada, populous states with many millions of voters. In 2020, Pennsylvania had 6.9 million voters, Michigan 5.5 million, Georgia 5 million, Arizona 3.3 million, and Wisconsin 3.2 million voters. Losing a couple percent of that many voters adds up to many lost votes.

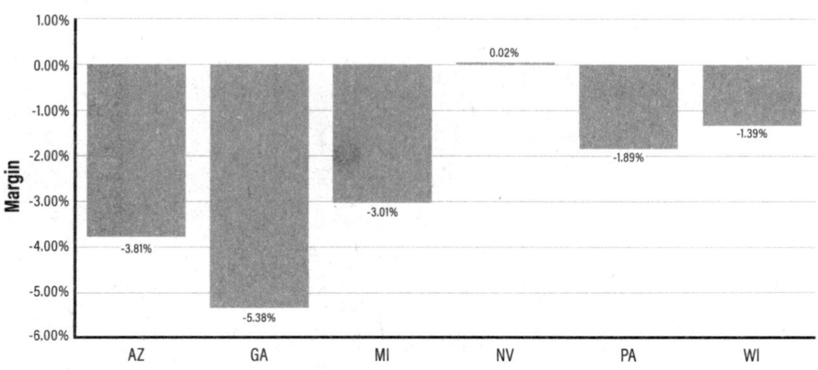

Raw data from MIT's Election Data and Science Laboratory. https://doi.org/10.7910/DVN/VOQCHQ

Chapter 18

SWING STATE COUNTY-LEVEL DATA ANALYSIS

Let's dissect what happened in the six purple states in 2020. I will gently remind you that I was paid by the Trump campaign to look for evidence of massive fraud in the election data and that I found nothing that came close to proving that large-scale voter fraud occurred in those six states. I have shown that Trump took a performance hit literally across the nation when looking at statewide election data.

By looking at county-level data, let's tackle each swing state separately.

Arizona

2016 Total Vote	2016 DEM Vote	2016 GOP Vote	Margin	2016 Libertarian Vote	2016 Green Vote	2016 Other Vote	2016 Write-in
2,604,277	1,161,167	1,252,401	91,234	106,327	34,345	0	18,883
2020 Total Vote	**2020 DEM Vote**	**2020 GOP Vote**	**Margin**	**2020 Libertarian Vote**	**2020 Green Vote**	**2020 Other Vote**	**2020 Write-in**
3,385,294	1,672,143	1,661,686	10,457	51,465	1,557	0	475

Arizona went for Trump in 2016 by 91,234 votes, or 3.78 percent over Clinton.

Arizona went for Biden in 2020 by 10,457 votes, or 0.31 percent over Trump.

Note that the Libertarian candidate, Jo Jorgensen, took 51,465 votes in 2020, nearly five times more than Biden's margin of victory. Had Trump's message better appealed to just a handful of Libertarian voters, he could have won. Also, note how the Green Party's votes almost completely disappeared in 2020 compared to 2016. Had the Green Party's candidate pulled as many votes in 2020 as they did in 2016, Biden could have lost.

I also find it remarkable that the number of write-in votes plummeted in 2020, from 18,883 in 2016 to just 475 in 2020. Many voters who cast "protest votes" in 2016 (the "vote them all out" crowd) appeared not to do so in 2020. More voters cast write-in ballots for president in 2016 than Biden's margin of victory in 2020.

The 2020 race in Arizona was amazingly close. The state endured an intense focus on voter and election fraud after the election, which found no substantial fraud (remember the Cyber Ninjas, who got paid millions and found nothing substantively wrong with the election?). There are plenty of viable reasons why Biden squeaked out a victory that do not include voter fraud.

The following chart shows how Trump underperformed in most Arizona counties in 2020 relative to 2016. Counties in red are counties that voted for Trump in both elections, blue voted Democrat in both years, and the one county that split is purple. The data behind this chart is displayed in the Appendix.*

For the remaining graphics in this chapter, the designations of red, blue, and purple states will be displayed using the grayscale colors as shown in this legend. The lightest color represents blue states, the darkest color red, and the color in-between represents purple states.

Blue **Red** **Purple**

County Margins for Arizona

Trump's change in the percentage of the vote from 2016 to 2020

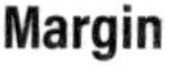

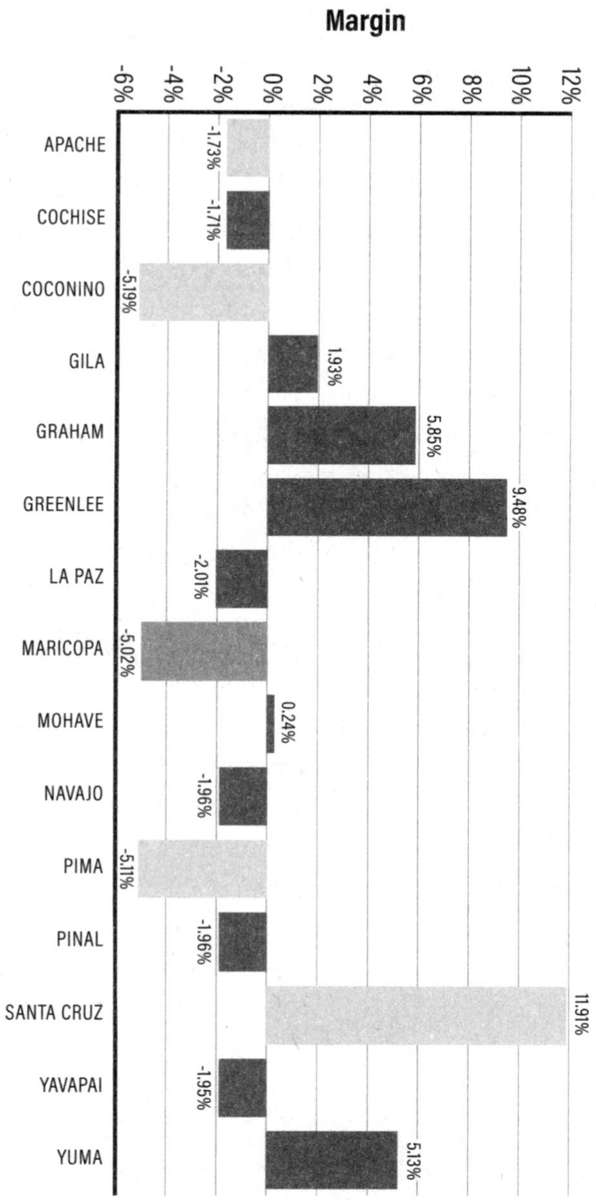
Margin
-6%
-4%
-2%
0%
2%
4%
6%
8%
10%
12%
APACHE -1.73%
COCHISE -1.71%
COCONINO -5.19%
GILA 1.93%
GRAHAM 5.85%
GREENLEE 9.48%
LA PAZ -2.01%
MARICOPA -5.02%
MOHAVE 0.24%
NAVAJO -1.96%
PIMA -5.11%
PINAL -1.96%
SANTA CRUZ 11.91%
YAVAPAI -1.95%
YUMA 5.13%

Raw data from MIT's Election Data and Science Laboratory. https://doi.org/10.7910/DVN/VOQCHQ

Maricopa County is most definitely an area of concern for Republican candidates: it has by far the largest population of any Arizona county, it is amongst the fastest-growing counties in the state, and it went from electing Trump in 2016 to electing Biden in 2020.

While Trump extended his margin of victory in some counties in 2020 versus 2016, most counties where he did this were relatively small. See Gila, Graham, and Greenlee counties. Yuma was the only larger county where Trump extended his margin of victory as a percentage of the vote cast. What happened in Arizona's other red counties in 2020 should give Trump heartburn. He lost ground in the percentage of his margin in Cochise, La Paz, Navajo, Pinal, and Yavapai counties. His total votes lost due to bleeding support comes to 8,623 votes—nearly Biden's overall margin of victory (10,457).

The only blue county where the Democrats lost ground is Santa Cruz.

Does this mean that Republicans are doomed in Arizona? Remember that Arizona's largest statewide vote-getter in 2022 was a Republican, the candidate for treasurer. While every statewide Republican who embraced election conspiracy theories lost their race in 2022, Kimberly Yee (a more moderate conservative who did not endorse election conspiracy theories) showed that Arizona as a state remains winnable for a Republican with a message geared toward a broader audience. More pointedly, Yee took Maricopa County in 2022—by 11 percentage points.

Georgia

2016 Total Vote	2016 DEM Vote	2016 GOP Vote	Margin	2016 Libertarian Vote	2016 Green Vote	2016 Other Vote	2016 Write-in
4,114,711	1,877,963	2,089,104	211,141	125,306	0	0	22,359
2020 Total Vote	**2020 DEM Vote**	**2020 GOP Vote**	**Margin**	**2020 Libertarian Vote**	**2020 Green Vote**	**2020 Other Vote**	**2020 Write-in**
4,998,482	2,474,507	2,461,839	12,670	62,229	1,013	0	1,231

Georgia went for Trump in 2016 by 211,141 votes or 5.13 percent.

Georgia voted for Biden in 2020 by 12,670 votes (I know this is off from pretty much every news account from Georgia, which says the margin was 11,779 votes, but this is what the data from the MIT Election Lab shows, so that is what I am going with) or 0.25 percent. The difference in vote totals is probably due to the timing of when the county vote totals were pulled. Or perhaps one or two counties provided their data in a way that the researchers who did the work did not expect. The difference does not worry me; it is by no means a smoking gun that fraud occurred. The MIT Data Lab's data show a bigger win for Biden in Georgia, not a smaller one.

Like the situation in Arizona, Libertarian presidential candidate Jo Jorgensen received enough votes in 2020 in Georgia to cover Biden's margin of victory five times over. It is far more likely that Trump's inability to peel Jorgensen's voters away was the deciding factor in his loss in Georgia rather than voter fraud.

Georgia's election results were thoroughly reviewed and audited multiple times, with no substantial fraud uncovered.[53]

The smallest Georgia county in votes cast was Taliaferro County, with 928 votes, a blue county. Quitman and Webster counties are the next smallest counties in vote counts, with 1,106 and 1,390 votes cast. They are both red counties. Trump lost ground in both in 2020. Here is their data.

State	County	Total 2020 Votes	DEM 2016 % of Vote	GOP 2016 % of Vote	DEM 2020 % of Vote	GOP 2020 % of Vote	GOP Margin Difference 2020 - 2016	Vote Difference
GA	TALIAFERRO	928	60.76%	38.91%	60.45%	38.79%	0.19%	2
GA	QUITMAN	1,106	44.16%	55.08%	44.94%	54.61%	-1.25%	-14
GA	WEBSTER	1,390	42.38%	56.45%	45.97%	53.81%	-6.23%	-87

53 Office of Georgia Secretary of State Brad Raffensperger, "2020 General Election Risk-Limiting Audit," https://sos.ga.gov/page/2020-general-election-risk-limiting-audit; Kate Brumback, "Georgia Again Certifies Election Results Showing Biden Won," AP News, December 7, 2020, https://apnews.com/article/election-2020-joe-biden-donald-trump-georgia-elections-4eee-a3b24f10de886bcdeab6c26b680a.

Quitman and Webster counties embody Trump's 2020 problem. He bled support in both places. If ever there was a perfect place to prove voter fraud happened, it would be in these two counties, which are small, red, and rural. What can explain his loss of support? Did 87 new voters fraudulently register to vote in Webster before the 2020 election? How many of the 2020 voters in Webster also cast ballots in 2016? Unfortunately, I do not have voter registration data from immediately after the 2016 election in Georgia, so I cannot conduct this analysis. But for any of the folks heavily invested in screaming about voter fraud in 2020, Webster County is your chance to prove it! Go to Webster; I'll go with you. Let's sift through the data and canvass the voters.

I am not kidding: Webster is interesting. Using voter registration data from November 18, 2019, 63 voters in Webster cast ballots in 2020 who were not registered to vote in 2019. Of those 63 voters, 43 cast their 2020 ballots by mail, and 24 were born after 1998, meaning they were likely students or underage in 2019. That leaves 39 potential fraudulent voters to track down. Heck, look at all 63. If fraud is the cause of Trump's bleeding support in Webster, it explains similar results nationwide. If no fraud can be found, it is beyond time to shut up.

Using graphics to depict voting data from Georgia's 159 counties is very difficult, so I decided to break Georgia's counties up by size. A total of 74 Georgia counties cast 10,000 or fewer votes in 2020, and 85 counties cast more than 10,000 votes.

The following five charts I display show how Trump's percentage of the vote changed from 2016 to 2020. I broke out the data by showing all the blue and purple counties in one chart, red counties with fewer than 10,000 votes spread across two charts, and red counties with more than 10,000 votes spread across the last two charts. I will display the small and large charts next to each other because their differences are significant.

County Margins for Georgia Blue and Purple Counties

Trump's change in the percentage of the vote from 2016 to 2020

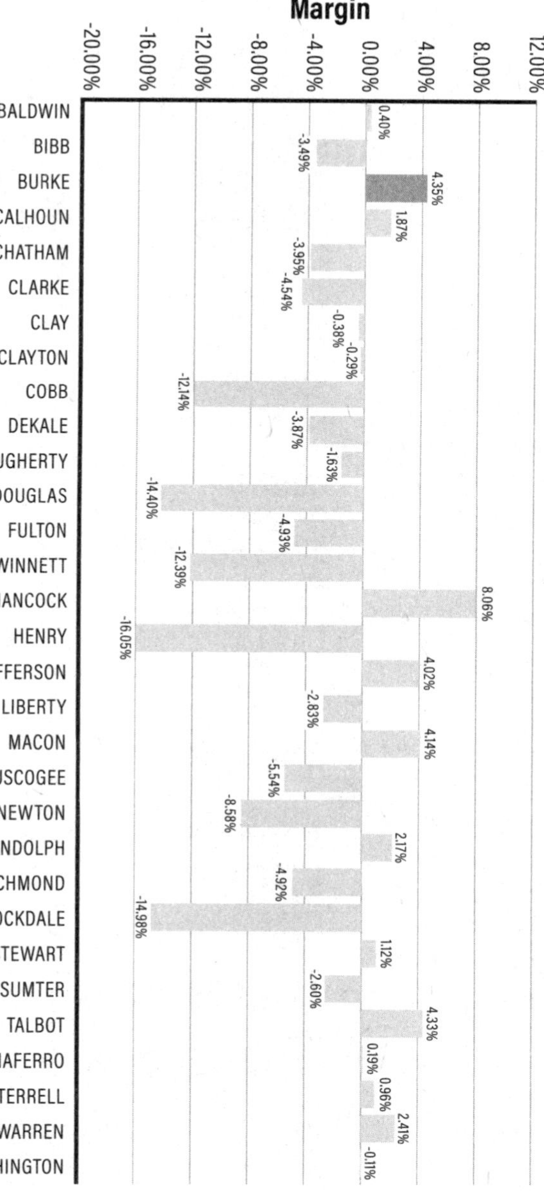

Raw data from MIT's Election Data and Science Laboratory, https://doi.org/10.7910/DVN/VOQCHQ

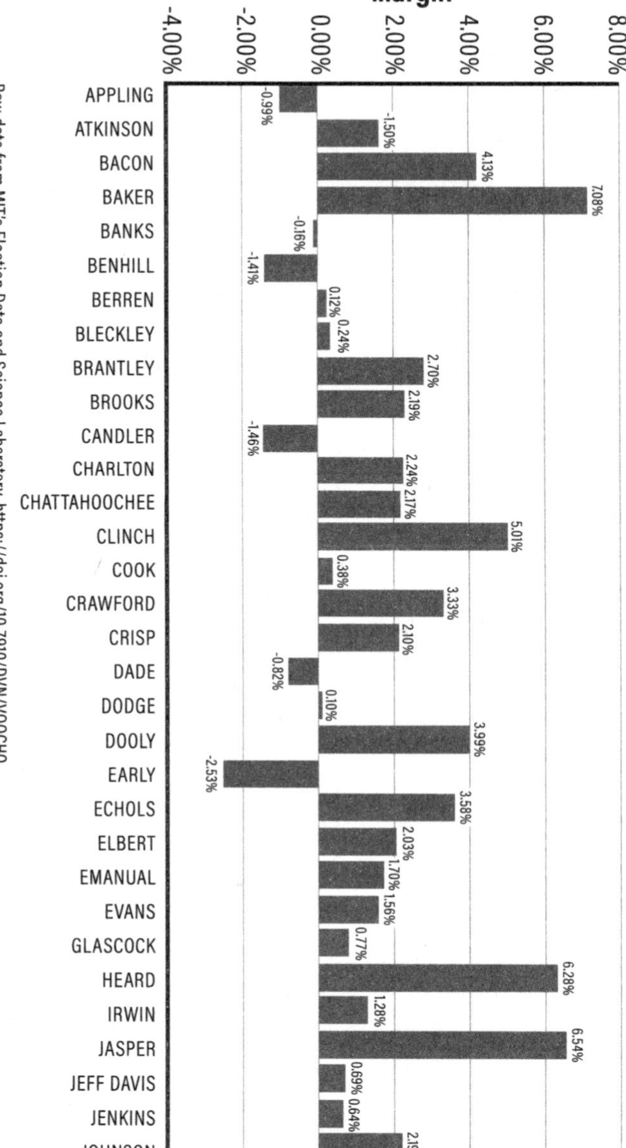
County Margins for GA Small Red Counties (A-J)
Trump's change in the percentage of the vote from 2016 to 2020
Margin
-4.00%
-2.00%
0.00%
2.00%
4.00%
6.00%
8.00%
APPLING
-0.99%
ATKINSON
1.50%
BACON
4.13%
BAKER
7.08%
BANKS
-0.16%
BENHILL
-1.41%
BERREN
0.12%
BLECKLEY
0.24%
BRANTLEY
2.70%
BROOKS
2.19%
CANDLER
-1.46%
CHARLTON
2.24%
CHATTAHOOCHEE
2.17%
CLINCH
5.01%
COOK
0.38%
CRAWFORD
3.33%
CRISP
2.10%
DADE
-0.82%
DODGE
0.10%
DOOLY
3.99%
EARLY
-2.53%
ECHOLS
3.58%
ELBERT
2.03%
EMANUAL
1.70%
EVANS
1.56%
GLASCOCK
0.77%
HEARD
6.28%
IRWIN
1.28%
JASPER
6.54%
JEFF DAVIS
0.69%
JENKINS
0.64%
JOHNSON
2.19%
Raw data from MIT's Election Data and Science Laboratory. https://doi.org/10.7910/DVN/VOQCHQ
©2024 Ken Block

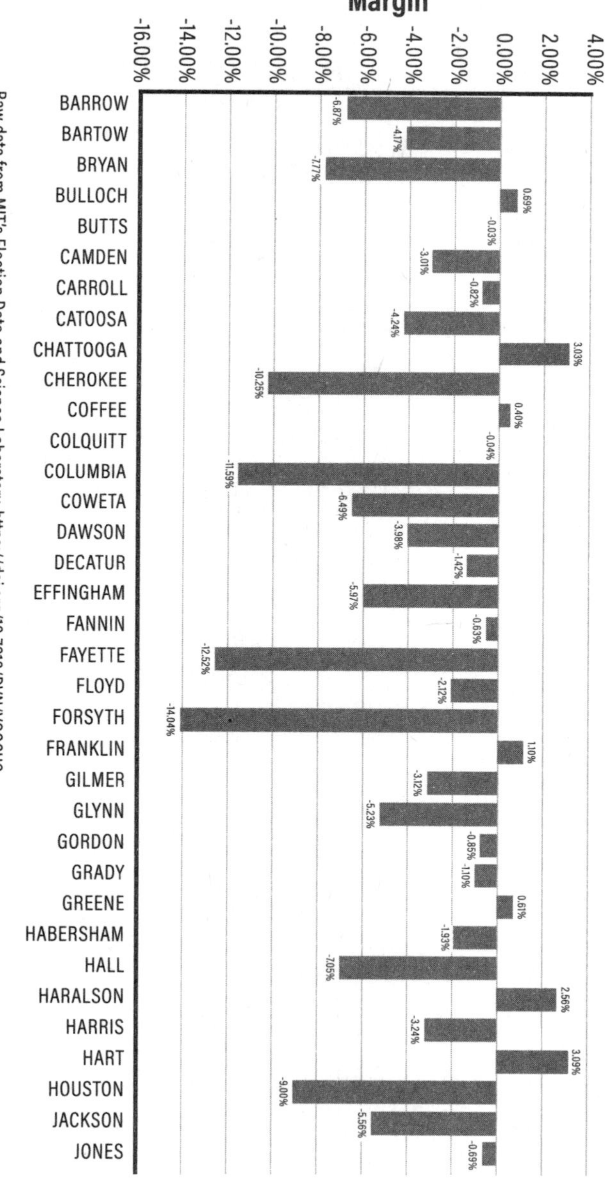
County Margins for GA Large Red Counties (A-J)
Trump's change in the percentage of the vote from 2016 to 2020
Margin
4.00%
2.00%
0.00%
-2.00%
-4.00%
-6.00%
-8.00%
-10.00%
-12.00%
-14.00%
-16.00%
BARROW -6.87%
BARTOW -4.17%
BRYAN -7.77%
BULLOCH 0.69%
BUTTS -0.03%
CAMDEN -3.01%
CARROLL -0.82%
CATOOSA -4.24%
CHATTOOGA 3.03%
CHEROKEE -10.25%
COFFEE 0.40%
COLQUITT -0.04%
COLUMBIA -11.59%
COWETA -6.49%
DAWSON -3.98%
DECATUR -1.42%
EFFINGHAM -5.97%
FANNIN -0.63%
FAYETTE -12.52%
FLOYD -2.12%
FORSYTH -14.04%
FRANKLIN 1.10%
GILMER -3.12%
GLYNN -5.23%
GORDON -0.85%
GRADY -1.10%
GREENE 0.61%
HABERSHAM -1.93%
HALL -7.05%
HARALSON 2.56%
HARRIS -3.24%
HART 3.09%
HOUSTON -9.00%
JACKSON -5.56%
JONES -0.69%
Raw data from MIT's Election Data and Science Laboratory. https://doi.org/10.7910/DVN/VOQCHQ
©2024 Ken Block

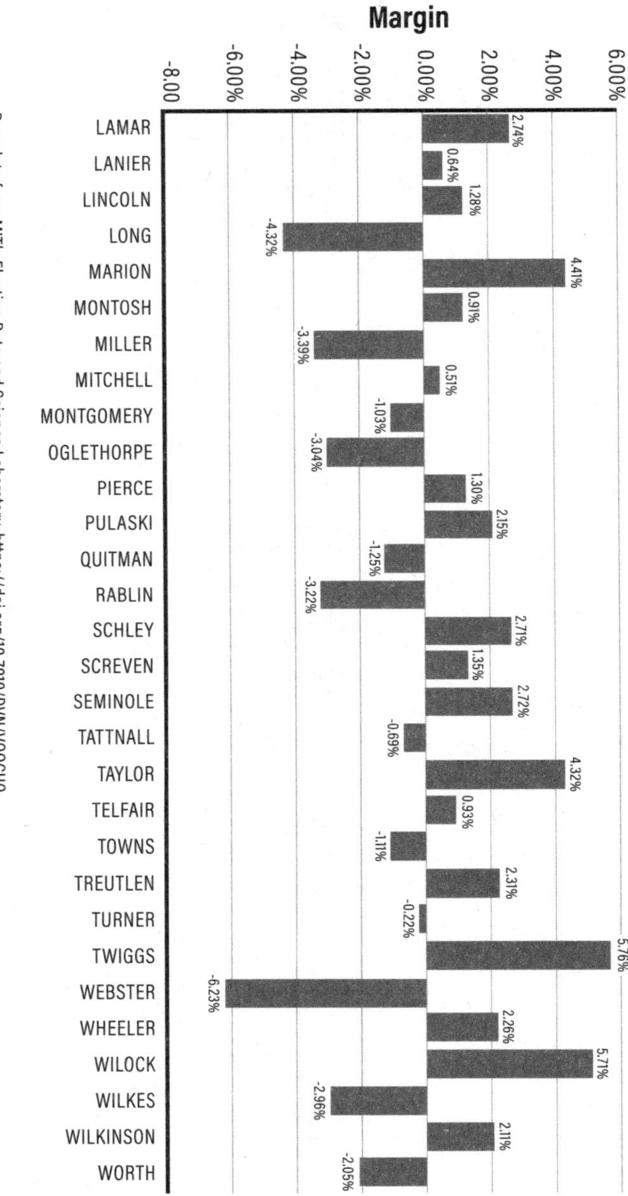
County Margins for GA Small Red Counties (K-Z)
Trump's change in the percentage of the vote from 2016 to 2020
Margin
-8.00
-6.00%
-4.00%
-2.00%
0.00%
2.00%
4.00%
6.00%
LAMAR 2.74%
LANIER 0.64%
LINCOLN 1.28%
LONG -4.32%
MARION 4.41%
MONTOSH 0.91%
MILLER -3.39%
MITCHELL 0.51%
MONTGOMERY -1.03%
OGLETHORPE -3.04%
PIERCE 1.30%
PULASKI 2.15%
QUITMAN -1.25%
RABLIN -3.22%
SCHLEY 2.71%
SCREVEN 1.35%
SEMINOLE 2.72%
TATTNALL -0.69%
TAYLOR 4.32%
TELFAIR 0.93%
TOWNS -1.11%
TREUTLEN 2.31%
TURNER -0.22%
TWIGGS 5.76%
WEBSTER -6.23%
WHEELER 2.26%
WILOCK 5.71%
WILKES -2.96%
WILKINSON 2.11%
WORTH -2.05%
Raw data from MIT's Election Data and Science Laboratory. https://doi.org/10.7910/DVN/VOQCHQ
©2024 Ken Block

County Margins for GA Large Red Counties (K-Z)

Trump's change in the percentage of the vote from 2016 to 2020

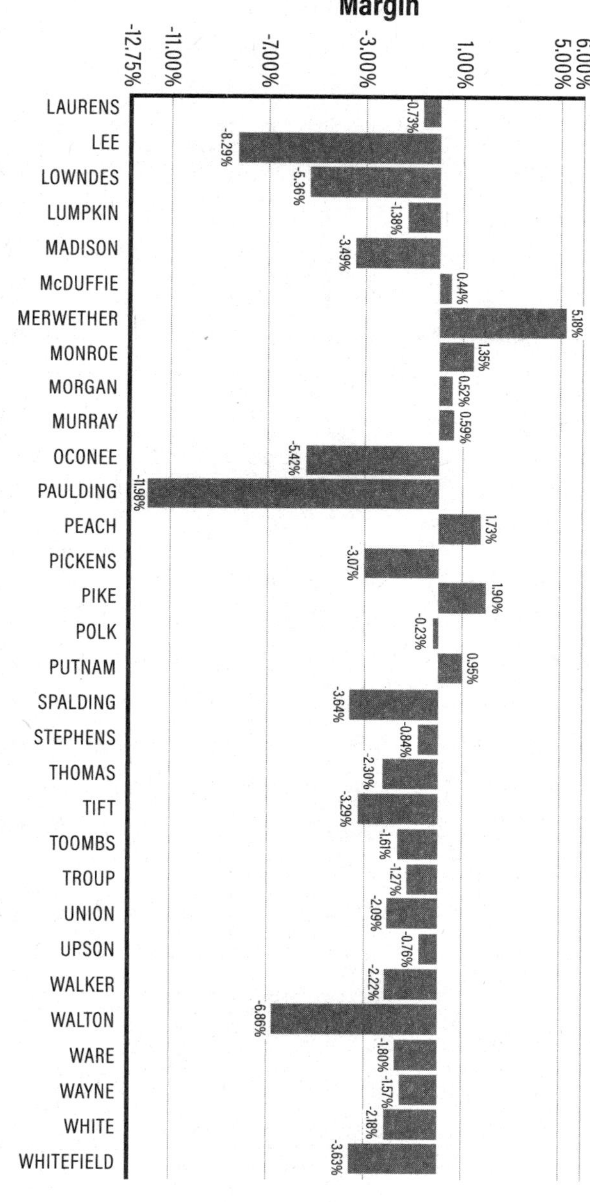

Raw data from MIT's Election Data and Science Laboratory. https://doi.org/10.7910/DVN/VOQCHQ

Trump did not perform uniformly poorly in the blue counties. While he did not win them, he did better in some of them in 2020 than in 2016.

The contrast between the four preceding GOP charts is incredible to me. Trump did far better in Georgia's tiniest red counties than he did in Georgia's larger red counties. There is no doubt in my mind that Trump lost Georgia due to his relatively poor performance in the larger red counties in 2020 compared to 2016.

Just like Arizona, Georgia's county-level data contains bad news for Trump. The overall result in Georgia is stunning. In the red counties that Trump won in 2020, he potentially left behind 107,599 votes due to the smaller size of his wins compared to 2016. When the swing in all counties is totaled, it adds up to more than 300,000 votes across the state.

Trump's bad news is clearly not the Georgia GOP's bad news. Incumbent GOP governor Brian Kemp won in 2022, winning 53.41 percent of the statewide vote against Democrat Stacey Abrams, who took 45.88 percent of the vote. Incumbent GOP secretary of state Brad Raffensperger won 53.23 percent of the vote against his Democrat challenger, who took 43.99 percent. And, of course, Herschel Walker lost his US Senate runoff election against the Democratic incumbent Raphael Warnock, 48.49 percent to 49.44 percent.[54]

What is the difference between Kemp, Raffensperger, and Walker? Only Walker wholly embraced election conspiracy theories. Republicans will likely continue to win elections in Georgia, assuming they have broad appeal.

The data behind these charts is displayed in the Appendix.*

54 Office of Georgia Secretary of State Brad Raffensperger, "Results," updated November 21, 2022, https://results.enr.clarityelections.com/GA/115465/web.307039/#/summary.

Michigan

2020 Total Vote	2020 DEM Vote	2020 GOP Vote	Margin	2020 Libertarian Vote	2020 Green Vote	2020 Other Vote	2020 Write-in
5,539,302	2,804,040	2,649,852	154,188	60,381	13,718	10,221	1,090
2016 Total Vote	**2016 DEM Vote**	**2016 GOP Vote**	**Margin**	**2016 Libertarian Vote**	**2016 Green Vote**	**2016 Other Vote**	**2016 Write-in**
4,799,284	2,268,839	2,279,543	10,704	172,136	51,463	18,348	8,955
2020/2016 increase	19.09%	13.97%					

Michigan has eighty-three counties, of which Trump won seventy-two in 2020, while Biden won eleven. Three of the counties Biden won in 2020, Trump won in 2016: Kent, Leelanau, and Saginaw.

In Michigan, Jo Jorgensen failed to take enough votes as the Libertarian Party's candidate to account for Biden's margin of victory in 2020: Jorgensen got 60,381 votes, Biden's margin was 154,188.

Trump barely eked out the win in 2016 by just 10,704 votes. Biden's margin in 2020 was 154,188. Does Michigan follow the same pattern as Arizona and Georgia when we look at county-level results? Did Trump bleed off enough support in red counties alone to cover Biden's margin of victory? In the case of Michigan, no. Trump lost 70,279 votes based on a declining margin of victory in red counties in 2020 as opposed to 2016.

Michigan has elected Democrats for president since 1992, except for Trump's extremely close win in 2016, when he squeaked by with a tiny margin the same size as Arizona's and Georgia's in 2020. Interestingly, Trump has never mentioned Michigan as a likely target of voter fraud based on the close results in 2016, which he won, but he contests the results in 2020, where he lost Michigan by many more votes than he won by four years before.

In 2020, Trump had trouble maintaining his margins of victory in red states and counties across the country. It is not the least bit

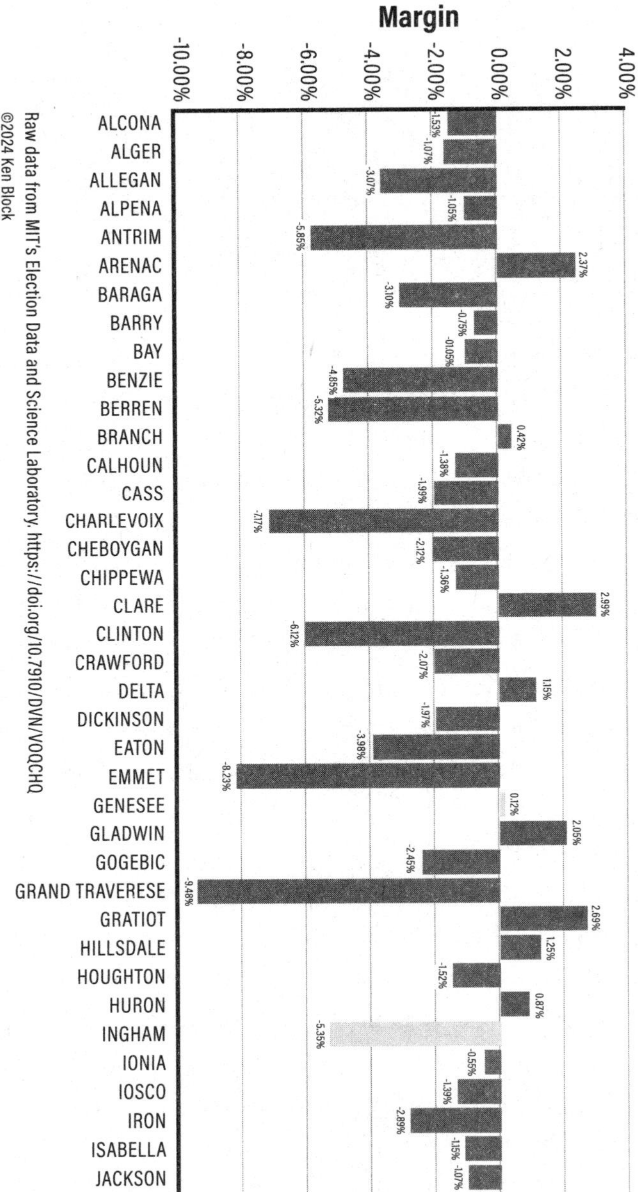
County Margins for Michigan (A-J)
Trump's change in the percentage of the vote from 2016 to 2020
Margin
4.00%
2.00%
0.00%
-2.00%
-4.00%
-6.00%
-8.00%
-10.00%
ALCONA -1.53%
ALGER -1.07%
ALLEGAN -3.07%
ALPENA -1.05%
ANTRIM -5.85%
ARENAC 2.37%
BARAGA -3.10%
BARRY -0.75%
BAY -01.05%
BENZIE -4.85%
BERREN -5.32%
BRANCH 0.42%
CALHOUN -1.38%
CASS -1.99%
CHARLEVOIX -7.17%
CHEBOYGAN -2.12%
CHIPPEWA -1.36%
CLARE 2.99%
CLINTON -6.12%
CRAWFORD -2.07%
DELTA 1.15%
DICKINSON -1.97%
EATON -3.98%
EMMET -8.23%
GENESEE 0.12%
GLADWIN 2.05%
GOGEBIC -2.45%
GRAND TRAVERESE -9.48%
GRATIOT 2.69%
HILLSDALE 1.25%
HOUGHTON -1.52%
HURON 0.87%
INGHAM -5.35%
IONIA -0.55%
IOSCO -1.39%
IRON -2.89%
ISABELLA -1.15%
JACKSON -1.07%
Raw data from MIT's Election Data and Science Laboratory, https://doi.org/10.7910/DVN/VOQCHQ
©2024 Ken Block

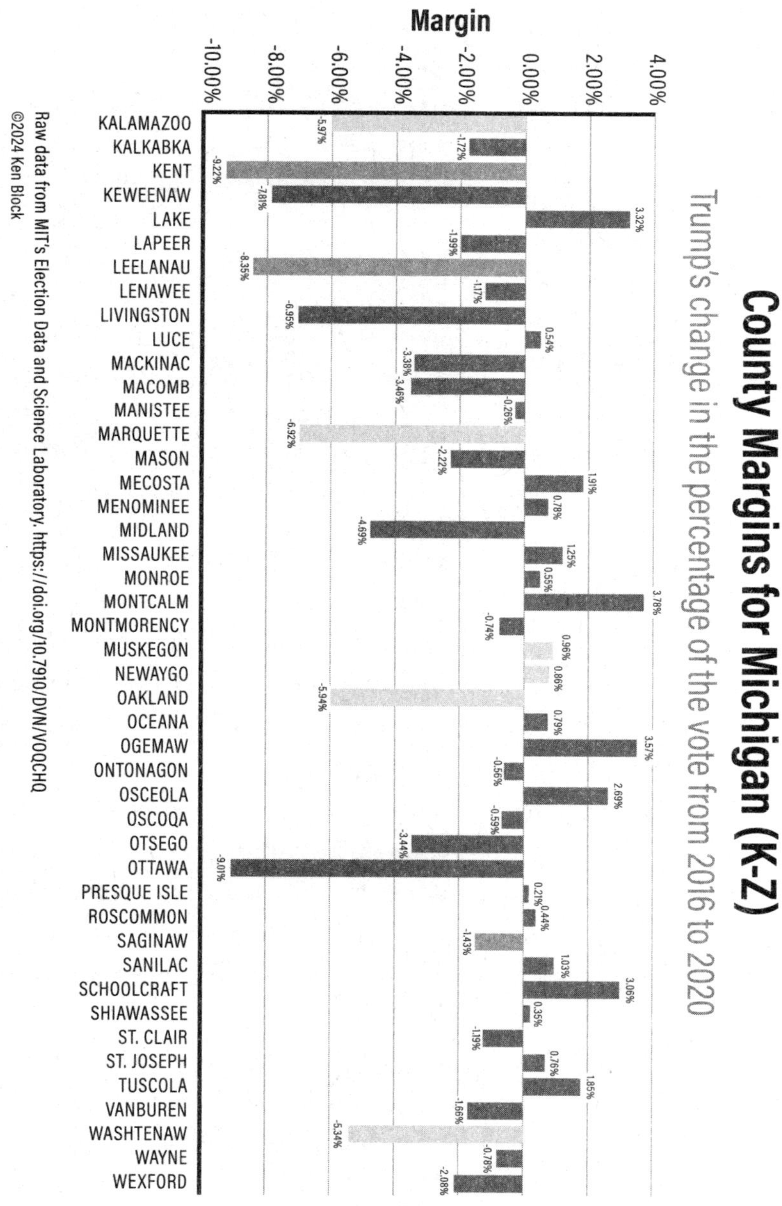

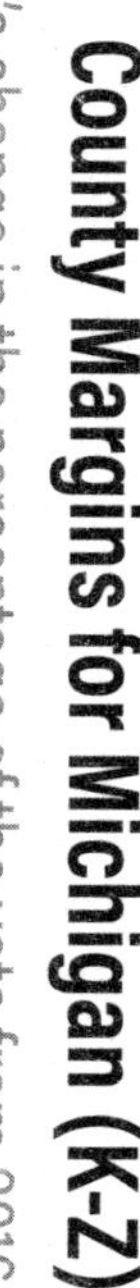

Margin

4.00% 2.00% 0.00% -2.00% -4.00% -6.00% -8.00% -10.00%

County	Margin
KALAMAZOO	-5.97%
KALKABKA	-1.72%
KENT	-9.22%
KEWEENAW	-7.81%
LAKE	3.32%
LAPEER	-1.99%
LEELANAU	-8.35%
LENAWEE	-1.17%
LIVINGSTON	-6.95%
LUCE	0.54%
MACKINAC	-3.38%
MACOMB	-3.46%
MANISTEE	-0.26%
MARQUETTE	-6.92%
MASON	-2.22%
MECOSTA	1.91%
MENOMINEE	0.78%
MIDLAND	-4.69%
MISSAUKEE	1.25%
MONROE	0.55%
MONTCALM	3.78%
MONTMORENCY	-0.74%
MUSKEGON	0.96%
NEWAYGO	0.86%
OAKLAND	-5.94%
OCEANA	0.79%
OGEMAW	3.57%
ONTONAGON	-0.56%
OSCEOLA	2.69%
OSCOQA	-0.59%
OTSEGO	-3.44%
OTTAWA	-9.01%
PRESQUE ISLE	0.21%
ROSCOMMON	0.44%
SAGINAW	-1.43%
SANILAC	1.03%
SCHOOLCRAFT	3.06%
SHIAWASSEE	0.35%
ST. CLAIR	-1.19%
ST. JOSEPH	0.76%
TUSCOLA	1.85%
VANBUREN	-1.66%
WASHTENAW	-5.34%
WAYNE	-0.78%
WEXFORD	-2.08%

Raw data from MIT's Election Data and Science Laboratory. https://doi.org/10.7910/DVN/VOQCHQ

surprising that the same dynamic that cost him in those places hurt him worse in areas that lean less Republican, like Michigan.

It is hard to find much good news for Republicans in Michigan. In 2022, Democrats swept all statewide offices.

The data behind these charts is displayed in the Appendix.*

Nevada

2016 Total Vote	2016 DEM Vote	2016 GOP Vote	Margin	2016 Libertarian Vote	2016 Green Vote	2016 Other Vote	2016 Write-in
1,125,385	539,260	512,058	27,202	37,384	0	36,683	0
2020 Total Vote	**2020 DEM Vote**	**2020 GOP Vote**	**Margin**	**2020 Libertarian Vote**	**2020 Green Vote**	**2020 Other Vote**	**2020 Write-in**
1,404,911	703,314	669,608	33,706	14,783	0	3,138	14,079

The last Republican elected for president by Nevada was Bush in 2004.

Nevada has seventeen counties, only two of which went for Biden in 2020. However, the fifteen red counties Trump won contained a grand total of only 180,000 or so votes, netting Trump only 122,146 votes, and most of the rest going to Biden.

Trump lost ground in the fifteen counties he won—a total of 1,454 votes compared to his performance in 2016. But incredibly, he gained ground in Clark County, the state's largest county that went blue in 2020 and 2016. Trump still lost in Clark County, but not as badly as he did in 2016. This fact argues strongly against any role voter fraud might have played in Clark County.

Libertarian candidate Jo Jorgensen's 2020 vote total came to roughly half of Biden's overall margin of victory in Nevada in 2020.

The data behind this chart is displayed in the Appendix.*

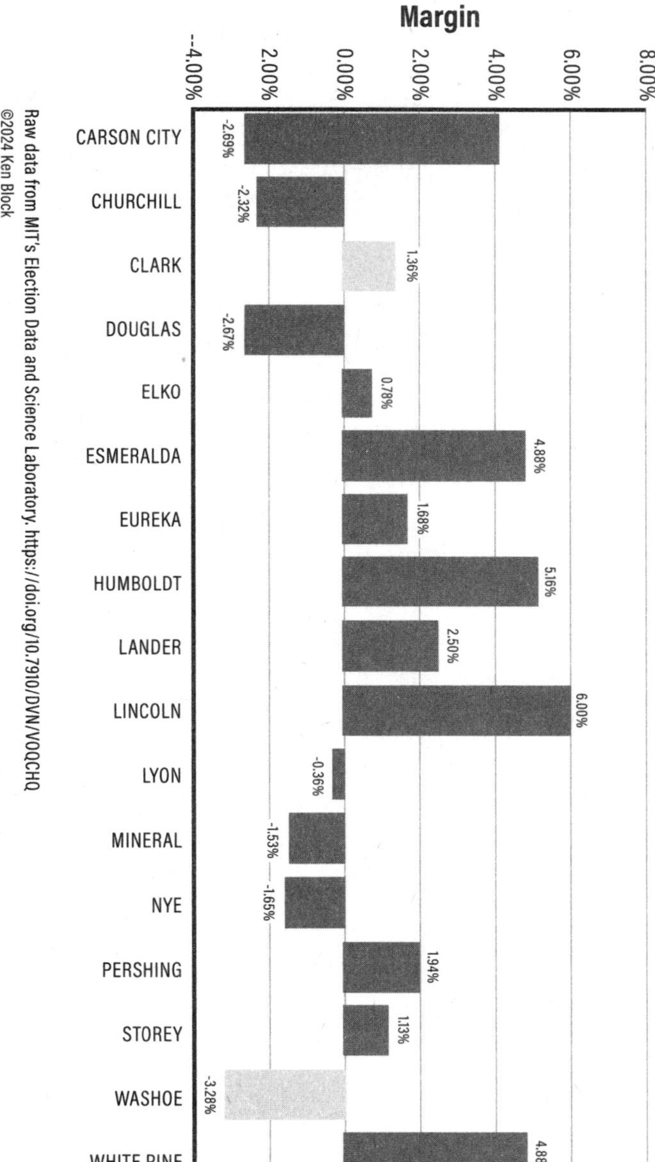
County Margins for Nevada
Trump's change in the percentage of the vote from 2016 to 2020
Margin
8.00%
6.00%
4.00%
2.00%
0.00%
2.00%
--4.00%
CARSON CITY
-2.69%
CHURCHILL
-2.32%
CLARK
1.36%
DOUGLAS
-2.67%
ELKO
0.78%
ESMERALDA
4.88%
EUREKA
1.68%
HUMBOLDT
5.16%
LANDER
2.50%
LINCOLN
6.00%
LYON
-0.36%
MINERAL
-1.53%
NYE
-1.65%
PERSHING
1.94%
STOREY
1.13%
WASHOE
-3.28%
WHITE PINE
4.88%
Raw data from MIT's Election Data and Science Laboratory. https://doi.org/10.7910/DVN/VOQCHQ
©2024 Ken Block

Pennsylvania

2016 Total Vote	2016 DEM Vote	2016 GOP Vote	Margin	2016 Libertarian Vote	2016 Green Vote	2016 Other Vote	2016 Write-in
6,115,402	2,926,441	2,970,733	44,292	146,715	49,941	21,572	0
2020 Total Vote	**2020 DEM Vote**	**2020 GOP Vote**	**Margin**	**2020 Libertarian Vote**	**2020 Green Vote**	**2020 Other Vote**	**2020 Write-in**
6,915,283	3,458,229	3,377,674	80,555	79,380	0	0	0

Jo Jorgensen strikes again! The Libertarian presidential candidate took nearly as many votes in Pennsylvania as Biden's margin over Trump in 2020. Please also note the potential impact of the Green Party's candidate on the 2016 election results. The Green Party candidate, Jill Stein, took more votes than Trump's margin over Clinton in 2016.

A very interesting situation arose in Pennsylvania in 2020 regarding the Green Party. The Democrats used Pennsylvania's ballot access laws to bar the Greens from the 2020 ballot. The case hinged on a technicality—that the Greens faxed a required form instead of submitting the original document.

According to an Associated Press article regarding the lawsuit, "Democrats have long gone to court to keep Green Party candidates off the ballot, worried that they will siphon otherwise liberal voters in close contests against Republicans in the politically polarized state."[55]

For all the Democrats' professed concern about voting and not disenfranchising a single voter, the party has no compunction about preventing people who are not Democrats from running for office. So maybe a new motto for the Democratic Party should be: "Everyone deserves to vote, but only Democrats should be allowed to run."

55 Marc Levy, "Green Party Candidate Is Ordered off Pennsylvania Ballot," AP News, September 17, 2020, https://apnews.com/cbd7947a020a1c5983a69e804ce3a5f8.

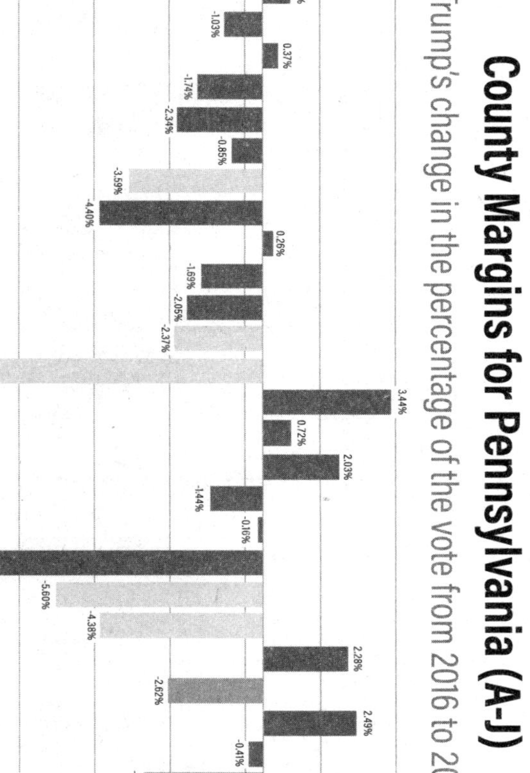

Raw data from MIT's Election Data and Science Laboratory. https://doi.org/10.7910/DVN/VOQCHQ

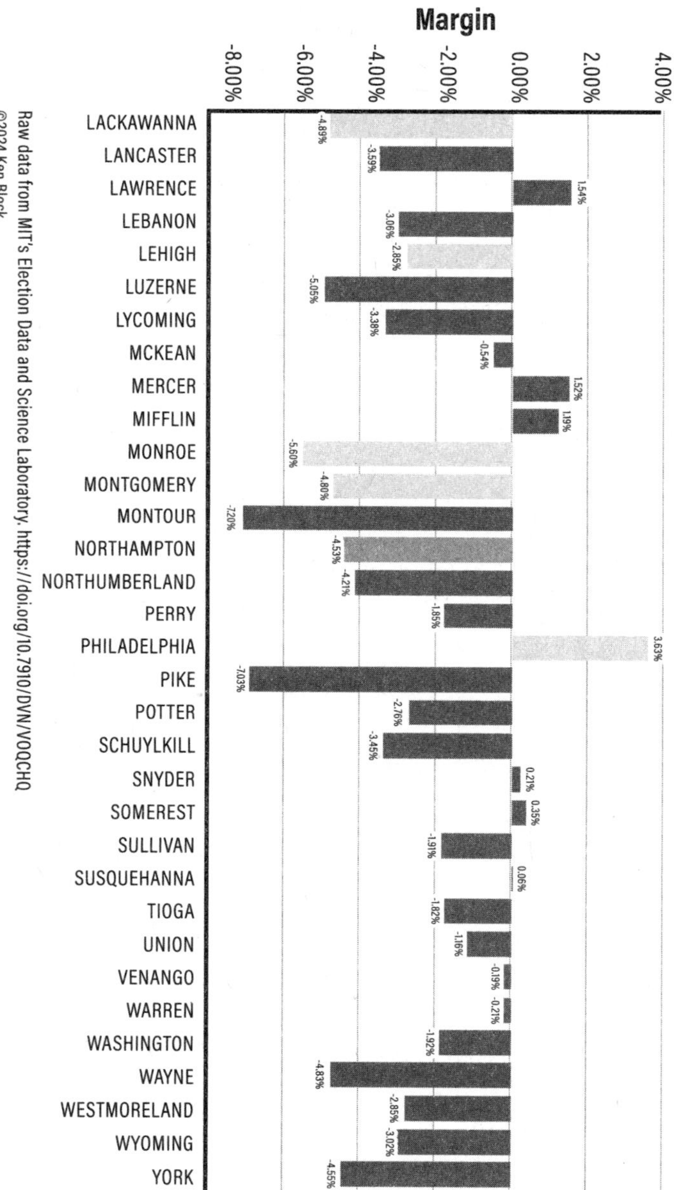
County Margins for Pennsylvania (K-Z)
Trump's change in the percentage of the vote from 2016 to 2020
Margin
4.00%
2.00%
0.00%
-2.00%
-4.00%
-6.00%
-8.00%
LACKAWANNA -4.89%
LANCASTER -3.59%
LAWRENCE 1.54%
LEBANON -3.06%
LEHIGH -2.85%
LUZERNE -5.05%
LYCOMING -3.38%
MCKEAN -0.54%
MERCER 1.52%
MIFFLIN 1.19%
MONROE -5.60%
MONTGOMERY -4.80%
MONTOUR -7.20%
NORTHAMPTON -4.53%
NORTHUMBERLAND -4.21%
PERRY -1.85%
PHILADELPHIA 3.63%
PIKE -7.03%
POTTER -2.76%
SCHUYLKILL -3.45%
SNYDER 0.21%
SOMEREST 0.35%
SULLIVAN -1.91%
SUSQUEHANNA 0.06%
TIOGA -1.82%
UNION -1.16%
VENANGO -0.19%
WARREN -0.21%
WASHINGTON -1.92%
WAYNE -4.83%
WESTMORELAND -2.85%
WYOMING -3.02%
YORK -4.55%
Raw data from MIT's Election Data and Science Laboratory, https://doi.org/10.7910/DVN/VOQCHQ
©2024 Ken Block

Pennsylvania endured several lawsuits contesting Trump's loss in the 2020 election. None of the lawsuits proved voter fraud occurred, and most were quickly tossed as meritless or lacking judicial standing.

Pennsylvania has sixty-seven counties. Trump won fifty-four, and Biden won eleven. Two counties in the state flipped from Republican to Democrat: Erie and Northampton. Like the rest of the country, many of Trump's county-level wins in Pennsylvania were in places with small populations.

Scanning the list of counties, it can readily be seen that in the red counties that went to Trump in both 2016 and 2020, Trump's margin of victory was smaller in 2020. Trump lost 78,640 votes due to his underperformance in 2020—nearly Biden's margin of victory.

Fascinatingly, Trump gained ground in Philadelphia, a city frequently at the center of discussions about voter fraud.

The data behind these charts is displayed in the Appendix.*

Wisconsin

2016 Total Vote	2016 DEM Vote	2016 GOP Vote	Margin	2016 Libertarian Vote	2016 Green Vote	2016 Other Vote	2016 Write-in
2,975,753	1,381,823	1,404,440	22,617	106,674	31,072	38,198	12,386
2020 Total Vote	**2020 DEM Vote**	**2020 GOP Vote**	**Margin**	**2020 Libertarian Vote**	**2020 Green Vote**	**2020 Other Vote**	**2020 Write-in**
3,297,352	1,630,673	1,610,065	20,608	38,491	1,089	17,034	8

Jo Jorgensen once again earned more votes in 2020 than Biden's margin over Trump.

Wisconsin has seventy-two counties: fifty-eight red, twelve blue, and two purple. In the red counties alone, Trump bled off more than 37,000 votes—more votes than he lost by in the election.

I feel like I am giving Wisconsin short shrift here in terms of descriptive language, but the dynamic at play has been well-documented in the states discussed here. Trump's across-the-board bleeding of

County Margins for Wisconsin (A-J)

Trump's change in the percentage of the vote from 2016 to 2020

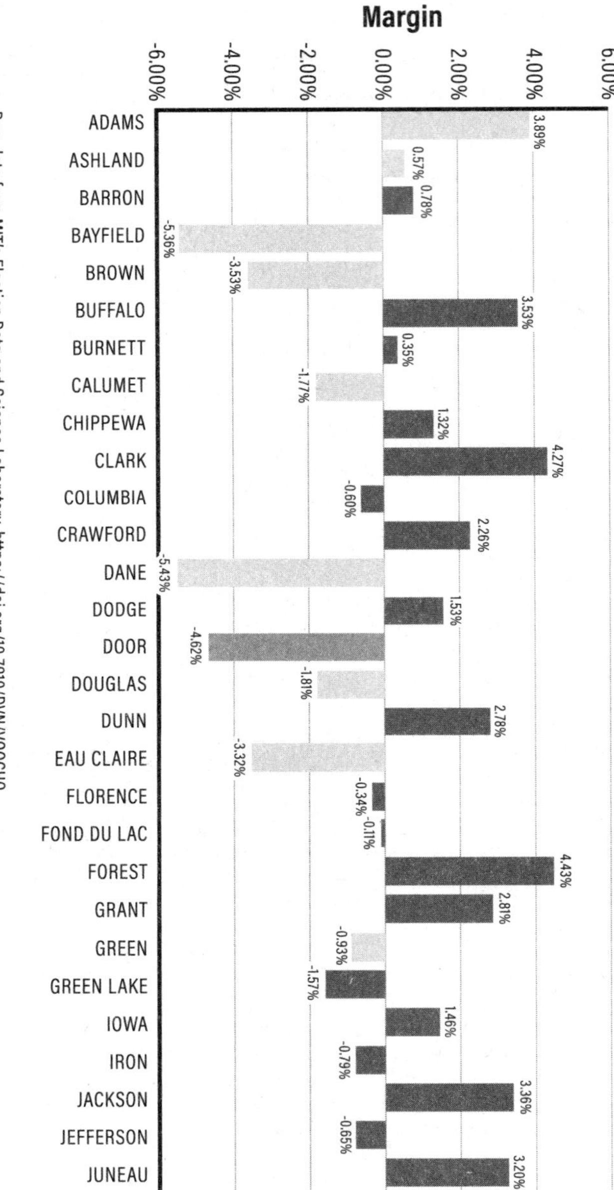

Raw data from MIT's Election Data and Science Laboratory. https://doi.org/10.7910/DVN/VOQCHQ

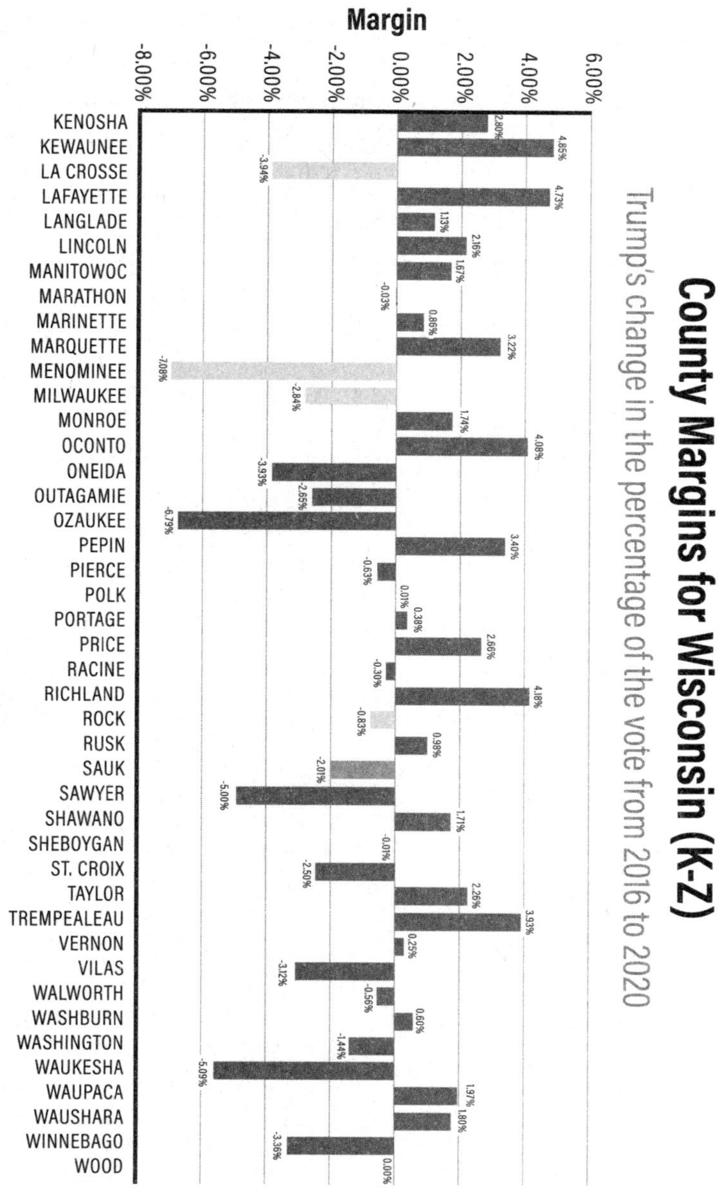

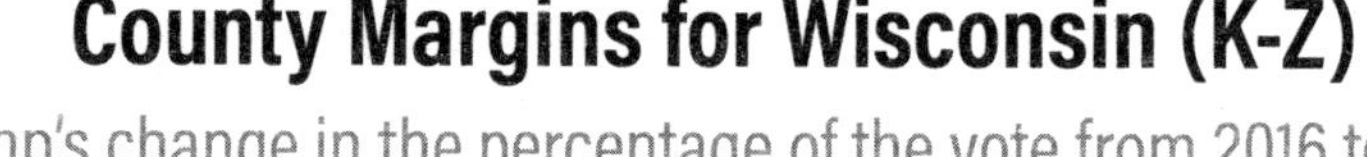

Raw data from MIT's Election Data and Science Laboratory, https://doi.org/10.7910/DVN/VOQCHQ
©2024 Ken Block

support cost him the election. Or maybe Trump's inability to appeal to Jo Jorgensen voters cost him the election. Either way, those probable causes of his loss are substantially more realistic than Trump's imagined, undefined, meritless, and thoroughly disproven claims of massive voter fraud.

For the stout of heart, the data behind the charts in this chapter is reproduced in the Appendix.*

Chapter 19

CAN TRUMP'S CLAIM OF MASSIVE MAIL BALLOT FRAUD BE DISPROVED? NO.

Former president Trump demonized mail ballots ahead of the 2020 general election. Trump understood that voting by mail was an activity more Democrats would undertake than Republicans, and he sharpened the divide between the two parties. Trump claimed that voting by mail was inherently fraudulent while instructing his followers to vote in person. After the election, Trump's lawyers tried to invalidate mail ballots in many swing states. Was Trump's targeting of mail ballots an attempt to win the 2020 election by making mail ballots a majority-Democrat voting mechanism, which he then tried to disqualify?

Trump continuously claims mail ballots were the mechanism by which the 2020 election was stolen. Is he right? This chapter was originally intended to answer that question. I almost did not write it due to the extraordinary difficulty in acquiring the data to perform the work. In hindsight, I should have trusted my instinct. Nonetheless, I decided to include this chapter because the background information on mail ballots is important for everyone to understand.

I wanted to perform the same kind of comparison I did in the previous chapter, looking at mail ballot data from 2016 and comparing it to the same data from 2020. A county-by-county look at mail ballot data across the two elections could have told us much about what happened. This is a good and necessary analysis to perform. It is also so challenging that I do not believe anyone has ever done it for any presidential election. How and what mail ballot data is reported differs dramatically from jurisdiction to jurisdiction, as does the data quality.

As I said, my original goal was to look at Trump's overall percentage of the mail ballot vote by county in 2016 versus 2020. Incredibly, I could only perform this analysis for five states due to bad and missing data. Unsurprisingly, Biden took a more significant percentage of the mail ballot vote in 2020 than Clinton in 2016. Trump's continuous messaging in 2020 telling Republicans to vote in person significantly impacted the partisan usage of mail ballots. Democrats used mail ballots heavily, and many Republicans heeded Trump's instructions to vote in person. Even with a complete and clean set of national mail ballot data, I would have had no way to separate the impact of Trump's messaging on mail ballot usage from any other cause, but, having said that, I believe that Trump's messaging was responsible for a large portion of the discrepancy in mail ballot usage between Democrats and Republicans in 2020.

It was not feasible for me to try to obtain mail ballot information from every election jurisdiction in the country. To do so for just the 2020 general election would involve acquiring 576 mail ballot files from across the country, figuring out each file layout, coding a program to process each file, and checking the validity of the final result. Even if all this work could have been done, differences in how jurisdictions reported the same data would make any analysis difficult, if not incorrect.

The effort for someone like me to obtain the 1,152 data files alone (I assume that the 2016 election would have as many files as the 2020 election) would take months unless those files could be obtained in their original forms from either the Democratic or Republican National Committees. I did have access to the Republican National Committee's data in 2020, so I know these files are collected all in one place. If I attempted to collect these files on my own, it could take some election jurisdictions months to respond to public data requests. Who knows how many of those jurisdictions would charge for the data? I estimate that as much as a full year of effort might be required to do this analysis. It needs to be done.

I spent weeks attempting to find quality nationwide data that could tell the story of mail ballots and their impact on the 2020 presidential election. Unfortunately, the data does not exist, which is surprising and terrible.

Every state implements mail ballots differently. Therefore, it is imperative to be able to compare data on how different mail ballot implementations impact elections. Do some jurisdictions have problems that others do not? The answer is yes.

You will find some interesting information in the following section that I was able to pull from two sets of mail ballot data. Unfortunately, neither of these data sets can be used to address the challenge of proving or disproving Trump's mail ballot fraud claims.

Trump's claims of massive mail ballot fraud have no foundation in fact. The data was unavailable in 2020 when I could not find the fraud in my work for the Trump campaign. And the data is not available now, based on the absence of any usable national database of mail ballot information. The lack of relevant data is not evidence of fraud, just as it does not disprove fraud.

Let's discuss the two very different sets of data I found that included county-level mail ballot information.

Introduction to US Election Assistance Commission Data

The US Election Assistance Commission (EAC) surveys every voting jurisdiction nationwide. In its own words, "The EAC is an independent, bipartisan commission charged with developing guidance to meet HAVA [Help America Vote Act] requirements, adopting voluntary voting system guidelines, and serving as a national clearinghouse of information on election administration."[56]

The survey is a detailed questionnaire that every election jurisdiction must complete. The data the EAC requests in its survey dives into many areas. For the 2020 general election, the survey was forty-one pages long.[57] There are a *lot* of data points buried in this survey.

My focus here is just on the section regarding mail ballot voting. The mail ballot data from this survey would provide great insight into mail ballot voting across the country, but only if every election jurisdiction provided all requested data. Many did not.

The EAC data requests also omit a critical piece of information: the presidential candidate for whom the mail ballot was cast. Without knowing for whom the vote was cast, it is impossible to address Trump's claim of partisan harm resulting from mail ballot fraud.

Unfortunately, the EAC seems to like to tweak its survey every election. For someone like me, who wants to compare data from election to election, finding the same data in two surveys was time-consuming. Also, the EAC fundamentally changed how the survey data was handled in the spreadsheet from 2016 to 2020. For anyone who wants to recreate my results or explore these data sets independently, be aware that the surveys frequently store *text* in data fields that are supposed to represent numbers. For example, a data element that is supposed to be the number of mail ballots

56 https://www.eac.gov.

57 US Election Assistance Commission (EAC), 2020 Election Administration and Voting Survey (EAVS), https://www.eac.gov/sites/default/files/Research/2020EAVS.pdf.

that were rejected for bad signatures contains the text string *was not supplied* instead. I spent much time cleaning up data to be able to do my analysis.

I describe the mechanics of voting by mail ballot elsewhere, so I won't repeat that information here. But be aware that the data points collected by the EAC relate directly to the various steps in the mail ballot voting process. If the EAC's data were complete and accurate, it would be a treasure trove of crucial information regarding voting in the United States.

The EAC's survey asks for all the data needed to understand how each election jurisdiction handles mail ballots. Some jurisdictions did not provide an answer to even basic questions, like how many mail ballots were mailed to voters. The EAC's incomplete mail ballot data highlights the lack of national standards for how essential elements of our elections work. It should not be optional for election jurisdictions to track the information the EAC requests. Every jurisdiction should be required to provide accurate data for every element the EAC requests. Unfortunately, many jurisdictions will probably have to change their systems and processes to track and provide the data that the EAC asks for.

More than 6,400 election jurisdictions are in the EAC's data for 2020. Fifteen jurisdictions did not provide data indicating how many mail ballots were mailed out to voters in 2020, with seven in Idaho and four in Alabama. These jurisdictions provided no data points regarding mail ballots for the 2020 election. Moreover, many more jurisdictions could not provide data points regarding other pieces of the mail ballot process.

In 2020, 664 election jurisdictions could not provide data on how many mail ballots mailed out came back as undeliverable. This is critical because when an official election mailing comes back as undeliverable, it legally allows officials to begin removing that voter from the rolls. Are the jurisdictions that failed to report this data not performing this task? How can list maintenance be done without information based on undeliverable mail ballots?

In addition, eighty-nine jurisdictions did not provide an answer for how many mail ballots were returned, accepted, and counted. One hundred did not answer how many mail ballots were rejected. In some cases, the data is available but from a different source. For example, all of Rhode Island's thirty-nine cities and towns appear as jurisdictions in the EAC's data, and all fail to provide details about rejected mail ballots. Rhode Island state election authorities track this information, but the EAC's data collection effort apparently does not attempt to obtain data from anywhere but the local jurisdictions.

So the data is incomplete, making any meaningful national comparative analysis difficult. As a result, the EAC's survey is not a useful tool in its current form and with the current level of data reporting. Jurisdictions that do not track the information requested should be required to change their systems and processes so that these questions can be answered.

How much money is spent on this election survey? It can easily take fifty hours to produce a survey response. With 5,519 surveys, at an estimated cost of $50 per hour, election officials might collectively expend almost $14 million responding to this survey. Employees of the EAC then must spend much time collecting the surveys and compiling the data. More than $20 million may be spent on this survey after every election. For that kind of taxpayer money, the data collected should be of much higher quality.

How Are Mail Ballots Handled?

Voting jurisdictions across the country handle mail ballots differently. Some states and counties carefully track every part of the mail ballot process for each vote cast, while others track little. It is maddening that there is so much variability in the voting process for a high-stakes race such as the presidential election in one of the most technologically advanced countries on earth.

For example, if you mail in an absentee ballot before Election Day but then die before Election Day, does your vote count? The answer depends on the state. I had trouble finding a definitive (and current) list of states and how they handle this situation. Still, as best as I could determine, twelve states allow this type of vote to count, sixteen states do not, and the remaining states appear to have no laws regarding this issue. It is bizarre that in the United States, whether your vote for president counts or not if you die after voting by mail depends, in the best case, on which state you were registered to vote in while you were alive. In the worst case, your state has not considered this situation and has no law governing how your vote should be handled. Could different election jurisdictions within the same state handle these deceased votes differently? Probably.

The differences in how states implement various aspects of mail ballots can yield shocking surprises in the data. For example, survey question C4L asks for the count of mail ballots rejected because the voter was deceased. Most states reported a few dozen of these rejections, but Michigan had 3,450, with hundreds reported in Wayne, Oakland, and Macomb counties. Was this an attempt at massive voter fraud? It was not. Michigan does not count the votes of voters who cast a mail ballot while living but who died before Election Day. Other states do count votes like this. Shouldn't these votes be treated the same way across the country in a national election?

Digging In

Considering the forementioned caveats, let's carefully get into the 2020 data. Here is the mail ballot data tracked in the EAC survey, what it can tell us, and highlights from the data available:

Total mail ballots mailed: The number of ballots mailed out to voters who applied for a mail ballot.

Total mail ballots returned by voters: The number of ballots either counted as good or rejected.

Total mail ballots marked as undeliverable: In some circumstances, when the United States Postal Service cannot deliver a letter, that letter gets marked as "undeliverable" and returned to the sender. High levels of undeliverable mailings can indicate obsolete voter rolls, voter error when applying for the mail ballot, or something worse.

The following states had no election jurisdictions that reported data on undeliverable ballots: Connecticut, Iowa, Kentucky, Mississippi, New Jersey, Rhode Island, and South Carolina. Are election authorities in these states tracking undeliverable mail ballots and taking action to clean up their voter rolls where appropriate?

The top ten states for mail ballots returned as undeliverable as a percentage of all mail ballots sent:

State	Number of jurisdictions	Number of jurisdictions not reporting data	Number of undeliverable ballots	Percentage of undeliverable ballots relative to ballots mailed
DC	1	0	45,072	10.817
NV	17	0	123,628	6.742
AZ	15	3	129,307	3.664
CO	64	0	115,709	2.964
MT	56	0	18,153	2.578
HI	5	3	16,499	2.203

State	Number of jurisdictions	Number of jurisdictions not reporting data	Number of undeliver-able ballots	Percentage of undeliverable ballots relative to ballots mailed
KS	105	0	7,970	2.196
GA	159	0	27,287	1.551
FL	67	1	89,189	1.470
CA	58	4	332,976	1.433

The Arizona counties that did not report undeliverable mail ballot data are Cochise, Santa Cruz, and Yuma. In Hawaii, they are Maui, Kauai, and Kalawao. California's nonreporting counties are Del Norte, Plumas, El Dorado, and Trinity. Gulf County is Florida's only nonreporting county.

> **Total mail ballots spoiled:** The EAC defines this as the number of ballots incorrectly marked or "surrendered" at the polling place in order to vote in person. It is unfortunate that this one data point describes two very different situations. Many mismarked ballots can indicate a ballot design issue or unclear instructions.

There are some monumental outliers in this data. North Carolina, Nevada, and Georgia all have double-digit percentages of spoiled or surrendered ballots. Seventeen states had fewer than 1 percent of mail ballots identified in the survey as spoiled or surrendered. Alaska, Alabama, Connecticut, Iowa, Kentucky, Missouri, Mississippi, New Jersey, Oklahoma, Rhode Island, and South Carolina reported no data for spoiled or surrendered ballots.

State	Number of jurisdictions	Number of jurisdictions not reporting data	Number of spoiled or surren-dered ballots	Percentage of spoiled or surrendered ballots relative to ballots mailed
NC	100	0	275,218	20.373
NV	17	0	216,446	11.803
GA	159	0	197,907	11.251
ID	44	18	39,348	9.677
TX	254	33	93,164	7.709
MN	87	0	93,878	6.075
MT	56	0	40,193	5.709
NM	33	0	18,711	5.009
WA	39	0	222,549	4.413
MI	83	0	118,346	3.932

Total mail ballots processed, counted, and included in overall vote totals: Some states clearly responded to this survey question with bad data. For example, Rhode Island's responses indicate that the state approved every mail ballot that was returned, while Kansas's responses show that 93.1 percent of all returned mail ballots were rejected. Both of these responses must be wrong.

Problems like this in the survey data force me to call into question all the data contained within the survey. It simply cannot be trusted in its current form and cannot be used for any serious analysis.

For what it's worth, here are the ten top and ten bottom states for the percentage of returned mail ballots approved as good votes according to the EAC survey. Incredibly, no jurisdiction in Alabama provided a response to this survey question.

State	Number of jurisdictions	Number of jurisdictions not reporting data	Number of counted ballots	Percentage of counted ballots relative to ballots returned
RI	39	0	318,313	100.000
IN	92	0	535,942	97.871
NH	320	0	253,932	96.388
ME	497	1	359,331	96.238
MO	116	0	899,695	96.156
NE	93	0	485,195	95.502
WY	23	0	85,454	95.437
SC	46	0	425,701	95.087
KY	120	0	631,497	94.752
WV	55	0	142,191	94.667

State	Number of jurisdictions	Number of jurisdictions not reporting data	Number of counted ballots	Percentage of counted ballots relative to ballots returned
GA	159	0	1,311,361	74.550
NY	62	1	1,763,448	74.527
LA	64	0	161,292	73.968
HI	5	1	548,636	73.264
NC	100	0	974,351	72.127

State	Number of jurisdictions	Number of jurisdictions not reporting data	Number of counted ballots	Percentage of counted ballots relative to ballots returned
NJ	21	0	4,178,875	69.035
CA	58	0	15,305,243	65.889
DC	1	0	234,758	56.343
NV	17	0	664,461	36.234
KS	105	0	24,924	6.867

Total number of mail ballots rejected: I am as skeptical about this data element as I am about the "good votes" element previously described. I believe these numbers to be so wrong that I won't bother showing you a top or bottom ten. None of these numbers adds up in a way that makes any sense.

Rhode Island had the tiniest percentage of mail ballots that were rejected, reporting only 0.03 percent. Arkansas had the highest rate, coming in at 6.28 percent.

None of the jurisdictions in Alabama reported any data for this data element either.

Mail Ballot Rejection Reasons

At this point, the survey gets granular, asking for counts of specific reasons that mail ballots were rejected. Unfortunately, for many rejection reasons, hundreds and sometimes thousands of jurisdictions supplied no data.

It is unacceptable that so many jurisdictions failed to supply data here. If fully and correctly filled out, this section would provide valuable insight into the impacts of mail ballot features like signatures, witness signatures, voters who died and voted by mail, and how states handle first-time voters who have not supplied required identification. Instead, we get election trivia that certainly highlights some areas of concern but does little to help us understand how mail ballots are handled nationally.

On account of this deficiency, I will abandon statewide comparisons here and will instead call out some figures that struck me as outlandish. I am going out on a limb and accepting at face value the counts each jurisdiction reported. This section of the survey is not hard to understand. It asks the responder to break out rejected ballots by the type of rejection.

Relatively high rates of error may indicate bad ballot design or poorly understood instructions.

Ballot Rejected Due to Missed Deadline

Only 34 percent of the election jurisdictions reported one or more rejected ballots due to arriving after the deadline, adding up to 66,957 rejected late ballots across the entire survey.

California and Illinois had the largest number of rejected late ballots, with 11,851 and 8,452, respectively.

Kane County, in Illinois, had by far the most rejected late ballots, with 6,214. Kane County outlies any other election jurisdiction with this figure. The next closest county is Riverside County, California, with 1,388 rejected late ballots. Kane County has a population of roughly half a million; Riverside County has a population of over 2.4 million. Either Kane County's reported data is wrong, or someone should be looking into what happened in Kane County in 2020.

Ballot Rejected Due to Missing Signature

Just 30 percent of jurisdictions reported one or more rejected ballots due to missing voter signatures. Survey-wide, 66,799 ballots were rejected for this reason.

California and New Jersey had the largest number of ballots rejected due to no signature, with 14,647 and 8,651.

Ballot Rejected Due to No Witness Signature

Some jurisdictions require witness signatures, while others do not. Some jurisdictions dropped witness requirements in 2020 due to the COVID-19 pandemic, but 8.8 percent of election jurisdictions reported one or more ballots rejected due to the lack of a required witness signature, which translates to 18,378 ballots.

North and South Carolina led the way regarding the total number of these rejected ballots, with 5,935 and 3,150, respectively.

Ballot Rejected Due to Bad Signature

Ensuring that a voter can be positively tied to a ballot mailed to election workers poses a challenge. Most places rely upon matching a signature on the mail ballot envelope with a signature on file with election authorities to confirm that the voter cast the ballot. This process is the one that I have the most concern about. From properly training election workers to correctly and reliably match signatures to handling huge volumes of mail ballots, ensuring election integrity via signature matching can be a weak link.

Everything I do and have done, in terms of communicating words on a page, has been done via a keyboard—for decades. I never had excellent, good, or even OK handwriting, but whatever I had has now atrophied to only slightly better than grammar school handwriting. My signature never looks the same way twice and it never has. If my life depended on it, I could not replicate my decades-old signature on file with election authorities. And yet, in the two elections in which I voted by mail, there were no issues with my signature.

When I explored signature data with Rhode Island election officials a few years ago, I learned that some voters in certain cities and towns lacked signature data with state election officials. With these challenges and the compressed time frame to count mail ballots, how well do election officials perform signature checking? Based on the overall data, the job is poorly done.

For example, North Carolina reports rejecting 28 ballots out of 981,816 cast due to mismatched signatures, and Ohio rejected 414 out of 2,144,504.

A mere 16.3 percent of election jurisdictions supplied data regarding signature matching, totaling 157,477 rejected ballots due to mismatched signatures. How is it that so many of our election jurisdictions provided no data on signature matching? Is data on rejections for signature matching not being kept, or is signature checking not happening in these jurisdictions? There were 741 counties that provided data on rejected ballots with no signatures but provided no data on rejected ballots due to mismatched signatures. What? Some of these nonreporting counties are large, such as Philadelphia County in Pennsylvania and Montgomery County in Maryland.

Some jurisdictions will try to reach voters with rejected mail ballots in an attempt to rectify problems with approving the ballot. The EAC should request data elements for this activity. For example, how many voters were contacted? How many resolved the issue with the ballot? What specific issue was resolved?

There is a real opportunity here for rejected mail ballots to become a partisan political weapon. As election work becomes increasingly politicized, partisan election workers might disproportionally reject mail ballots from those registered to the opposing party. The only real protection from this outcome is for election officials to provide clean and detailed data so that outside eyes can watch for this sort of problem.

Ballot Rejected Due to Multiple Ballots in an Envelope

When a mail ballot is returned to election workers through the mail, that ballot must be sent in the official mail ballot envelope. Only one mail ballot can be placed into an official envelope marked with (or that is supposed to be marked with) the voter's signature. If multiple mail ballots are sent in one official envelope, election workers cannot determine which ballot is associated with the signature on the envelope and must discard all the ballots contained within.

This seems like a straightforward requirement—one that all voters should be able to understand. I did not expect to see an issue with many invalidated ballots due to multiple ballots in an envelope. And then, along came Kings County. Kings County is the borough of Brooklyn in New York City. More than 2.7 million people live in Kings County.

Across *all* survey responses, 8,257 mail ballots were identified as rejected because they were included with other ballots returned in the same envelope—7,531 mail ballots were rejected due to multiple ballots in an envelope in Kings County alone.

What the heck is going on in Kings County? Are the mail ballot instructions there unclear about including only one ballot per envelope? Are many of these rejected ballots from individuals who speak the same language? Does Kings County not pay the postage for mail ballots, causing thrifty voters to attempt to save money by putting multiple ballots in one envelope?

If the Kings County data has been correctly reported, someone must dig into what has gone wrong there.

Ballot Rejected Because a Vote Had Already Been Cast

Many election jurisdictions allow three forms of voting: voting by mail, voting early (before Election Day) by casting a ballot in person, and voting in person on Election Day. All election jurisdictions need safeguards to prevent voters from casting a vote using more than one of these voting mechanisms.

The survey asks jurisdictions for a count of mail ballots rejected because a vote had already been cast. Across the survey, 49,016 mail ballots were rejected because they represented a duplicate vote.

One county stands apart as an outlier for these rejected duplicate votes. Lake County, Illinois, reported 14,633 rejected duplicate mail ballots. Lake County has a population of roughly 700,000. Seven hundred counties reported this data element, with the vast majority reporting less than one hundred ballots rejected for this reason.

Does Lake County stand out because it did a great job identifying duplicate votes? Or was there a coordinated push in Lake County by more than 14,000 voters to attempt to commit voter fraud? Or was something else going on in the county that did not go on in other Illinois counties to cause voter confusion? By way of comparison from the same state, the city of Chicago reported 332 rejected duplicate ballots.

Ballot Rejected Because Required Identification Was Not Provided

Federal law makes it a crime for noncitizens to vote in federal elections. The law and its intent are clear—at least to me.

The Help America Vote Act, passed in 2002, places requirements on election officials to collect Social Security numbers or driver's license numbers from newly registered voters if either of those forms of identification has been issued to the voter. If neither of those forms of identification has been issued, election authorities may give the voter a "voter number," which serves as identification for election purposes.

The Help America Vote Act places an additional requirement on election officials for voters who register without a driver's license or a Social Security number. Before those voters can cast a mail ballot as their first vote, they must provide documentation to election workers. It is this requirement that is behind this survey question.

Only 224 jurisdictions reported that one or more mail ballots were rejected because of missing identification. There are states with vast numbers of voters in their voter registration systems that lack both Social Security numbers and driver's licenses. For example, New York State had nearly two million votes cast in 2020 by voters without this information in the voter registration database. How is it that New York election authorities reported no rejected ballots due to missing identification? Is New York not enforcing this federal requirement?

The Help America Vote Act only mandates that Social Security numbers or driver's licenses be collected from newly registered voters after 2004. This helps to explain why states such as New York can have so many voters in their databases without these forms of identification. I don't understand why election authorities would not try to collect this information from voters not covered by the Help America Vote Act mandate. Without a Social Security number, it can be challenging to determine if a voter has died.

Fewer than half of states report at least one rejection due to the lack of required identification. I wonder what, if anything, the remaining states are doing to conform to the Help America Vote Act's requirement to disallow mail ballot votes for newly registered voters who did not supply required documentation.

Ballot Rejected Because Voter Was Deceased

The following table shows the states that allow a vote to count from a voter who properly casts a mail ballot but dies before the election. Question C4L asks jurisdictions to supply a count of *rejected* mail ballots because the voter was determined to be deceased. States with * for the count had no jurisdictions providing the requested data.

The data in this table is interesting because, if the information was provided correctly, these states are documenting rejected votes due to voter fraud: someone tried to cast a vote in the name of a deceased person, and the ballot was intercepted and rejected.

Arkansas	36
Connecticut	*
Idaho	8
Florida	108
Louisiana	*
Maryland	*
Massachusetts	50
Minnesota	119
Missouri	130
New Mexico	0
North Dakota	0
Ohio	3

I don't display statistics from any other state for this data point because those states either reject mail ballots received from someone who died before the election or do not have a readily discernable policy. These other states can reject mail ballots from deceased voters who die before Election Day. That is not fraud.

The following states reject votes cast by a mail ballot voter who dies before Election Day: Colorado, Delaware, Hawaii, Illinois, Indiana, Iowa, Kentucky, Michigan, Missouri, New Hampshire, New Jersey, Pennsylvania, South Dakota, Tennessee, Virginia, and Wisconsin.

Chapter 20

THE MIT ELECTION AND DATA SCIENCE LABORATORY'S VOTING DATA

MIT's Election and Data Science Laboratory came through for me again with two sets of presidential returns from the 2016 and 2020 elections.[58] Anyone looking at this data who would like to explore it differently or try to recreate my findings must know that the county names differ from election to election. Be sure to look for the same county across multiple elections using the county FIP code, not the county name.

This data set should have solved my problem of finding county-level election returns that included which candidate received the vote, breaking out the count of mail ballot votes. I was looking for the total number of mail ballots cast for each candidate in each county, and this file was set up to accommodate that data. Unfortunately, some counties did not provide data that included a breakdown of votes cast per candidate, instead only supplying the total number of votes cast

58 MIT Election Data and Science Lab, 2018, "US President Precinct-Level Returns 2016," https://doi.org/10.7910/DVN/LYWX3D, Harvard Dataverse, V11; MIT Election Data and Science Lab, 2022, "US President Precinct-Level Returns 2020," https://doi.org/10.7910/DVN/JXPREB, Harvard Dataverse, V4.

in the election. Other counties did not provide a breakdown of mail ballot votes.

I could only find five states with usable data that allowed me to compare mail ballot performance between 2016 and 2020—not nearly enough to draw any conclusions about what happened in 2020. Worse, none of the states that reported the data I needed were swing states in 2020.

As with the EAC's survey data, the data provided by election officials documenting election results should be consistent across the country. All data should be reported the same way and mean the same thing. The data should be as detailed as possible to facilitate election research. This data should include tallies by different voting mechanisms and the candidates for whom the votes were cast. The federal government should create a data portal for election officials to report this information. That portal should ensure that the data entered is consistent across jurisdictions.

Election data is not rocket science. The collection of this data is the problem, and it is only a problem because no formal requirements guide those who provide the data. If an election system cannot produce the data I am discussing, that system should be deemed obsolete and replaced immediately.

After looking at the small set of meaningful data with information about mail ballots and candidates in 2016 and 2020, I can draw no conclusions beyond obvious facts.

Many more mail ballots were cast in 2020 than in 2016, for which we can thank COVID-19. President Trump received more mail ballot votes in 2020 than in 2016, although as a percentage of the vote, he got a smaller share in 2020 than in 2016.

Trump's lower percentage of the mail ballot vote in 2020 was likely because he exhorted his base not to vote by mail. (As with many things, the simplest explanation is usually correct.)

No data exists to prove or disprove claims of massive mail ballot fraud. Nevertheless, deficient lawsuits using the flimsiest of data were filed in 2020 that attempted to insinuate fraud occurred. Yet former president Trump continues to rail about mail ballot fraud, knowing that attempts to prove that fraud existed failed in 2020.

It should be unacceptable to every American voter that our election infrastructure cannot deliver the data needed to assess how our elections are run and to allow a thorough analysis of their results.

PART III

HOW WE CAN IMPROVE OUR ELECTION INFRASTRUCTURE

Chapter 21

A POLITICAL/LEGAL/MORAL/ INFRASTRUCTURE PROBLEM

We have federal elections with federal laws that set the rules for those elections. A few basic examples: A person may only vote once in a federal election. A voter must be at least eighteen years of age to vote in a federal election. A dead person may not vote in a federal election.

For most complex activities that have been computerized, rules such as these are enforced by the computer systems that were developed to support them. That is not the case for our federal elections.

The Constitution makes the implementation of voting the responsibility of the states. As a result, we have a loose network of thousands of computer systems that implement our federal elections. We do not have a single national voting or voter registration system. Of course, our nearly 250-year-old constitution was written well before anyone could imagine computers.

The Founders also did not consider the mobility that comes with modern life. One of the biggest data challenges in our federal elections is that people constantly relocate. (Estimates are that as much as 12 percent of our population moves yearly.) When Americans move from one state to another, voter registrations often remain active in the states they left. Sometimes, people are tempted to vote in the state they left *and* the state to which they moved. There is nothing in place to stop them from committing this voting crime.

The problem is that state-based and county-based election systems are strictly programmed to implement that state's or county's elections. As a result, they can't do much to enforce some national election laws, like ensuring that an individual voter only votes once. No system exists that enforces this requirement. Some patchwork efforts have been made that attempt to fill the gap, but those efforts leave much to be desired.

The multistate aspect of voter data is where a federalized solution should come into play. We need a way to ensure that one active voter registration exists for every individual across all states. The absence of a system that ensures that a person can only be registered once leads to many issues, including distrust and, sometimes, fraud.

There are additional problems that the state-based implementation of our elections brings to our federal elections. Those problems can be grouped into three main categories:

- States implement the same voting functionality differently. For example, who can choose to vote by mail in a federal election and under what circumstances they can do so can vary dramatically from state to state. Also, some states correctly enforce rules like a minimum voting age requirement of eighteen years, while other states sometimes mistakenly allow seventeen-year-olds to vote.
- States have vast differences in the quality of the data used as the foundation of their elections.
- Some states are even exempt from federal laws that provide guardrails for how our federal elections must be run.

Another critical area of deficiency in our federal elections is legal in nature. We have a web of laws and more than a hundred years of legal findings that leave us with an overly complex framework for implementing something that, at its core, is quite simple: a national election in which citizens vote for who their leaders should be.

Politicians and political parties use election laws to gain an advantage whenever they can. Why do we only have two major political parties? One reason is that many states have enacted laws that make successfully launching a new political party impressively difficult. Furthermore, Democrats and Republicans both engage in gerrymandering, redrawing the boundaries of political districts to the benefit of some candidates and the detriment of others. Worse, there is a body of legal precedent that legalizes the efforts of partisan legislatures to disadvantage new political parties.

I have firsthand experience with how state laws impede the ability of alternative political parties to take root. When I first had the idea to create a centrist political party in Rhode Island, I dove into the laws governing how a new party could gain "recognition" by the state. Along with recognition came fundraising benefits, ballot placement, and many other legal necessities. Rhode Island law gave political parties two ways to be recognized: 1) a party's gubernatorial or presidential candidate wins 5 percent of the vote (this is how the Democrat and Republican parties keep their recognition), or 2) the party submits signatures equivalent to 5 percent of the last general election vote. In the latter case, the process of collecting signatures could not begin until January 1 of the election year in which party recognition was desired.

Of course, a new political party seeking state recognition can't rely upon winning 5 percent of the last vote—especially when the party does not yet exist. That leaves signatures. Collecting tens of thousands of signatures when the weather is nice, and people congregate at parades and festivals, is one thing. It is quite another to get those signatures going door-to-door in the middle of a New England winter.

Worse, Rhode Island's deadline for candidates to declare for statewide and local offices is near the end of June. Any new party would have to collect a ton of signatures, get them certified, and then start recruiting candidates and raising money—all within six months. The party cannot raise money for campaign purposes under Rhode Island's campaign finance laws until it is recognized by the state. What candidate would commit to running under the banner of a nascent political party that had to meet such a high burden to launch? The state's nested laws all but ensured that a new political party could not be successfully launched with enough time left to do all the things necessary to build grassroots, develop candidates, and execute winning campaigns.

I pulled all the facts together and brought them to the attention of a former Rhode Island attorney general, Arlene Violet. Arlene has become a mentor and a friend. Her courageous and successful efforts to take down the mafia in Rhode Island provide no hint of her background: she left the Sisters of Mercy Convent to run for office. Arlene agreed with my assessment that Rhode Island's ballot access laws were unfair and connected me with the Rhode Island chapter of the American Civil Liberties Union (ACLU).

The ACLU took my case and provided an outstanding attorney, Mark Freel. Mark and I have developed a close friendship, and he has become my personal and corporate attorney. I have dragged him into several interesting situations over the years.

The Office of the Attorney General of Rhode Island defended the state against my federal lawsuit challenging the constitutionality of these laws. I was deposed for more than four hours by the state's attorney, who was fixated on the thought that the idea for the Moderate Party emerged from a meeting of like-minded people who sat around a coffee table. He tried using this phrase to malign the not-yet party, dismissing the idea that a political party could be created in such a way. It was.

We went to trial. Mark told me not to worry about the fact that I was scheduled to take the stand; he was sure I would do just fine.

I had never been inside a courtroom before. Mark sat at a table, and Arlene Violet was one of the few people sitting in the audience. The state's attorney interrogated me for nearly an hour. Near the end of my session, he sprung what I suspect he considered a trap. He seized on a statement I had made in my deposition and spent what felt like a very long time trying to get me to impeach myself. We went around and around and around while I refused to give him what he wanted. Eventually, the judge stopped us and, in so many words, asked the state's attorney what the heck he was doing. During all of this, I managed to slip a peek over at my attorney, who sat stone-faced.

The bench trial ended after a truly inspired speech by Mark. As we walked out of the courtroom, Arlene came up to me and congratulated me. I turned to Mark and asked him why he left me hanging while I was being bombarded. He said with a big smile that he knew I would be OK and was counting on the fact that the state's attorney would aggravate the judge.

Judge William E. Smith rendered his verdict on May 29, 2009.[59] I let out a war whoop as I put my head around the courtroom win. Smith's closing paragraph read: "There is no question '[t]he American song is one best sung by a plurality of voices.' R.I. Chapter of Nat'l Women's Political Caucus, Inc. v. Rhode Island Lottery Comm'n, 609 F. Supp. 1403, 1413 (D.R.I. 1985). Without justification, a January 1 start date unduly silences would-be singers in Rhode Island at a critical stage of the democratic process. Thus, in accordance with the foregoing, JUDGMENT will be entered (1) declaring that the January 1 start date for petition signature collection in R.I. Gen. Laws § 17-1-2(9)(iii) is unconstitutional; and (2) permanently enjoining Defendants from enforcing or applying the start date set forth in § 17-1-2(9)(iii) as a ground for rejecting or refusing to certify signatures collected by the Moderate Party for inclusion on the official Rhode Island election ballot in 2010."

59 *Block v. Mollis*, 618 F. Supp. 2d 142 (D.R.I. 2009), https://casetext.com/case/block-v-mollis.

But the State of Rhode Island was not yet done with me. The Moderate Party was about to embark on something that had not, to the best of my knowledge, been done before in the state. We needed to collect more than 22,000 validated signatures to qualify the party. We had one hundred volunteers, none of whom had spent much time collecting signatures, but they all favored a new choice on the ballot. One day, I received a secret heads-up from an employee at Rhode Island's Board of Elections (BoE), who told me to move quickly on getting the signatures because the BoE was considering passing new regulations regarding signature collection that would have caused us many problems. With the help of some extremely generous donors (without whose support the party would never have been launched), we hired a dozen professional signature collectors who gathered the lion's share of the 35,000 signatures we collected from around the state. We collected those signatures in seven weeks.

The party was formally recognized in September 2009. I walked away from it in 2013 to run as a Republican in the 2014 gubernatorial election. Getting traction with candidates, voters, and donors was just too hard. The signature fight instantly established a toxic relationship between me and the BoE. The BoE's executive director was very political and ultimately was fired from his job.[60] My decade of interactions with the BoE have convinced me that the board has acted to slow down political competition and frustrate attempts to address dirty voter data. The BoE has dragged its feet when asked to investigate potential voting abuses. In one circumstance, a board member smirked as he indicated that the BoE could not do anything about a possible voting crime because the state's one-year statute of limitations had expired. The BoE had known of this issue for many months.

60 Brian Crandall, "RI Board of Elections Fires Executive Director Kando," turnto10.com, August 31, 2016, https://turnto10.com/news/local/ri-board-of-elections-fires-executive-director-kando.

More than one politically connected person has told me that "the powers that be" regret not trying harder to keep me from establishing the new party. I have no problem at all believing this statement. Those who enjoy a stranglehold on political power will do anything to keep that power. Disadvantaging political opposition is the surest path to holding on.

Depressingly, the Libertarian Party in New Hampshire encountered a similar problem in 2014 when their state shortened the period in which it could collect signatures to qualify their party—from twenty-one months to seven. They sued in federal court in New Hampshire, where the judge determined that the state law was constitutional and was properly used in the state's exercise of its power to "avoid ballot clutter." How is it possible that two more or less identical situations in two different states yielded polar opposite legal verdicts? Why do our laws and legal findings allow partisan politicians to enact laws that disadvantage new political parties? Can anyone explain to me why it is considered ballot clutter when new party options appear on the ballot? On appeal to the First Circuit Court of Appeals in Boston, the court did not overrule the New Hampshire case. My lawsuit was never mentioned in the appeals decision.[61]

Our legal system has set a precedent that allows for the systematic suppression of new political parties. How did this ever happen and how do we fix it?

We don't have a great mechanism for putting election officials into positions of power. Officials put into office via elections deal with partisan pressures. Appointed officials are often put in place by partisan politicians, leading to more of the same. In Rhode Island, our appointed Board of Elections had no Republicans on the

61 *Libertarian Party of New Hampshire v. Gardner*, 843 F.3d 20 (1st Cir. 2016), https://casetext.com/case/libertarian-party-of-new-hampshire-v-gardner-8.

seven-member board until Democratic governor McKee took heat for not putting at least one Republican into a seat.

I have seen firsthand how elected officials sometimes deal with voter fraud through the prism of partisanship. For example, I was discussing voter fraud with senior members of the governor's office in a red state. As we discussed people casting duplicate votes in that state and other states, I was asked about the breakdown of the political parties of those voters. When I said that the fraud skewed more frequently toward Republicans than Democrats, the shocking response was, "Why would we do anything about this then?"

Voter fraud is unacceptable to some politicians unless it benefits their own party.

Chapter 22

HOW STATES BOTCH VOTER DATA

Before I get going on the many things that can go wrong with states' voting data, I would be remiss not to praise one state that makes its data reasonably available and avoids most of the problems many other states suffer from. Nevada's voter data is very clean—notably better than most other states. I have looked carefully at Nevada's voter data several times and have not seen significant problems.

New York State has the most extreme example of how county-based differences negatively impact the integrity of a state's voting data. New York's sixty-two counties recorded votes cast in the 2022 general election in thirty different ways. New York State's voter history file contains many tens of millions of votes. Anyone trying to dig out all the votes cast in 2022 from that file must look for votes cast with an election described as: "20221108 GE," "2022 GENERAL ELECTION," "GE 20221108," "GENERAL ELECTION 2022," "GENERAL ELECTION, 2022," "GENERAL 2022," and on and on and on.

Most states identify votes cast in a specific election simply with the (correct) election date. New York's statewide voter file has a lot of corrupted data, with nearly 6,500 votes cast in the 2022 general election labeled with the wrong date. Those votes are identified as being cast in the "2022108" election instead of the "20221108" election. That missing "1" will interfere with many computerized queries. I wonder if state election officials know of this issue and if their systems account correctly for these mislabeled votes.

Different states and counties implement the same laws and rules differently, yielding a chaotic result for our national elections. None of this means our elections are corrupt, or that an election loss can be blamed on these inconsistencies. However, a well-implemented technical solution for our federal elections could guarantee that every registered voter and every vote cast in these elections is subject to the same vetting process, regardless of where that voter lives. Some data standards should also be insisted upon—what New York is doing is silly and easily resolved. It is unfathomable to me that statewide election officials in New York have not insisted that every county report on votes cast in a specific election the same way.

Dead Voters on the Rolls

Federal law requires most states (though not all—I'll get into it) to remove deceased registered voters from the voter rolls. Some states do this job exceedingly well, and others carry tens of thousands of dead registered voters on the rolls.

There are multiple likely reasons why voter roll maintenance differs dramatically from state to state. Based on my work with some states and their data, some of the worst states for maintenance of their voter rolls also have the worst data with which to work. For example, based on voter data acquired in January of 2023, New Jersey has 25,783 registered voters with a date of birth of 01/01/1800. Of those registered voters, 7,896 cast ballots in the 2022 general election. It will be tough for New Jersey election officials to determine if any of these 25,783 voters are deceased because an accurate date of birth, along with name and address, are critical components used to identify a person uniquely.

The fact that thousands of voters without valid dates of birth on the voter rolls cast ballots in New Jersey in the 2022 general election is not evidence of voter fraud. It is evidence of a very poorly maintained voter list. Unfortunately, New Jersey is not alone regarding poorly maintained voter lists. I use New Jersey's data here because the state had the misfortune of its data coming across my desk while I was writing this chapter.

When presented with evidence that deceased voters are on the rolls, some states will gladly accept the help and investigate. Rhode Island is a star example of this. Using the process I described here, I identified nearly 2,000 deceased registered voters on Rhode Island's rolls a few years ago. State election officials asked for the list, went through it, and, last I knew, had removed more than 75 percent of the identified voters because they were confirmed as deceased. Some of those voters had died many years in the past.

When presented with lists of tens of thousands of deceased voters, other states will lash out and fight rather than engage in what should be a no-brainer task—removing dead voters from the rolls. An example of this knee-jerk, ideological reaction to outside interest in the voter rolls is seen in Pennsylvania, which in 2020 was presented a list of almost 22,000 deceased registered voters that I produced. Rather than evaluate the list for accuracy and take action where appropriate, Pennsylvania did nothing.

The state was eventually sued for not properly maintaining its voter rolls. Burning money and time, a legal fight needlessly played out over an essential list-maintenance activity. Pennsylvania settled the case and promised to evaluate my list. Ultimately, nearly 90 percent of the voters I had identified as deceased were removed from the voter rolls or marked as "inactive"—an excellent outcome. That said, 189 of the voters I had identified as deceased before the 2020 general election cast votes in 2020, with several of those votes making the news as people were charged and convicted of voter fraud for casting ballots in the name of the deceased.

Does It Matter?

Why should anyone care whether a state carries tens of thousands of dead voters on its rolls? In Pennsylvania's case, some of those dead registered voters had fraudulent votes cast in their name in the 2020 election. Sloppy data opens the door to unwanted results, such as the dead casting ballots or people taking multiple bites of the electoral apple. We don't clean up the data because massive fraud is occurring. We clean up the data because voting is at the core of our republic and is mission-critical. We clean up the data to ensure that no one games the system, whether to gain one vote or many.

Should we care about voter fraud if the number of fraudulently cast votes is relatively small? George Bush's margin of victory over Al Gore in Florida in 2000 was 537 votes. Florida's outcome determined our country's president in 2000. I confirmed that more than 2,000 duplicate votes were cast in Florida and some other states in the 2016 general election. In Virginia in 2018, a tied legislative race was broken by drawing a name out of a canister. The outcome of that drawing determined control of Virginia's House of Delegates.[62] If proven voter fraud was produced in either of the above situations, it would be extraordinarily difficult to say with certainty how that fraud may have impacted the result. We want our voter registration data to be as clean as possible, so that we are as protected as possible from a situation in which an election is decided by a few votes when fraudulent votes were cast.

Cleaning up our voter registration data is not rocket science. We should care about even a small amount of voter fraud because it should be unacceptable to everyone that even one vote has been made fraudulently.

62 Sarah McCammon, "Virginia Republican David Yancey Wins Tie-Breaking Drawing," npr.org, January 4, 2018, https://www.npr.org/2018/01/04/573504079/virginia-republican-david-yancey-wins-tie-breaking-drawing.

Chapter 23

ACCESS TO VOTER DATA IN THE UNITED STATES

It is illegal to obtain voter registration files from some states in the US. If this statement feels wrong to you—it should. But it is true. There are states in our country that will not provide to a member of the public, for any price, a file of who is registered to vote and who voted in that state's election. So several states conduct their elections without providing public transparency regarding who can and who does vote.

For the states that will provide their voter data upon request, the range of costs charged for this data is astonishing, ranging from free to over $37,000.

North Dakota is the only state in the country that does not have voter registration and is exempt from a federal law that requires it, since the state did not have voter registration in place when the National Voting Rights Act was passed in 1993. As a result, a fundamental requirement of our federal elections—that you must be registered to vote—does not apply to voters in North Dakota. North Dakota's exemption leads to many data challenges for federal election integrity.

There needs to be more consistency between states regarding what data is offered in voter registration files, how much the data costs, and who can access this data.

What does it say about our federal elections when the public cannot obtain a complete list of who can vote and who voted? Unfortunately, that is the current sad state of affairs regarding federal election data and transparency in the United States.

Why are some states charging members of the public to see the data that underpins our elections? American taxpayers, via federal tax dollars, have spent more than $5 billion on election infrastructure in our states. Do these states really need a couple of thousand dollars more in fees generated by selling voter data to the public who paid to generate it?

The states that charge for the data may use those fees to limit who can access the data. You must genuinely want to see a state's data if you are willing to pay thousands of dollars to obtain it.

Granted, some awful things have been done with voter data over the years. For example, someone in New England got voter files from Rhode Island and Connecticut and put those files up on a website for all to see. Some companies acquire voter data from states and then resell that data or, worse, monetize the data in marketing applications. Registering to vote should not result in a barrage of junk mail. I believe these are not acceptable uses of a voter registration file. At the same time, using high costs to limit the misuse of voter data is an unacceptable solution. There are far better ways to limit how voter data can be used, such as sensible nondisclosure agreements and terms of use.

Alabama is the hands-down winner when it comes to the most expensive voter data in the country. Alabama charges a penny for each voter record that it delivers electronically.[63] With over 3.7 million registered voters, it costs over $37,000 to acquire Alabama's full voter regis-

63 Office of Alabama Secretary of State Wes Allen, "Public Inspection of Voter Registration Information," https://www.sos.alabama.gov/sites/default/files/voter-pdfs/VoterListRequestForm.pdf.

tration database. What possible explanation can Alabama provide to justify the cost of its data relative to the cost of every other state's?

Arizona had costly voter data a few years ago—also in the $30,000 range. Today, Arizona's cost for its data is under $1,000 because the state was pressured to lower the price.

The Help America Vote Act of 2002 provided substantial funding to help states pay for new voting infrastructure mandates like fully computerized, statewide voter registration lists. Every state must now maintain its statewide voter registration database in a computer system by federal law.

This means, for example, that Alabama elections officials are not printing out reams of paper to provide their voter rolls, nor are they making photocopies of them—they are clicking a computer key to produce an electronic file of their statewide voter registration database. They should provide a secure website for the public to download their purchased data. The entire transaction should take an Alabama elections worker 10–15 minutes. Thirty-seven thousand dollars is a lot for those 10–15 minutes of work.

The information I am providing here was current as of early 2021. States can, and do, modify what they charge for data and what information is provided. These modifications can be driven by legislative changes at the state level, executive fiat by election officials, or even in response to legal challenges.

What each state charges for its voter registration data, what information each state provides with its voter registration, whether or not a state makes its voter registration data available to the public, and the file format of the data provided are all moving targets. Any list with this data should be assumed to have some out-of-date information.

How can large states such as California, Florida, New York, and Pennsylvania possibly offer their data for free or less than $50 while a state such as Alabama charges over $37,000? What is Alabama trying to hide? Why is Alabama able to get away with this? Alabama can charge $37,000 for its voter registration file because federal law is silent on putting sensible boundaries on what a fair cost to the public should be for the data.

Here is a chart of what each state charges for its voter registration data. The states marked with a cost of "N/A" have something else going on, which I will explain.

State	Cost
AL	$37,000
AK	$20
AZ	$621
AR	$0
CA	$0
CO	$100
CT	$300
DE	$28
FL	$0
GA	$250
HI	N/A
ID	$21
IL	N/A
IN	N/A
IA	$1,100
KS	$200
KY	$2,000
LA	$5,005
ME	N/ A

State	Cost
MT	$1,000
ND	N/A
NE	$500
NV	$0
NH	N/A
NJ	$375
NM	$5,034
NY	$0
NC	$0
OH	$0
OK	$0
OR	$500
PA	$20
RI	$25
SC	$2,500
SD	$2,500
TN	$2,500
TX	$5,481
UT	$1,050

State	Cost
MD	N/A
MA	N/A
MI	$23
MN	$51
MS	$1,100
MO	$0

State	Cost
VT	$0
VA	$9,943
WA	$0
WV	$500
WI	$12,500
WY	$0

"N/A"

Massachusetts

By far, Massachusetts has the most abusive policy regarding making its statewide voter database available. State law mandates that the statewide voter registration file not be made available to the public except to state party committees, statewide candidates, and "any other individual, agency or entity that the state secretary designates."

A request for the statewide list yields a response from the secretary of state's office stating that state law makes the statewide list "not public" but that every Massachusetts municipality can be contacted individually and that municipality's list may be purchased. I know this because I asked the Massachusetts secretary of state's office for statewide voter data, and this is the response I received.

There are 351 municipalities in Massachusetts. Contacting each one to purchase its voter list is many times more difficult than the effort required to reach every other state combined to request their voter lists.

Worse, Massachusetts municipalities have different voting systems. In looking at the voter registration files from just twenty or so towns, I found six different file formats, meaning six different sets of code were needed to process those files. I am sure many more file formats are scattered around the other Massachusetts municipalities.

What is the purpose of a state law that makes the statewide voter file not public but makes voter registration data at the municipal level public? What state purpose is served by making it five to eight times harder to acquire a statewide voter file in Massachusetts than the combined effort to obtain the data from every other state in the country?

Hawaii

Hawaii does not provide a statewide voter registration file to a member of the public. Even though federal law under the Help America Vote Act requires states to maintain a single database with all registered voters, Hawaii will not provide a copy of statewide voting data upon request. Hawaii instead requires anyone who wants to acquire a statewide file of voters to request files from each county in the state.

I don't have insight into why Hawaii operates this way. Is it possible that Hawaii does not keep a current statewide database of voters and that if you want a current statewide file, the only way to get one is by going to each county? If this is the case, I would argue that Hawaii is not entirely in conformance with the Help America Vote Act's requirements.

There are four counties in Hawaii. Someone who wants a statewide file of registered voters in the state must do four times more work to obtain that data than to obtain the data from New York State or Florida. As of 2021, the four Hawaiian counties share the same data format, meaning one set of programs can be used for all four counties.

The Public Interest Legal Foundation has sued Hawaii over this issue.[64]

64 Public Interest Legal Foundation, "*PILF v. Nago*," https://publicinterestlegal.org/cases/pilf-v-nago.

Illinois

Illinois will only provide its statewide voter registration file to "state political committees" and government entities. The state will provide access to the voter registration list via a computer screen at the Board of Elections office, but the list cannot be copied or printed. Making a voter list available via a computer screen without being able to store the list as a file is an empty gesture when you consider that Illinois has more than 8 million registered voters.

Illinois's basic premise, that election transparency is accomplished by forcing someone interested in looking at the voter rolls to come to a specific office and then only read data on a screen, is a farce. Unfortunately, several other states follow this playbook, as we will see.

As an aside, while Rhode Island does provide a voter file to the public for $25, the state stopped giving full dates of birth a few years ago in a move made by then secretary of state Nellie Gorbea. I had been evaluating Rhode Island's voting data and found it lacking in several areas, which I brought to their attention. Now, anyone who wants to access full dates of birth in Rhode Island voter registration data must drag themselves to the Rhode Island secretary of state's office, where full birth dates can be viewed on a screen but not exported. This move reduced the ability of anyone to evaluate the state's voter data fully.

Indiana

Indiana will only provide its statewide voter registration file to political parties, the media "for publication in a news broadcast or newspaper," and members of state legislative leadership.

Maine

Maine will only provide its statewide voter registration file to political parties, "get out the vote" efforts, law enforcement, and current office holders.

The language above would seem to seriously disadvantage a candidate for office who is not affiliated with a political party, denying that candidate access to the voter rolls.

This situation has been contested in a long-running federal lawsuit filed by the Public Interest Legal Foundation. Interestingly, the Department of Justice recently entered the case, submitting a "friend of the court" filing in support of the case that Public Interest Legal has made.[65]

Maryland

Maryland will only allow voters registered in the state to request the voter file for $125.

New Hampshire

New Hampshire will only allow political parties, political committees, and candidates to obtain the state's voter rolls. However, anyone can go to the state records and archives office to view the entire voter roll of over 1,000,000 voters on a computer screen—but they may not print, duplicate, or transmit the data. Another gesture that is intended to provide a veneer of transparency but is useless in practice.

New Hampshire does not want anyone looking at its voter data.

North Dakota

Only North Dakota does not register its citizens to vote. Every other state registers its voters for federal elections. Therefore, no one can request a voter registration file because one does not exist. However, a file of who cast votes (called "the central voter file") can be requested by candidates, political committees, and political parties.

65 Public Interest Legal Foundation, "*PILF v. Bellows*," https://publicinterestlegal.org/wp-content/uploads/2023/07/DOJ-Amicus-Brief-1.pdf.

Voter registration was mandated in a voting law passed in 1993 called the National Voter Registration Act (NVRA). However, four states were exempted from the NVRA because they did not have voter registration when the bill passed: Minnesota, North Dakota, Wisconsin, and Wyoming.

North Dakota's representatives in Congress work to keep North Dakota free from voter registration. Significant legislation to reform our elections passed the House in 2021 (called HR 1) but failed to pass the Senate. Congressman Kelley Armstrong (R-ND) added an amendment that guaranteed that North Dakota would not be made subject to the requirement to register voters.[66]

Why does it matter that North Dakota lacks voter registration? In our federal election, where a person may only vote once by federal law, it is currently impossible to determine if someone in North Dakota can also vote in another state. Consequently, the voting infrastructure implemented in North Dakota prohibits any proactive screening from determining where duplicate registered voters exist. Instead, only a reactive look after the fact can determine if a duplicate vote occurred. But, since North Dakota severely limits who can see their central voter file, even this after-the-fact look is impossible.

We should not have a federal election system in which some states are exempted from following the rules other states must follow. This situation weakens the integrity of our federal elections.

It is time to remove all state exemptions to all federal election laws. Every state should be mandated to follow every law. It is incredible that our national election infrastructure has devolved this far.

66 KX Conversation, "Rep. Kelly Armstrong on HR1", KXNET.com, March 9, 2021, https://www.kxnet.com/news/local-news/kx-conversation-rep-kelly-armstrong-on-hr-1/.

Chapter 24

WHAT IS IN EACH STATE'S VOTER DATA?

The data elements in each state's publicly available voter data vary remarkably. This, too, is an issue when considering our elections from a top-down view: we have a federal election with federal laws and rules.

As elected election officials and legislatures change ideologically over time, one can see how more left-leaning officials have acted to limit the voting data available to the public, with states such as Rhode Island, Massachusetts, and Maine aggressively taking actions to limit access to voting data or limiting the data that is made publicly available. To be fair, red states such as Indiana also hide their data from public examination. I fail to see how this protects our elections. On the contrary, it makes them far less transparent.

Some key elements in voter registration data are necessary to understand how states conform to our various election laws. These elements are critical when auditing whether deceased voters are on the rolls or duplicate votes have been cast, be it between states or within the same state.

Why is it necessary for the public to be able to audit election data? Because there is tremendous variability in the quality of state data. Transparency and accountability demand that state election officials do not hide evidence that they are performing their jobs poorly. In the absence of any oversight at the federal level and what amounts to the Wild West in terms of data across the country, the only accountability comes from public review of the data. Audits cannot be credibly conducted by the same people maintaining the data being audited.

Some ideologues will insist that list maintenance somehow infringes on someone's right to vote. The Help America Vote Act takes care of any list maintenance error that mistakenly removes someone from the voter rolls by implementing "provisional voting." Provisional voting permits someone who encounters a problem with casting their ballot due to registration issues to be able to cast a provisional ballot anyway. Once the vote is cast, a multiday window starts during which whatever problems stand in the way can be resolved.

Granted, the provisional ballot process is inconvenient, requiring potential voters to address an issue with their voter registration data before their vote is counted. But—there is a problem with those voters' registration data! A mission-critical system has rules that define how that system works. If the rules are not enforced, system integrity is compromised. Remember Judy Presto? Not following required voter registration data mandates—such as looking for and removing deceased voters—allowed a dead person to cast a vote.

Of course, states need to exercise care to ensure that list maintenance only removes voters who, as can be shown with a high degree of certainty, should no longer be on the voter rolls. Being dead is a rational reason for a voter to be removed from the voter rolls and can be determined with a high degree of certainty—not a perfect degree, but high. No database is perfect! A person with multiple voter registrations in different states should be contacted to determine which registration should be active, and the other registrations should be removed. These are basic concepts, and they are not being effectively implemented in far too many circumstances.

Basic Data Needs

To uniquely identify a voter and perform basic auditing tasks, one needs:

- Full name including first name, middle name, last name, and any suffix such as Junior, Senior, or III.
- Full address where the voter resides. Ideally, states should maintain address data conforming to US Postal Service standards. Many do not.
- Out-of-state mailing address information. Again, this address information should conform to US Postal Service standards.
- Full date of birth.
- Registration date.

Additionally, it is necessary for states to provide the voter identification number that they assign to every registered voter. States must provide this number because this number is how the state uniquely identifies each voter in its system. When a voter's address or name changes for whatever reason, the voter identification number remains the same. Without a voter identification number, anyone looking at the data will be faced with the birthday problem for every single voter.

The different states are all over the place regarding providing this basic identifying information in the voter rolls, but birth date information is the most frustratingly inconsistent data element provided by the states. Roughly half the states provide a full date of birth: day, month, and year; nearly half only give a year of birth. Several states offer no piece of the date of birth.

Some state election officials twist themselves into pretzels to justify limiting birth date information, claiming that somehow providing birth date information represents an identity theft risk. These officials apparently have never looked at social media, where many people willingly provide full birth dates for all to see. They also have not looked at other websites where people freely offer up their dates of birth. You can Google just about anyone's date of birth. Pretty much everyone of a certain age has received birthday congratulations from the AARP, along with a solicitation to join.

I want to mention an important caveat regarding voters who are victims of domestic abuse. Many states offer these voters anonymity in the public voter rolls—with good reason. I am not arguing that voters who have filed domestic abuse complaints should have their voting data exposed. There is a place for anonymity when someone's life is in danger.

The SSN Myth

Regarding our collective protection from identity theft . . . we have no protection. Our most theoretically secure and confidential piece of data—our Social Security number—is not secure and is no longer confidential. Please excuse me for taking a few paragraphs to talk about this.

The massive fraud committed against state unemployment insurance systems during the first year of COVID-19 shows just how badly Social Security numbers have been compromised. In my home state of Rhode Island, where roughly half a million people work, more than half a million unemployment insurance claims were filed.[67] A great many of those claims were fraudulent. I had a fraudulent claim filed in my name. I found out when I was notified as the owner of my business that one of my employees—me—had filed a claim. The claim tried to have the check sent to an address in Kentucky. Whoever attempted this fraud somehow added the address in Kentucky to my file at one of the three large credit bureaus.

You must provide a Social Security number to file an unemployment insurance claim. I know very few people in Rhode Island who

67 Tim White, "More than 40% of RI Unemployment Claims Flagged as Fraudulent during Pandemic," WPRI.com, March 5, 2021, https://www.wpri.com/target-12/more-than-40-of-ri-unemployment-claims-flagged-as-fraudulent-during-pandemic.

did not have a fraudulent unemployment insurance claim filed in their name. Were the state's computer systems hacked?

Across the country, it is estimated that up to $135 billion in unemployment insurance benefits were fraudulently taken.[68] That is a lot of Social Security numbers when considering that the average unemployment insurance benefit is a couple of hundred dollars a week.

Massive data breaches have exposed most of our Social Security numbers to hackers. Small data breaches have exposed our Social Security numbers to hackers. On the dark web, you can buy everything you need to commit identity theft, including Social Security numbers.

The United States needs to replace Social Security numbers with something else.

Sorry for the digression. But speaking of Kentucky . . .

The Kentucky Problem

Kentucky poses a much different challenge with the voter data that the state provides to the public. Kentucky does not offer the voter identification number the state uses to identify a voter uniquely. As far as I know, Kentucky is the only state that withholds this critical data element.

As justification, the state mumbled something about how providing this number could somehow pose a risk to the operations of the state's elections. Every other state in the country that provides voter registration data provides the voter identification number with that data.

I suppose Kentucky may have a very odd system that does not assign voter registration numbers to voters. If that is the case, the state should fess up and address this system shortcoming because there is no other way to identify a voter uniquely.

68 US Government Accountability Office, "Unemployment Insurance: Estimated Amount of Fraud During Pandemic Likely Between $100 Billion and $135 Billion," September 12, 2023, https://www.gao.gov/products/gao-23-106696.

Alternatively, Kentucky may have a system that uses Social Security numbers as the unique identifier in the voter registration system. If that is the case, Kentucky's system violates one of the key best practices in system design: you do not uniquely identify people in a system using highly confidential information such as Social Security numbers.

If the state does assign voter identification numbers to voters, then refusing to provide that number amounts to an effort on the state's part to hinder access to critical public data regarding elections.

It should not be necessary to fight fifty different states over what data they do or do not provide with their voter registration information. Federal dollars pay for these systems. Congress should mandate what data every state must provide.

What comes after Kentucky's attempt to stifle inquiry by withholding voter identification numbers? Some state deciding to withhold last names? There is nothing to stop a state from doing this, except filing yet another lawsuit with an uncertain outcome.

Out-of-State Addresses

Out-of-state mailing addresses also provide a critical window into how our federal elections are conducted. An out-of-state mailing address in a voter's registration data is used if a person at one address wants election-related material sent to a different address.

It occurred to me to try to match up out-of-state mailing addresses in a voter registration in Rhode Island with the residential address for a voter with the same name and age in, say, North Carolina. In this analysis, I exclusively used a voter's address information provided by that voter in their voter registration data in two states to prove that the registrations belong to the same person. It is easiest to explain this visually. (See the graphic on the following page.)

In looking at the data acquired in April of 2023 from only seven states, 180,023 matched pairs of registrations were found using the abovementioned matching technique. Of the 180,023 matched pairs

Voters Who Voted in Two Different States in the 2022 General Election
One state's address is the out-of-state mailing address in the other state's registration data

	RI		NC
Voter ID:	11111	Voter ID:	22222
Last Name:	BOGUS	Last Name:	BOGUS
First Name:	NAME	First Name:	NAME
Middle Name:	FAKE	Middle Name:	
Street Number:	123	Street Number:	678
Street:	EASY ST	Street:	MAIN ST
City:	SOMETOWN	City:	ANYWHERE
State:	RI	State:	NC
Zip Code:	99999	Zip Code:	99998
Party:	DEM	Party:	REP
Date of Birth:	3/11/1949	Date of Birth:	
Year of Birth:	1949	Year of Birth:	1949
Vote Type:	ABSENTEE	Vote Type:	EARLY
Out of State Address Information		**Out of State Address Information**	
Street Number:	678	Street Number:	
Street:	MAIN ST	Street:	
City:	ANYWHERE	City:	
State:	NC	State:	
Zip Code:	99998	Zip Code:	

of registrations, the data indicates that in 77 matched pairs, a duplicate vote was cast against each registration. For these 77 duplicate votes, the individual's voter registration data is all that is needed to prove that these votes are illegal.

Chapter 25

MAIL BALLOTS: VITAL VOTING MECHANISM, TOOL FOR EVIL, OR SOMETHING ELSE?

Former president Trump skillfully made mail ballots a controversial issue during and after the 2020 general election. His arguments caused many of his followers to distrust mail ballots. The former president made the case (echoed by some other losing candidates in 2020) that mail ballots should not be counted, that they are not legal, and that no self-respecting Republican should vote by mail.

Trump's likely motivation for demonizing mail ballots is pretty apparent: thanks in no small part to his messaging during the campaign, many Republicans were going to vote in person on Election Day while many other voters were going to vote by mail during that first year of COVID-19. If you consider his electoral situation strategically, he segmented a considerable chunk of his opponent's votes so that he could attempt to nullify them—a bold, if unsound, strategy.

The 2020 election saw a record number of voters cast ballots by mail. I voted by mail in 2020 for only the second time in my life. I first voted by mail in 2014, when my town had many proposed changes to the town charter on the ballot. There was much talk about long lines expected at polling places as voters slogged through pages of legalistic language in proposed charter changes. I spent an hour casting my ballot at my kitchen counter.

So what is the real story behind mail ballots? Are they good or evil? Are they inherently less secure than voting in person? Are they illegal? As with anything to do with voting, the answers depend on what state is involved, the specific rules in question, and the person you ask.

Although I have laid out, in general terms, how mail ballots work, I will describe the process again here. I do this because you should not discuss—or argue about—mail ballots without fully understanding how they function and how they are implemented.

The order of steps in the mail ballot process in many states go something like this:

1. A registered voter requests a mail ballot.
2. That request is received by election officials.
3. A mail ballot is sent out to the voter at the address provided in the request—which might not be the residential address in the voter registration.
4. The mail ballot is mailed back to election workers if the voter votes. The ballot itself has no markings that indicate who the voter was who cast the vote. Instead, the ballot is enclosed in an envelope that contains the voter's biographical information, signature, and possibly, depending on the state, a witness signature or even a requisite notary stamp. That envelope is enclosed in an outer envelope used for mailing purposes.
5. Election officials receive the envelope in the mail.
6. The inner envelope is removed from the mailing envelope, and election workers try to confirm the information on the inner envelope. The confirmation process can include verifying the signature, ensuring that witness signatures or notary stamps are provided, and confirming that the requested information on the envelope is there, like dates of birth, full name, and the correct address corresponding to the voter registration.

7. Once the inner envelope has passed all the checks, the envelope can be opened and the ballot removed. This happens at different times in the process, depending on the state. When the ballot is separated from the envelope, the vote is considered officially cast.
8. If the information on the inner envelope fails the checks, election workers might begin trying to contact the voter to remedy whatever is wrong.

If an argument is to be made against mail ballots, it must be about the implementation of one of the steps above.

Voting by mail is legal in every state in the country. However, there are differences among the states regarding who can vote by mail and whether or not those voters need an acceptable excuse to do so. I am struck once again by how a difference in the way states handle one specific voting issue can impact how or whether a US citizen can vote in our federal elections, depending on where they live. For example, how can a citizen in one state cast a vote for president by mail for any reason, while a citizen in another may not unless they have an acceptable reason as defined by the state? This is yet another example where all states should have the same set of rules for the conduct of our federal elections.

It is impossible to have a generalized debate about whether or not mail ballots are secure, because mail ballot security differs from state to state. Also, how a state confirms a voter's identity matters more when it comes to mail ballot voting than it might with in-person voting—especially if in-person voting requires a voter to provide some form of identification.

If you are frustrated by all of the caveats I am throwing your way before getting to the meat of this subject—join the club. We are in the most complex area of election law, where state laws and rules—and all states differ from one another—define and regulate how our federal elections are run.

I will preface everything that follows with this: state-based voting laws change continuously. Therefore, compiling a list of state laws for a specific election issue takes time and effort. I am relying on the work of others as I describe how many states observe one law or another. Since the totality of voting laws in the country is constantly in flux, one or more of the data points I refer to in the following section will likely have changed since the data was compiled.

Ballot Harvesting

Let's jump right to one of the most contentious aspects of mail ballots. Ballot harvesting is the activity of collecting mail ballots from voters and returning them to election workers. Harvesting usually refers to the collection of many ballots—not just one or two—by someone who is not a close connection to the voter.

According to Ballotpedia,[69] as of August 2022, only Alabama bans anyone from turning in someone else's ballot. Twenty-five states allow anyone selected by the voter to turn in their ballot (which makes unrestricted ballot harvesting possible). Eleven states restrict who can turn in ballots on behalf of another to family members, caregivers, or other household members. Thirteen states do not address whether someone else can turn in a ballot on behalf of an individual.

Allowing someone else to deliver a voter's mail ballot makes sense for people with health issues, mobility challenges, and so on. Of course, if someone is receiving mail at their home, it seems likely that person should also be able to return the mail ballot by mail.

In the interest of full disclosure, in my 2014 campaign for governor, I hired Rhode Island's "mail ballot king" to do whatever he does regarding mail ballots. I was never told what he did or what kind of impact his operation had on my campaign. In Rhode Island, harvesting mail ballots is legal. Generally, mail ballot operations in

69 Ballotpedia, "Ballot Harvesting (Ballot Collection) Laws by State," August 2023, https://ballotpedia.org/Ballot_harvesting_(ballot_collection)_laws_by_state.

Rhode Island tend to focus on senior living facilities and densely populated areas. It is commonly understood that you are likely to lose your race if you do not engage fully in such mail ballot operations in Rhode Island. I still lost that race, but I do not blame you, Eddie—although I think you should be regulated out of your job.

Should partisan players (candidates, campaign workers, anyone paid to collect ballots, or volunteers for a campaign) be allowed to handle other voters' ballots? Remember that collecting someone else's ballot often means being in the room with the voter while the ballot is filled out.

Some states have mind-numbingly different rules regarding how candidates and campaigns can interact with voters on Election Day versus how they can interact with mail ballot voters. For example, in Rhode Island, no candidate or campaign worker can stand within one hundred feet of the entrance to a voting location on Election Day. This is meant to prevent campaigns from unduly influencing voters. Great. However, Rhode Island does not prevent candidates and campaign workers from standing over the shoulder of someone filling out a mail ballot. I cannot reconcile these two very different rules—it makes no sense.

In the 2022 general election, some candidates for the Rhode Island state legislature handed in eight or more mail ballots on behalf of others. In a recent election (pre-COVID-19), one notary public collected and notarized more than two hundred mail ballots in Newport, Rhode Island, earning $15 per hour for her work.[70] (Post-COVID-19, the state no longer requires mail ballots to be notarized.)

Every one of these harvested mail ballots includes votes for federal offices. The net effect is that some states deliver harvested votes in our

70 Jennifer Bogdan, "Board of Elections Votes to Allow 230 Mail Ballots Notarized by Same Person," *Providence Journal*, August 28, 2017, https://www.providencejournal.com/story/news/politics/2017/08/28/board-of-elections-votes-to-allow-230-mail-ballots-notarized-by-same-person/19104356007.

federal elections and others do not. Inconsistency and integrity are oppositional ideas.

The Trump campaign asked me to look for evidence of harvested mail ballots in Pennsylvania nursing homes in the 2020 general election. I purchased a list of more than three hundred nursing homes in the state, which included address information. Using that information, I found all mail ballots cast from those addresses in the election.

In terms of scale, not all that many nursing home mail ballots were cast in Pennsylvania in 2020—just 2,903 out of 4,482 voters registered to vote at nursing home addresses. In nearly every case, the total number of mail ballots received by date was pretty evenly distributed. However, in three cases a large percentage of the mail ballots from one nursing home were cast on the same day. In one circumstance, 226 votes were cast from the same facility on the same day. In another, 160 votes were cast from a different facility on the same day. Remember that ballot harvesting was legal in Pennsylvania during the 2020 election.

Mail ballot harvesting runs counter to the goal of running transparent and fair elections. Mail ballots provide a reasonable way (if the identity issues described in the following are well-handled) for voters to vote when they cannot get to a polling place or want to avoid dealing with long lines or other problems that can be associated with voting in person. No partisan actor should have the ability to be near anyone about to cast a vote—whether in person or by mail ballot.

Mail Ballot Security

A fundamental issue with mail ballots is how the vote is made: in private, without interacting with election workers, and in many states without providing strong proof of identity. So how do we confirm the identity of who cast a mail ballot?

Before COVID-19, to vote by mail, a Rhode Island voter had to prove their identity to a notary, who would then stamp their mail ballot.

In response to the COVID-19 crisis, the state removed the requirement that a mail ballot must be notarized or have witness signatures. Much partisan arguing accompanied this change, with folks on the right stating that this change weakened election integrity and folks on the left arguing that the change augmented election accessibility. Both arguments are correct.

My issue with the change is that Rhode Island election officials have not confirmed all of their registered voters' identities. If registered voters have unconfirmed identities, how can a state eliminate the only check to stop a fraudulent vote from being cast by mail?

Some folks will argue that matching the signatures on the mail ballot with the signatures attached to the voter registration record is a sufficient check to verify identity. But that presumes that the voter registration has been appropriately confirmed in the first place. When I last checked, many tens of thousands of Rhode Islanders whose identity the state did not verify managed to cast ballots. How do I know? I asked the state to identify voters on the rolls who did not have Social Security numbers or driver's license information (let's call this PII, Personally Identifiable Information) in the voter registration database. When I first asked for this information in 2018, the state had more than a hundred thousand votes cast by voters without PII—one third of the total ballots cast.

The Help America Vote Act of 2002 requires states to confirm the identities of new voters with the state's department of motor vehicles or the Social Security Administration. This is done by using the PII supplied in the voter registration application. Unfortunately, the Help America Vote Act fails to address what states should do about voters who registered to vote before 2004. And, perhaps worse, hundreds of newly registered voters in Rhode Island without PII voted in 2020. What a mess.

Rhode Island is by no means the worst state for not confirming who its voters are. For example, in 2020, New York State had over

1,800,000 votes cast by voters whom the state identified to me as not having PII.

Election officials cannot properly remove a deceased voter from the rolls who has incorrect or no PII attached to the voter record. It is difficult to look up a voter in the Social Security Death Master File if you do not know that voter's Social Security number. If a project is funded to process New York's voter file, I expect they will find many deceased registered voters in New York State.

What Is an Appropriate Window for Voting in Advance of an Election?

Mail ballots and early voting introduce the weird scenario in which a vote can be cast in advance of an election (in some cases, many weeks in advance) by a voter who dies before Election Day. Some states have laws that explicitly acknowledge this situation and clarify whether votes cast in this circumstance are valid or invalid. Other states are silent on the topic.

What is a reasonable window to allow for voting before an election? What is to stop a state from creating a multimonth voting window? Why does it matter? At what point does voting and dying within an extremely long voting window become voting from the grave?

In my experience as a candidate for governor, the messaging calendar was a critical part of my election strategy. We wanted my most important message points to come out close to the election. The reason for this was twofold: 1) most normal people (and I do not consider myself in this category) only start paying attention to campaigns close to the date of the election, and 2) excellent message points brought out too early lose their impact over time.

A campaign's messaging at the end of the race is called by many the "final argument." A lot of thought, time, and (often) money is poured into creating and broadcasting a campaign's final argument. Long early voting windows greatly complicate campaigns' final argument considerations. Candidates want their message to be heard and considered by as many voters as possible. So how do you reach the earliest of early voters with your final argument *and* effectively communicate that message to the many voters who are not yet tuned in to the noise the different campaigns deluge them with?

I lay out these challenges from my perspective as a candidate for statewide office. The complications of many different early voting windows for presidential campaigns are mind-boggling. Long early voting windows can leave the earliest of early voters regretting their vote if substantive issues arise after they cast their ballot.

Many early voters tend to be the most partisan. They are either self-motivated to vote for or against a candidate, or they vote for a party and could never bring themselves to vote for any candidate not in that party. They may be readily identifiable by campaigns and bombarded with phone calls, mailings, and even in-person visits to cast their vote early.

There is a place for early voting. It is good to make voting as convenient as possible for as many voters as possible. However, long early voting windows combined with legal ballot harvesting can make elections about something other than ideas and messaging; it turns it into a race for who can collect the most mail ballots the fastest. We are all the poorer for that. The country is worse off if the determining factor in our elections is what campaign can harvest the most mail ballots.

Have Harvested Mail Ballots Caused Election Problems?

Yes, but only locally—and rarely, from what I can find.

In the 2018 primary election in North Carolina's 9th Congressional District, McCrae Dowless organized a ballot harvesting operation violating North Carolina election law.[71] He was accused of fraudulently signing some of the ballots that were harvested or filling in some of the ballots himself. He died before he could be tried. Dowless's harvesting operation was conducted on behalf of a Republican candidate. The voting results for this race were nullified, and a new election was held. Four other individuals who worked with Dowless on the harvesting operation pleaded guilty to the charges against them.

There are dozens of recent examples of individuals convicted of voter fraud for voting by mail on behalf of one or two others.[72] Bear in mind that it can be difficult to get law enforcement to investigate and prosecute voter fraud of this magnitude.

I am not claiming that mail ballot fraud is prevalent. However, as I hope you have seen from our discussions of mail ballot data, a lot is left to be desired in terms of good data to help us assess how mail ballots are working. Anyone claiming that there is no fraud involving mail ballot voting does so in the absence of good data to make that claim. Anyone relying upon numbers of convictions to make their case ignores the fact that there is little in the way of an organized law enforcement effort to look for mail ballot fraud.

71 Fox8 Digital Desk, "McCrae Dowless Arrested Amid NC Absentee Ballot Investigation in 9th District Congressional Race," MyFox8.com, February 27, 2019, https://myfox8.com/news/politics/your-local-election-hq/mccrae-dowless-arrested-amid-nc-absentee-ballot-investigation-in-9th-district-congressional-race.

72 Jeremy Bernfeld, "Rhode Island Man Pleads No Contest to Voter Fraud Charges," thepublicsradio.org, May 19, 2022, https://thepublicsradio.org/article/rhode-island-man-pleads-no-contest-to-voter-fraud-charges; Office of Public Affairs, US Department of Justice, "Woman Arrested for Voter Fraud Scheme," January 12, 2023, https://www.justice.gov/opa/pr/woman-arrested-voter-fraud-scheme; Associated Press, "Wisconsin Activist Who Ordered Absentee Ballots in Others' Names Charged with Election Fraud, ID Theft," NBCNews.com, September 2, 2022, https://www.nbcnews.com/politics/2022-election/wisconsin-activist-ordered-absentee-ballots-others-names-charged-elect-rcna46019; Ed Shanahan, "Former New York Election Official Admits to Vote Fraud Scheme," *New York Times*, January 11, 2023, https://www.nytimes.com/2023/01/11/nyregion/voter-fraud-election-official-guilty.html.

There are two or three recent examples where someone was convicted of fraudulently casting a dozen or so mail ballots.[73] Mail ballots provide a tantalizing and theoretically low-risk way to commit voter fraud. The most partisan among us are most likely to commit this fraud. The issue is similar to leaving your keys in a parked car with the windows rolled down. While most people will leave the car alone, there are always those seeking to take advantage if the risk of getting caught is low. The least we can do in our national elections is help honest people stay honest.

73 NBCCT News Room, "Former Stamford Democratic Party Official Sentenced for Absentee Ballot Fraud," nbcconnecticut.com, November 14, 2022, https://www.nbcconnecticut.com/news/local/former-stamford-democratic-party-official-sentenced-for-absentee-ballot-fraud/2915636.

Chapter 26

THE MASTER LEVER: SINGLE-PARTY VOTING

One of my proudest political moments to date was the day in 2014 when the Rhode Island legislature, after years of my advocacy and fifty years of thwarted efforts by others, voted to eliminate single-party voting from the Rhode Island ballot. Another name for this voting mechanism is (or at least was in Rhode Island) the "master lever," a term whose origins go back to when we voted on mechanical machines.

The master lever is a terrible form of voting, where voters cast ballots for a party instead of a person. When I first engaged in the advocacy effort in 2009, Rhode Island was one of only thirteen states still using the master lever.

Only six states still have the single-party voting mechanism on their ballots today. According to the National Conference of State Legislatures,[74] those states are Alabama, Indiana, Kentucky, Michigan, Oklahoma, and South Carolina. All are red states except for Michigan.

74 National Conference of State Legislatures, "Straight-Ticket Voting," January 20, 2023, https://www.ncsl.org/elections-and-campaigns/-straight-ticket-voting.

The reason it took fifty years to eliminate the master lever in Rhode Island is that the Democratic Party is dominant at all levels of government, and eliminating the master lever was not in the Democrats' collective interests. Also, in Rhode Island there is no way to move a bill through the general assembly without the buy-in of Rhode Island's politically powerful speaker of the house and senate president. Rhode Island has no form of ballot initiative, which means the public cannot get a change made unless the speaker and president endorse that change. Rhode Island Democrats have controlled the state for more than seventy years.

The story of how I helped the advocacy effort achieve victory is entertaining and a great example of using data to bring about change. It is also important to highlight that a small number of states still cling to this terrible form of voting.

I first testified to a Rhode Island Senate legislative committee in 2009 in favor of a perennial bill to eliminate the master lever. I will never forget the aggressive admonishment I received from one of the senators on the committee, who claimed that my efforts to eliminate single-party voting amounted to racism. He asserted without evidence that people of color would be somehow disadvantaged at the polls if they could not vote using the master lever. I was not allowed to respond to his statements because he was "commenting" on my testimony and not engaging in dialogue. I was put off by the senator and offended by his allegation. This was one of my earliest experiences dealing with Rhode Island's legislature and legislators.

Up to this point, the problem with the advocacy effort was that the same collection of "good government" types and Republican sponsors of the bills were the only people coming out to put pressure on the legislature. Republicans are the party of opposition in Rhode Island, so most efforts to reform how the government works come via the GOP here. I decided to try to get more people involved in making change through social media and email campaigns. The challenge was educating enough people about the issue, making them care, and then getting them to come out in person to appear before the legislature. The state's primary newspaper, the *Providence Journal*, was instrumental in helping to address these issues. The *Journal*'s editorial pages consistently attacked the master lever and Rhode Island's entrenched politicians who were unwilling to make a needed change because it ran counter to their political self-interest. It is beyond sad that today the *Providence Journal* no longer editorializes. An important megaphone has been silenced because the state's newspaper could no longer afford a full-time editorial pages editor.

Arguing that Rhode Island was an outlier relative to most other states (one out of thirteen that still had the master lever) was an effective talking point for advocates, as was the idea that when we vote, we should be voting for a human being and not a political party. But it wasn't enough.

Larger crowds began to show up in person for the annual hearings, first a few dozen and, by the end, hundreds. Unfortunately, legislative leadership made life very difficult for the members of the public who cared enough to show up. Long committee agendas inevitably stuck the master lever legislation at the end, meaning everyone who showed up had to wait, often for three or four hours or more, sitting on the floor in hallways. Also, by addressing the master lever legislation after 7 or 8 p.m., the media would not cover the issue due to deadlines.

The breakthrough came in 2012 in the basement of Burrillville's (a small, rural community) town hall. Rhode Island has a state law that orders all ballots from an election to be sealed for twenty-two months once certified. Once sealed, the only way to access the ballots is to get the Board of Elections to agree to unseal them (forget about it) or go to court.

I got a phone call from a Burrillville town employee who told me that the 2010 ballots were due to be discarded because the twenty-two months under seal had elapsed. They asked me if I wanted to look at them prior to their discarding them. Did I ever!

I was on the 2010 ballot, running as a third-party candidate for governor. It would be amazing to see how the master lever was used in that election. Burrillville was an ideal place to do this analysis because just over 5,000 ballots had been cast in 2010—a manageable amount of paper to review. What I did not realize was that Burrillville had a two-page ballot in 2010, so we had to sift through 10,000 pieces of paper, not 5,000.

The executive director of Rhode Island's chapter of Common Cause, John Marion; a board member of Operation Clean Government, Beverly Clay; and a few other people came in and helped to sort through all that paper, identifying more than six hundred master lever ballots cast in the 2010 general election. We spent all day in the basement.

Once we had separated out the master lever ballots, the town official scanned them for us, and we were in business! Bev Clay went through every one of those ballots, calculating vote totals for each candidate on the ballot by hand, sorted by which master lever party had been indicated.

There were some incredible examples of voters not understanding how this relatively simple voting mechanism worked. For instance, in the ballot shown on page 233, the voter did not identify a single party for the single-party voting mechanism. Instead, they marked all three parties listed.

In the example on page 234, the voter failed to correctly mark the ballot—twice. Because the voter failed to connect the arrow, the ballot reader could not determine how the vote was cast. As a result, this ballot likely yielded no vote cast unless election workers went back and manually determined that the master lever mechanism should have been selected.

Precinct ID 0302
Congressional District 1
Representative District 47
Voting District 2
Senate District 23

Ballot 1

OFFICIAL ELECTION BALLOT
STATE OF RHODE ISLAND
TOWN OF BURRILLVILLE
TUESDAY, NOVEMBER 2, 2010

0 22

1. To vote:
Complete the arrow(s) pointing to your choice(s) with a single bold line, like this .

2. To vote for a write-in candidate:
Print the name of the person on the blank line labeled "Write-In" for the office and complete the arrow pointing to your write-in choice like this .

3. To cast a straight party vote:
Complete the arrow pointing to the party of your choice in the straight party section of the ballot. If you cast a straight party vote and also vote for an individual candidate or candidates for a certain office on the ballot, the straight party vote will not be counted for that office and only the individual candidate or candidates voted for will be counted for that office.

STRAIGHT PARTY
To vote a "Straight Ticket" complete the arrow pointing to the party of your choice.

- MODERATE
- DEMOCRAT
- REPUBLICAN

REPRESENTATIVE IN CONGRESS
DISTRICT 1
TWO Year Term
Vote for 1

- David N. CICILLINE — DEMOCRAT
- John J. LOUGHLIN, II — REPUBLICAN
- Gregory RAPOSA — Vigilant Fox
- Kenneth A. CAPALBO — Independent
- Write-in

GOVERNOR
FOUR Year Term
Vote for 1

- Kenneth J. BLOCK — MODERATE
- Frank T. CAPRIO — DEMOCRAT
- John F. ROBITAILLE — REPUBLICAN
- Lincoln D. CHAFEE — Independent
- Joseph M. LUSI — Independent
- Ronald ALGIERI — Independent
- Todd GIROUX — Independent
- Write-in

LIEUTENANT GOVERNOR
FOUR Year Term
Vote for 1

- Elizabeth H. ROBERTS — DEMOCRAT
- Robert P. VENTURINI — Hour With Bob
- Robert J. HEALEY, JR. — Cool Moose
- Write-in

SECRETARY OF STATE
FOUR Year Term
Vote for 1

- A. Ralph MOLLIS — DEMOCRAT
- Catherine Terry TAYLOR — REPUBLICAN
- Write-in

ATTORNEY GENERAL
FOUR Year Term
Vote for 1

- Christopher H. LITTLE — MODERATE
- Peter F. KILMARTIN — DEMOCRAT
- Erik B. WALLIN — REPUBLICAN
- Keven A. McKENNA — Independent
- Robert E. RAINVILLE — Independent
- Write-in

GENERAL TREASURER
FOUR Year Term
Vote for 1

- Gina M. RAIMONDO — DEMOCRAT
- Kernan F. KING — REPUBLICAN
- Write-in

SENATOR IN GENERAL ASSEMBLY
DISTRICT 23
TWO Year Term
Vote for 1

- Paul W. FOGARTY — DEMOCRAT
- Julian P. FORGUE — REPUBLICAN
- Write-in

REPRESENTATIVE IN GENERAL ASSEMBLY
DISTRICT 47
TWO Year Term
Vote for 1

- Cale P. KEABLE — DEMOCRAT
- Donald A. FOX — REPUBLICAN
- Write-in

TOWN COUNCIL
FOUR Year Term
Vote for 4

- Kevin M. BLAIS — MODERATE
- Wallace F. LEES — DEMOCRAT
- Nancy L. ANGELL — REPUBLICAN
- Edward J. BLANCHARD — DEMOCRAT
- Stephen N. RAWSON — REPUBLICAN
- Norman C. MAINVILLE — DEMOCRAT
- David J. PLACE — REPUBLICAN
- John Michael KARMOZYN, JR. — DEMOCRAT
- Jacqueline ZAHN — Independent
- Cynthia J. LUSSIER — Independent
- Write-in
- Write-in
- Write-in
- Write-in

NON-PARTISAN SCHOOL COMMITTEE
FOUR Year Term
Vote for 4

- Raymond J. TRINQUE
- Mary Margaret KARMOZYN
- Aaron J. COUTU
- Paul J. COUTURE
- Peter F. LAMBERT
- Write-in
- Write-in
- Write-in
- Write-in

STATE QUESTIONS ON BACK

LOCAL QUESTIONS ON SEPARATE BALLOT

VOTE BOTH FRONT AND BACK OF BALLOT

Precinct ID 0304
Congressional District 1
Representative District 47
Voting District 4
Senate District 23

Ballot 1

OFFICIAL ELECTION BALLOT
STATE OF RHODE ISLAND
TOWN OF BURRILLVILLE
TUESDAY, NOVEMBER 2, 2010

0 24

1. To vote:
Complete the arrow(s) pointing to your choice(s) with a single bold line, like this.

2. To vote for a write-in candidate:
Print the name of the person on the blank line labeled "Write-in" for the office and complete the arrow pointing to your write-in choice like this.

3. To cast a straight party vote:
Complete the arrow pointing to the party of your choice in the straight party section of the ballot. If you cast a straight party vote and also vote for an individual candidate or candidates for a certain office on the ballot, the straight party vote will not be counted for that office and only the individual candidate or candidates voted for will be counted for that office.

STRAIGHT PARTY
To vote a "Straight Ticket" complete the arrow pointing to the party of your choice.

MODERATE
DEMOCRAT
REPUBLICAN

REPRESENTATIVE IN CONGRESS DISTRICT 1
TWO Year Term
Vote for 1

David N. CICILLINE — DEMOCRAT
John J. LOUGHLIN, II — REPUBLICAN
Gregory RAPOSA — Vigilant Fox
Kenneth A. CAPALBO — Independent
Write-in

GOVERNOR
FOUR Year Term
Vote for 1

Kenneth J. BLOCK — MODERATE
Frank T. CAPRIO — DEMOCRAT
John F. ROBITAILLE — REPUBLICAN
Lincoln D. CHAFEE — Independent
Joseph M. LUSI — Independent
Ronald ALGIERI — Independent
Todd GIROUX — Independent
Write-in

LIEUTENANT GOVERNOR
FOUR Year Term
Vote for 1

Elizabeth H. ROBERTS — DEMOCRAT
Robert P. VENTURINI — Hour With Bob
Robert J. HEALEY, JR. — Cool Moose
Write-in

SECRETARY OF STATE
FOUR Year Term
Vote for 1

A. Ralph MOLLIS — DEMOCRAT
Catherine Terry TAYLOR — REPUBLICAN
Write-in

ATTORNEY GENERAL
FOUR Year Term
Vote for 1

Christopher H. LITTLE — MODERATE
Peter F. KILMARTIN — DEMOCRAT
Erik B. WALLIN — REPUBLICAN
Keven A. McKENNA — Independent
Robert E. RAINVILLE — Independent
Write-in

GENERAL TREASURER
FOUR Year Term
Vote for 1

Gina M. RAIMONDO — DEMOCRAT
Kernan F. KING — REPUBLICAN
Write-in

SENATOR IN GENERAL ASSEMBLY DISTRICT 23
TWO Year Term
Vote for 1

Paul W. FOGARTY — DEMOCRAT
Julian P. FORGUE — REPUBLICAN
Write-in

REPRESENTATIVE IN GENERAL ASSEMBLY DISTRICT 47
TWO Year Term
Vote for 1

Cale P. KEABLE — DEMOCRAT
Donald A. FOX — REPUBLICAN
Write-in

TOWN COUNCIL
FOUR Year Term
Vote for 4

Kevin M. BLAIS — MODERATE
Wallace F. LEES — DEMOCRAT
Nancy L. ANGELL — REPUBLICAN
Edward J. BLANCHARD — DEMOCRAT
Stephen N. RAWSON — REPUBLICAN
Norman C. MAINVILLE — DEMOCRAT
David J. PLACE — REPUBLICAN
John Michael KARMOZYN, JR. — DEMOCRAT
Jacqueline ZAHN — Independent
Cynthia J. LUSSIER — Independent
Write-in
Write-in
Write-in
Write-in

NON-PARTISAN SCHOOL COMMITTEE
FOUR Year Term
Vote for 4

Raymond J. TRINQUE
Mary Margaret KARMOZYN
Aaron J. COUTU
Paul J. COUTURE
Peter F. LAMBERT
Write-in
Write-in
Write-in
Write-in

STATE QUESTIONS ON BACK

LOCAL QUESTIONS ON SEPARATE BALLOT

VOTE BOTH FRONT AND BACK OF BALLOT

The ballot I'll show you on page 235 demonstrates the issue that destroyed the master lever in Rhode Island. This ballot represents a master lever vote for the Moderate Party. The Moderate Party had three candidates on the Burrillville ballot: me for governor, Chris Little for attorney general, and Kevin Blais for town council. Even though

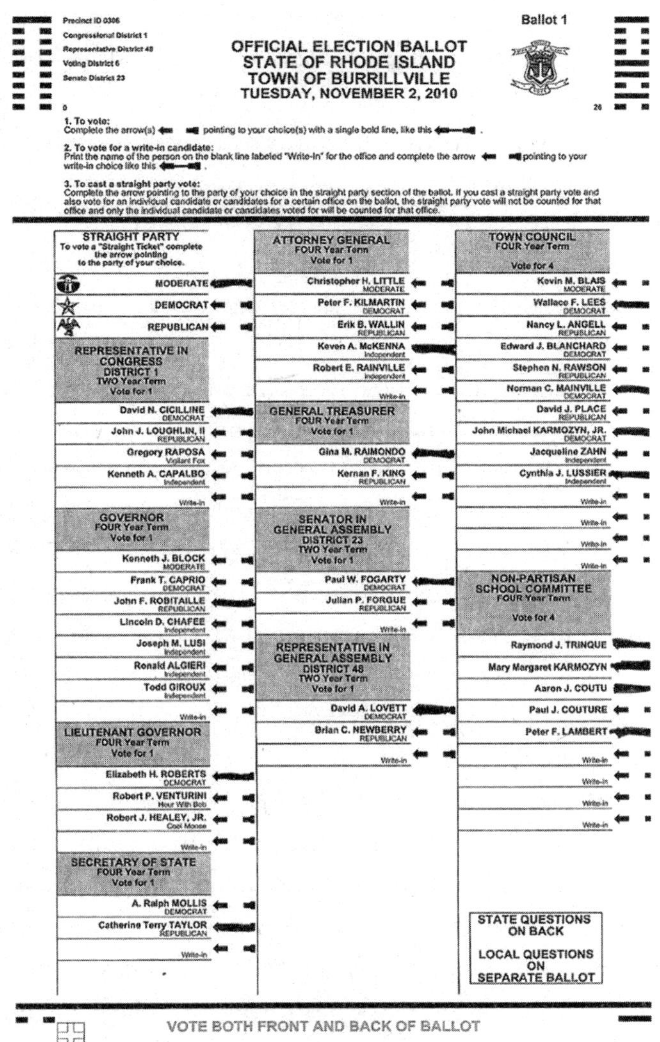

Precinct ID 0306
Congressional District 1
Representative District 48
Voting District 6
Senate District 23

Ballot 1

OFFICIAL ELECTION BALLOT
STATE OF RHODE ISLAND
TOWN OF BURRILLVILLE
TUESDAY, NOVEMBER 2, 2010

0 26

1. To vote:
Complete the arrow(s) pointing to your choice(s) with a single bold line, like this .

2. To vote for a write-in candidate:
Print the name of the person on the blank line labeled "Write-In" for the office and complete the arrow pointing to your write-in choice like this .

3. To cast a straight party vote:
Complete the arrow pointing to the party of your choice in the straight party section of the ballot. If you cast a straight party vote and also vote for an individual candidate or candidates for a certain office on the ballot, the straight party vote will not be counted for that office and only the individual candidate or candidates voted for will be counted for that office.

STRAIGHT PARTY
To vote a "Straight Ticket" complete the arrow pointing to the party of your choice.

- MODERATE
- DEMOCRAT
- REPUBLICAN

REPRESENTATIVE IN CONGRESS DISTRICT 1
TWO Year Term
Vote for 1

- David N. CICILLINE — DEMOCRAT
- John J. LOUGHLIN, II — REPUBLICAN
- Gregory RAPOSA — Vigilant Fox
- Kenneth A. CAPALBO — Independent
- Write-in

GOVERNOR
FOUR Year Term
Vote for 1

- Kenneth J. BLOCK — MODERATE
- Frank T. CAPRIO — DEMOCRAT
- John F. ROBITAILLE — REPUBLICAN
- Lincoln D. CHAFEE — Independent
- Joseph M. LUSI — Independent
- Ronald ALGIERI — Independent
- Todd GIROUX — Independent
- Write-in

LIEUTENANT GOVERNOR
FOUR Year Term
Vote for 1

- Elizabeth H. ROBERTS — DEMOCRAT
- Robert P. VENTURINI — Hour With Bob
- Robert J. HEALEY, JR. — Cool Moose
- Write-in

SECRETARY OF STATE
FOUR Year Term
Vote for 1

- A. Ralph MOLLIS — DEMOCRAT
- Catherine Terry TAYLOR — REPUBLICAN
- Write-in

ATTORNEY GENERAL
FOUR Year Term
Vote for 1

- Christopher H. LITTLE — MODERATE
- Peter F. KILMARTIN — DEMOCRAT
- Erik B. WALLIN — REPUBLICAN
- Keven A. McKENNA — Independent
- Robert E. RAINVILLE — Independent
- Write-in

GENERAL TREASURER
FOUR Year Term
Vote for 1

- Gina M. RAIMONDO — DEMOCRAT
- Kernan F. KING — REPUBLICAN
- Write-in

SENATOR IN GENERAL ASSEMBLY DISTRICT 23
TWO Year Term
Vote for 1

- Paul W. FOGARTY — DEMOCRAT
- Julian P. FORGUE — REPUBLICAN
- Write-in

REPRESENTATIVE IN GENERAL ASSEMBLY DISTRICT 48
TWO Year Term
Vote for 1

- David A. LOVETT — DEMOCRAT
- Brian C. NEWBERRY — REPUBLICAN
- Write-in

TOWN COUNCIL
FOUR Year Term
Vote for 4

- Kevin M. BLAIS — MODERATE
- Wallace F. LEES — DEMOCRAT
- Nancy L. ANGELL — REPUBLICAN
- Edward J. BLANCHARD — DEMOCRAT
- Stephen N. RAWSON — REPUBLICAN
- Norman C. MAINVILLE — DEMOCRAT
- David J. PLACE — REPUBLICAN
- John Michael KARMOZYN, JR. — DEMOCRAT
- Jacqueline ZAHN — Independent
- Cynthia J. LUSSIER — Independent
- Write-in
- Write-in
- Write-in
- Write-in

NON-PARTISAN SCHOOL COMMITTEE
FOUR Year Term
Vote for 4

- Raymond J. TRINQUE
- Mary Margaret KARMOZYN
- Aaron J. COUTU
- Paul J. COUTURE
- Peter F. LAMBERT
- Write-in
- Write-in
- Write-in
- Write-in

STATE QUESTIONS ON BACK

LOCAL QUESTIONS ON SEPARATE BALLOT

VOTE BOTH FRONT AND BACK OF BALLOT

the single-party vote was for the Moderate Party, this voter marked their ballot for other candidates instead of Moderate candidates, overriding the master lever. As a result, not a single Moderate candidate received a vote on this ballot.

In fact, of 116 Moderate Party master lever votes cast in Burrillville in 2010, I received only 18 votes. Chris Little did a little bit better, netting 32 votes. What went on here? Voters used the master lever section of the ballot to indicate their *political leanings* instead of using it as a voting mechanism.

With this information, I could make the case that voters misused the master lever voting mechanism. By 2013, we were getting hundreds of people to attend the state house to push for eliminating the master lever.

Once it became known how I obtained access to the Burrillville ballots, the Board of Elections changed its policies and no longer allowed Rhode Island's cities and towns to warehouse sealed ballots, instead requiring those ballots to be warehoused at the Board of Elections. This decision flies in the face of serving the public interest. It ensures that a careful examination of physical ballots cannot be performed—under any circumstances. Had I not been allowed to bend the rules and look at Burrillville's unsealed ballots, no one would have known that Rhode Island's ballots had a serious issue with how voters used them.

The pressure on the general assembly to eliminate the master lever was now extraordinary. In early 2014, I was again a candidate for governor, running as a Republican. During a campaign stop, I bumped into Speaker of the House Gordon Fox, a nice guy sitting in a position of power that seems to invite corruption. Rhode Island's speaker is the most powerful elected official in the state, enjoying far more power than Rhode Island's governor, who is constitutionally weak. Moreover, Rhode Island's speaker enjoys far more power than many speakers in other states. I remember talking with a former Massachusetts speaker who envied how completely Rhode Island's speaker controls the general assembly and the state. Speaker Fox pulled me aside and told me I had done a "masterful" job with the master lever. I thanked him and asked him if that meant we could move the bill to the floor for an up or down vote. A smirk replaced his smile, and we parted ways.

In March 2014, Speaker Fox was arrested for accepting bribes, at least one of which came as a check.[75] A chaotic process quickly ensued where wannabe speakers made promises to members of the House, essentially buying speaker votes. Finally, a new speaker emerged, Nicholas Mattiello. We soon had our largest turnout to a committee hearing to advocate for eliminating the master lever, close to 250 people—for a "good government" issue! The unexpected change in leadership was the last element needed to topple the master lever, and before the 2014 legislative session ended, the master lever in Rhode Island met its demise.

During a debate later in 2014, a reporter asked me what I had accomplished in politics aside from the recent master lever victory, implying that I had not done much else. I could have pointed to my successful constitutional challenge to Rhode Island's restrictive ballot access laws, my success in earning 6.5 percent of the vote in 2010 to keep the new political party I founded on the ballot, or waste and fraud findings I made in Rhode Island's Department of Health and Human Services. Instead, I rejected the premise of his question and thoroughly enjoyed taking a master lever victory lap.

Perhaps some of you were wondering how the Moderate Party candidates wound up being displayed first in every race. For every election, Rhode Island determines ballot position via a lottery. Recognized political party candidates are positioned first on the ballot, with one drawing for the political parties determining the positions of every party candidate. Then, unaffiliated candidates, sometimes called "independent" candidates, participate in a second lottery for ballot positions underneath party candidates.

75 GoLocalProv News Team, "The History of Gordon Fox: From Camp St. to Speaker to Prison," GoLocalProv.com, June 11, 2015, https://www.golocalprov.com/news/the-history-of-gordon-fox-from-camp-st.-to-speaker-to-prison.

The Moderate Party was incredibly lucky to have gained the first ballot position. The positioning of unaffiliated candidates after the party candidates is just one of many examples of how the Democrats and Republicans make life difficult for any candidate who runs outside of those parties.

There are issues here relevant to the conduct of elections across the country. Voted ballots should be made available for public review. They should not be hidden under seal. I don't know how many states seal their ballots after an election, but that practice is bad for transparency and should be ended everywhere. Transparency makes for better elections.

Single-party voting should be eliminated across the country. We vote for individuals, not parties. The master lever ballot design and voting function confused voters. The concept is not difficult to understand—mark one place on the ballot to vote for every candidate running as a candidate for that political party. And yet, the physical ballots showed us that a considerable percentage of voters misused the master lever voting mechanism.

In states such as Rhode Island, where just two people (the speaker and the senate president) tightly control the legislature and the state, election reforms cannot be left to the whims of elected officials. Incumbent politicians and dominant political parties will use the lawmaking and legal processes to solidify their advantages whenever possible. It should not take fifty years of advocacy, thousands of hours wasted sitting in the legislature's halls, and a speaker's arrest to make election reforms happen.

Chapter 27

RANKED CHOICE VOTING

Several states and municipalities are experimenting with ranked choice voting (RCV), sometimes called Instant Runoff Voting. With this ballot style, voters can vote for multiple candidates for the same elected office, ranking their preferences as first choice, second choice, and so forth. Advocates for this form of voting say that RCV:

- enhances voter participation
- improves the voting experience
- resolves the "problem" of an election with more than two candidates in which the victor does not win the majority of votes
- is easy to understand
- encourages candidates outside of the two major parties to run
- decreases negative campaigning

Those opposed claim that RCV:

- benefits extremist candidates
- confuses voters
- causes some votes not to be counted
- may not be worth the cost to implement

There are academic studies supporting both sides of the debate. Different groups that support RCV often use the same language in their materials, with the same talking points. Some of those opposed provide data from actual elections to bolster their arguments.

In short, there is not a lot of hard data on which to make decisions about RCV. But the data that is out there should give everyone pause.

Pushback against RCV is not necessarily ideological. A ballot initiative in Washington, DC, to implement RCV has been challenged by a lawsuit filed by the DC Democratic Party.[76] The District's Republican Party also opposes RCV. Support for voting reforms like RCV and top-two elections comes only from the two major parties when the reform benefits the party in a specific situation.

Let's start with what a ranked choice ballot might look like. This image is a sample ballot from Maine's 2020 First Congressional District election.

76 Michael Brice-Saddler, "DC Democrats Sue to Block Ranked-Choice Voting Ballot Measure," *Washington Post*, August 8, 2023, https://www.washingtonpost.com/dc-md-va/2023/08/08/dc-ranked-choice-ballot-measure-open-primaries-lawsuit.

SS District 35 SR District 3 York District 5 Style No. 309

State of Maine Sample Ballot
General Election, November 3, 2020

Instructions to Voters

To vote, fill in the oval like this ⬬

To rank your candidate choices, fill in the oval:

- In the 1st column for your 1st choice candidate.
- In the 2nd column for your 2nd choice candidate, and so on.

Continue until you have ranked as many or as few candidates as you like.

Fill in no more than one oval for each candidate or column.

To rank a Write-in candidate, write the person's name in the write-in space and fill in the oval for the ranking of your choice.

President Vice President	1st Choice	2nd Choice	3rd Choice	4th Choice	5th Choice	6th Choice
Biden, Joseph R. Harris, Kamala D. Democratic	O	O	O	O	O	O
De La Fuente, Roque "Rocky" Richardson, Darcy G. Alliance Party	O	O	O	O	O	O
Hawkins, Howard Walker, Angela Nicole Green Independent	O	O	O	O	O	O
Jorgensen, Jo Cohen, Jeremy Libertarian	O	O	O	O	O	O
Trump, Donald J. Pence, Michael R. Republican	O	O	O	O	O	O
Write-in	O	O	O	O	O	O

U.S. Senator	1st Choice	2nd Choice	3rd Choice	4th Choice	5th Choice
Collins, Susan Margaret Bangor Republican	O	O	O	O	O
Gideon, Sara I. Freeport Democratic	O	O	O	O	O
Linn, Max Patrick Bar Harbor Independent	O	O	O	O	O
Savage, Lisa Solon Independent	O	O	O	O	O
Write-in	O	O	O	O	O

Rep. to Congress District 1	1st Choice	2nd Choice	3rd Choice
Allen, Jay T. Bristol Republican	O	O	O
Pingree, Chellie M. North Haven Democratic	O	O	O
Write-in	O	O	O

Turn Over for Additional Contests

Voters are asked to rank their choices for president, US senator, and First Congressional District representative. Assuming that a voter ranks all four candidates for the US Senate race, let's discuss how vote counting works in Maine.

Imagine that the Senate race was extremely close and that none of the four candidates had enough first-choice votes to win the election with more than 50 percent of the vote. Our imaginary voter ranked Independent Lisa Savage first, Max Patrick Linn second, Susan Collins third, and Sara Gideon fourth.

After counting all the first-place votes, Savage had the fewest votes of the four candidates and would be eliminated. For all voters who picked Savage as their first choice, their second-choice candidates would be counted in the second round. Our voter cast a second-choice ballot for Linn. None of the three remaining candidates in the second round of counting had more than 50 percent of the vote, and Linn had the fewest votes and was eliminated. For Linn's first- and second-choice voters, the next candidate down each voter's list would get the next vote. In my example, that would be Collins. At this point, only two candidates remain, and the candidate with the most votes would be declared the winner.

Got it? Yeah . . . it's not simple.

Worse, the ballot design shown is doomed to be misunderstood by some voters. In the chapter on single-party voting, I display some ballots where the simpler-to-understand mechanism of choosing all candidates for one party was prolifically misunderstood and misused. RCV is much more challenging to understand and use than single-party voting.

Without scientific evidence, I believe the first candidates for each race on an RCV ballot will have a more significant advantage than the first candidates on a non-RCV ballot. It has been shown that ballot position can give a candidate in the first position an advantage in winning the vote from certain voters. Adding language such as "first choice," "second choice," and so on, seems likely to add to that advantage. I looked for any academic study that looked into this and could not find one.

How many voters will mismark the rankings, for example, casting votes for two second-choice candidates?

What happens in my scenario above if my imaginary voter only made a first- and second-choice vote, failing to mark a third-choice candidate? After Linn was eliminated, my voter's ballot would be considered "exhausted." As a result, my voter's ballot no longer counts in the election. The implications of this are that the victorious candidate in the third round would win with fewer votes counted in the overall election than the number of votes cast in the first round. In Maine, some races saw a 6 percent rate of ballot exhaustion.[77]

Are our elections better if fewer voters' ballots count in the second and third rounds of vote tallies compared to the first round?

It is not at all unreasonable to imagine that a voter would refuse to vote for several candidates in a multicandidate race. For example, highly partisan conservative voters would never vote for any candidate perceived to be "on the left," and highly partisan liberal voters would never vote for any candidate perceived to be "on the right."

Academic Arguments against RCV

The MIT Election and Data Science Laboratory published a study in 2021 by Jesse Clark[78] that showed, through surveys, that voters found that RCV ballots were challenging to fill out, had lower levels of confidence and satisfaction with the voting experience, and believed RCV ballots were "slanted against the respondent's party [meaning that the voter felt that the RCV ballot design conferred an advantage, somehow, to the other party]." This study also found that incivility in

77 Matt Vasilogambros, "Nearly 9,000 Ballots Were Not Counted in Maine's New Election System," *Stateline*, June 27, 2018, https://stateline.org/2018/06/27/nearly-9000-ballots-were-not-counted-in-maines-new-election-system.

78 Jesse Clark, "The Effect of Ranked-Choice Voting in Maine," MIT Election Data & Science Lab, March 18, 2021, https://electionlab.mit.edu/articles/effect-ranked-choice-voting-maine.

RCV elections increased, directly contradicting what RCV advocates claim. However, Clark does confirm that "non-major party candidates saw a 6 percent increase due to RCV."

It seems unlikely that ballot styles impact the civility of a race. Unfortunately, negative campaigning works, at least in some circumstances. A losing candidate will likely "go negative" to make up ground.

The Pew Charitable Trusts published a story by Matt Vasilogambros[79] that documented the thousands of voters whose ballots were exhausted in the 2018 Maine elections that used RCV. Also noted was the number of ballots that were "spoiled," a situation where the voter made a mistake on the ballot egregious enough that the vote could not be counted. Hundreds of ballots were spoiled in the 2018 election just in the city of Bangor.

The Hill ran an opinion piece from Nathan Atkinson, an assistant professor at the University of Wisconsin Law School, and Scott C. Ganz, an associate teaching professor at Georgetown University's McDonough School of Business. This piece made the case that RCV makes it more possible for extremist candidates to win elections.[80] For example, in a race with RCV where a far left, far right, and moderate candidate are on the ballot, the extreme candidates are likely to garner more first-round votes than the moderate candidate, causing the moderate candidate to be eliminated. This would happen even though the moderate candidate was a more palatable choice for most voters and would have won based on second-choice rankings.

79 Matt Vasilogambros, "Nearly 9,000 Ballots Were Not Counted in Maine's New Election System," *Stateline*, June 27, 2018, https://stateline.org/2018/06/27/nearly-9000-ballots-were-not-counted-in-maines-new-election-system.

80 Nathan Atkinson and Scott C. Ganz, "The flaw in ranked-choice voting: rewarding extremists," *The Hill*, October 30, 2022, https://thehill.com/opinion/campaign/3711206-the-flaw-in-ranked-choice-voting-rewarding-extremists.

My Take on RCV

As someone who believes that third-party candidates are good for our elections, I should embrace RCV as a good thing. But I cannot. I don't believe RCV solves any of the problems advocates claim it solves.

Does it matter if a candidate wins a four-person race with 45 percent of the vote in a non-RCV election or 50.1 percent in the third round of an RCV election? I don't believe so. Putting a candidate over the top with second- and third-choice rankings does not confer a mandate on that candidate. Not at all. Mandates come from overwhelming popular support, not a contrived vote-counting mechanism.

From a third-party candidate perspective, ranked choice voting is *not* the magic bullet to level the playing field with the major-party candidates. To overcome the disadvantages of running outside the two-party system and have voters believe that an outside candidate can succeed, the systemic roadblocks Democrats and Republicans erect to disadvantage other candidates must be disassembled.

From seemingly benign issues like ballot placement to ballot access (qualifying a party or a candidate to be on the ballot), campaign finance, and gerrymandering, the two major parties have constructed a legal rat's nest of laws that combine to disadvantage nontraditional candidates.

It is worth a brief look at how incumbents use seemingly sensible laws to squelch competition, using as an example state-enacted campaign finance laws. Many states (but not all) place limits on how much money candidates can raise from donors. These limits are usually calendar year–based or set a limit within the term of the office being sought. For example, Rhode Island's governor serves a four-year term. The state has an annual campaign finance limit of $2,000 per year. Over a four-year term, Rhode Island's governor can raise $8,000 from each donor—$2,000 per year. The same is not true for anyone who wants to challenge the incumbent governor for their seat in the next election, unless those candidates undertake a four-year campaign.

Most serious candidates for governor start their campaigns within two years of the election, meaning that a contender can legally raise only $4,000 per donor under Rhode Island's campaign finance law, while the incumbent can raise up to $8,000.

States that have enacted term-based limits have enacted a much more level playing field for nonincumbent candidates. Rhode Island should enact a campaign finance limit of $8,000 for four-year offices, but it probably will not. Getting incumbent office holders to enact a law that removes a political advantage that they enjoy is a very heavy lift.

There will be voters who struggle with any ranked choice ballot design. Some mistakes will be made that will invalidate a voter's ballot in some races. Is it acceptable for a voting mechanism to disenfranchise a voter?

I believe the benefits of ranked choice voting are dubious, but the cost of RCV should be considered too high for the benefit it may or may not deliver.

Chapter 28

TOP-TWO PRIMARIES AND ELECTIONS

George Washington warned us about political parties. In his farewell address on leaving the presidency, he said:

> The alternate domination of one faction over another, sharpened by the spirit of revenge, natural to party dissension, which in different ages and countries has perpetrated the most horrid enormities, is itself a frightful despotism.[81]

Washington could not have been more prescient. For decades, Americans have bemoaned "partisan gridlock" in Congress. Now we have tit-for-tat calls for impeachment, apocalyptic language in our political discourse, and constant demonization of members of the other political party. The "aisle" across which politicians used to reach to work together and get things done is now more like a World War I trench than a carpeted walkway.

The consequence of a top-two election system, intended or not, is that candidates outside the two major parties are effectively shut out

81 George Washington, "Farewell Address to the People of the United States," *Daily American Advertiser*, September 19, 1796, https://www.senate.gov/artandhistory/history/resources/pdf/Washingtons_Farewell_Address.pdf.

as viable general election candidates. The last thing our country needs is a method of voting that shuts down candidates who reject the major party duopoly.

A handful of states run a "top-two" election. Top-two is an open primary where anyone competing for an elected office can run—but only the top two vote-getters in the primary move on to the general election. Typically, write-in candidates are not allowed on the general election ballot in a top-two election. Top-two election primaries can yield weird results, like two members of the same party making the general election ballot.

In California, one stated goal of implementing a top-two election system was to lessen the extremism of candidates,[82] and some articles indicate that general election candidates in California are somewhat less extreme due to top-two. Other articles are less sure.[83] Of course, quantifying extremism is a very subjective undertaking.

A truism in American politics is that far fewer voters participate in primary elections than in general elections. Those who vote in primaries tend to be motivated partisans, delivering major party nominees who swing out to the extreme end of the ideological spectrum. In midterm primary elections, 80 percent of voters do not participate.[84]

Only 20 percent of voters pay attention to primary campaign politics and candidates. Most voters only tune in to the general election. When third-party candidates are eliminated in top-two primaries where a fraction of voters participate, those candidates' messages are simply never heard by general election voters.

82 Dan Walters, "Has California's top-two primary system worked?" CalMatters.org, June 13, 2022, https://calmatters.org/commentary/2022/06/has-californias-top-two-primary-system-worked.

83 John Myers, "News Analysis: Ten Years Later, California's 'Top Two' Primary Isn't Always What It Seems," *Los Angeles Times*, June 9, 2022, https://www.latimes.com/california/story/2022-06-09/california-top-two-primary-tenth-anniversary-offers-few-promised-results-news-analysis.

84 Joshua Ferrer and Michael Thorning, "2022 Primary Turnout: Trends and Lessons for Boosting Participation," Bipartisan Policy Center, March 6, 2023, https://bipartisanpolicy.org/report/2022-primary-turnout.

Candidates outside the Democrat and Republican parties are essentially shut out of participation in general elections by top-two. As a result, third-party candidates and their parties will never gain the exposure necessary to raise name recognition and political viability in top-two voting systems.

There is not as much research on top-two elections as I had hoped. While some articles say top-two made elections somewhat less extreme, no report says top-two should be rolled out everywhere as a game-changer.

Top-two election systems are an attempt, like ranked-choice voting, to force our elections into a situation where the winner of a general election is guaranteed to win more than 50 percent of the vote. This goal is silly—and wrong.

The goal of an election is not to deliver a mandate to the winner. The goal is to allow voters to decide who temporarily holds a seat of power and responsibility.

Our country is nearly evenly divided ideologically. Whether a candidate wins a multicandidate election with 40 percent of the vote or a one-on-one election with 50.1 percent, neither situation means the winner has a "mandate" to ignore the will of the many voters who did not vote for them.

Hyperpartisanship has led us to a place where "elections have consequences." The two major parties now go all out to win by any means necessary to govern as if half of the country does not exist.

Hyperpartisans consider *compromise* a filthy word. Campaign cash is more likely given to politicians who embrace confrontation and invective rather than statesmanship. Primary election voters want fighters who brawl for the sake of the conflict—not leaders who work to create consensus.

George Washington's accuracy in forecasting the perils of party politics is uncanny. We cannot ignore his warning of the dangers of party politics by allowing the two major political parties to enact voting mechanisms that squelch political competition.

Competition in free markets has made our economy one of the strongest and most productive in the world. Unfettered political competition is the best remedy for the political dysfunction destabilizing our country today.

PART IV

BETTER ELECTIONS

Chapter 29

WE CAN AND SHOULD IMPROVE OUR ELECTIONS

Our election processes and legal foundations have evolved over the centuries. Americans conduct their lives very differently now than they did hundreds of years ago, and our election infrastructure has not kept up with technological advances. Our election systems fail to adequately address integrity issues with our federal elections because states are responsible for their own elections, with no requirements placed on them to ensure that federal election integrity issues are handled uniformly.

Some states maintain their voter registration data well. More states have terribly maintained voter data. There are few federal mandates setting requirements for how states must maintain their data. Over the years, legal decisions have helped to make a hash out of it. Legal fights over access to voter data, maintenance of voter data, and even whether or not all states must follow the same rules have clogged our court systems with lawsuits over how our elections are conducted.

We have federal laws that make it a crime to cast more than one vote in a federal election. However, no governmental body is tasked with systematically looking for and addressing violations or voter registration issues like an individual being registered to vote in more than one state. Dramatic differences in how states administer elections can make the experience of voting in federal elections in America quite different from state to state and sometimes county to county.

Democrats and Republicans have passed laws to gain election advantage over each other and all other political parties. Voting districts are often gerrymandered—created, in most cases, via a crass political process designed to provide an election advantage to the party in power.

The mechanics of our elections, warped by partisan jockeying for political advantage, provide an uneven playing field for both voters and candidates.

It is not surprising that we have ended up here. Two hundred years ago, voters seldom moved from their homes, and no one could have imagined today's technology. It made sense to administer elections at the lowest governmental level possible—because that was the easiest thing to do. While we have made some efforts to improve election administration over the last two decades, we are still hamstrung by a mindset inherited from long ago.

America needs to refresh everything about its elections. The good news is that a mechanism exists to make this happen: Congress. The bad news is, politics.

There are ideas I discuss in the following sections that offer every political ideology something to love and something to loathe. Suppose our decision-makers can leave their party-dominated views of elections behind and instead focus on what is best for the country. In that case, we can make significant changes.

My proposed changes directly relate to the issues I have discussed in this book. Many other changes are needed. Some case law decided decades or centuries ago addressed problems of the day, but changes in technology and other voting laws have made those old laws irrelevant or, worse, chaotic. A book could be written exclusively about how our election operations should be redesigned to account for modern technology and changes in how we live our lives. Were we to design an elections infrastructure based on technological best practices and our current technological capabilities, we would never design anything like what we are stuck with today.

Let's start by trying to find some common ground.

Principles for Change

American elections should be free, fair, and impartial for voters and candidates.

Transparency in our elections is fundamental to keeping the electorate's trust.

Robust political competition is crucial to the health of our form of democracy.

The question of whether or not a vote is discarded should yield the same result for the same set of circumstances in every state.

Federal election rules, laws, and regulations should apply to every state—without exception.

Voter registration data is foundational to the operation of our elections. Clean voter registration data is critical to election integrity.

Our elections allow voters to evaluate candidates and vote for those they deem best suited for the job. Elections are about individual decision-making. The most capable winners of an election will be those candidates who convince the most voters to vote for them. Races that hinge on vote-collection strategies are not about convincing voters who the best candidate will be.

A voter's choices on their ballot must be kept confidential and anonymous.

All election data used to conduct an election and document final election results must be made available to candidates and the public before the certification of those election results. Certification of election results without this data being made publicly available is not transparent. It denies candidates the ability to contest an election result based on a complete set of election data.

Election rules, laws, and regulations should not confer an advantage to one candidate or party or disadvantage one candidate or party. A change in how we conduct our elections whose purpose is to benefit or disadvantage a candidate or party is antithetical to free and fair elections.

Chapter 30

PROPOSALS FOR CHANGE

Now that the basic principles are established and we have beyond the shadow of a doubt established the fact that our current system is deeply flawed, it's time for the lightning round portion of our journey to better elections. Let's go.

Access to Voting Data

The National Voting Rights Act of 1993 (NVRA) requires states to make voting records, including voter registration data, available for public inspection. What the NVRA fails to do is comprehensively describe the data that states must provide. As a result, the data that states provide run the gamut from fully transparent (names, addresses, full dates of birth, and voter history) to fully opaque (several states provide no voter registration information to the public on demand).

An affordable, complete record of who is registered to vote in our elections is crucial to election integrity and transparency.

A few states will likely argue that full birth dates are confidential information and that providing this information somehow presents a risk of identity theft. The reality is that full dates of birth for nearly everyone are already available online for free. People willingly share their dates of birth on social media and genealogy websites. Almost everyone's most confidential personal data, including Social Security numbers, have been obtained by hackers and are available for sale on the dark web. Full dates of birth are not a primary vector for identity theft. Without full dates of birth, it is extremely difficult to audit the accuracy of voter registration data.

Proposal

Every state must minimally make available to the public an electronic copy of the state's voter registration database, on demand. Data to be provided must include complete name, full address, full out-of-state mailing address, full date of birth, registration date, and voter registration status.

Voter registration numbers, assigned by state election officials for each voter, must also be provided. Two individuals with the same name and date of birth are only uniquely identified in public voter registration data with different voter registration numbers. A small number of states currently withhold voter registration numbers from the public.

States are strongly encouraged to provide more information than what is detailed above.

The public must be able to acquire a statewide voter registration file with a single transaction. Requiring the public to piece together a statewide voter registration file county by county or town by town represents a serious obstacle to transparency.

States may only charge for the cost of delivering the statewide voter registration file to the requestor. Such fees may not include the recoupment of the cost of building, maintaining, or operating the voter registration system. Taxpayer dollars have already paid for these systems.

Fees charged for electronic voter registration files may not be based on how many voter records are in the file. Charges based on a per-record basis made sense when the voter list had to be printed on paper, but not when the data is provided electronically.

Every state must implement a method for the public to download an electronic copy of the voter registration file. Some states only make their electronic files available on CD or DVD, dated technology with which almost no new computer is sold.

A standard file format will be defined to which every state is expected to conform. Some states have wildly complex data formats far beyond the capabilities of many spreadsheet users.

Those who obtain voter registration data from states should be prohibited from reselling the raw data for profit or using the data in a for-profit endeavor like marketing databases. An individual or organization may not place a full or partial voter registration file online that discloses the names and addresses of specific voters without the express consent of election officials.

Approved uses of voter registration files should include all election-related activities.

Attempts by election authorities to hinder or limit the ability of the public to use voter registration data to assess election integrity issues should be prohibited.

Every state must archive a copy of its voter registration database as of the night of every election, and it must provide that archived copy on demand if requested. This is an important reform, as voter databases change daily. For those who wish to study a specific election, most states do not have the ability to provide a copy of what the voter rolls looked like on Election Day.

No state is exempt from these requirements.

The intent of this law is to ensure that the public may acquire complete, statewide voter registration data at an affordable cost from every state in the country.

Bloated Voter Rolls

Many voter registration records for voters who are no longer eligible to vote remain on the voter rolls of most states. I don't ascribe this situation to nefarious intent. We ended up like this, in part, because:

1. There is no formal governmental mechanism that allows states to share data for the purposes of maintaining voter rolls.
2. There is no requirement that states work cooperatively to ensure that when voters move between election jurisdictions, old voter registration data is accurately removed in a timely way.
3. The process to remove ineligible voters often relies upon election mail marked "return to sender." Many mailings that are improperly addressed never get returned to the sender. As a result, many ineligible voters who have moved away are not removed from the voter rolls.
4. Some states cannot uniquely identify many of their voters. Although the Help America Vote Act asks states to obtain Social Security numbers for their registrants, some newly registered voters end up on the voter rolls without Social Security numbers. As an extreme example, New York State admitted that its voter registration database lacked Social Security numbers for nearly 2 million registrants who cast votes in 2020. Many of these voters registered to vote before the passage of the Help America Vote Act.
5. When a state does not have a voter's Social Security number, it becomes very difficult to determine when that voter has died, especially if the voter dies out of state.

A voter registration system loaded with voters who are no longer alive or are otherwise ineligible to vote creates a hardship for candidates who rely upon the voter files to conduct their campaigns. The two major political parties invest millions of dollars each to clean up voter data and remove voters deemed ineligible to vote from their private databases. Candidates outside the two major parties are left with the official voter rolls; these candidates waste money and time trying to communicate to and with voters who are no longer eligible to vote—courtesy of bloated rolls.

Proposal

The US Election Assistance Commission (EAC) should be tasked with creating a computer system and supporting infrastructure to assist states with cleaning up their bloated voter rolls.

All states must routinely transmit their voter files to the new system and expect to receive a list of voter registrations no longer eligible to vote. States must include Social Security numbers for the data they transmit to the EAC. The EAC takes this information and looks for individuals registered to vote in multiple election jurisdictions. The EAC should also be tasked with determining if any of these voters are deceased according to the Social Security Administration's Death Master File. States must remove dead voters from the rolls. For voters that the EAC determines to be registered to vote in multiple jurisdictions, states must research the situation and, as quickly as possible, remove the invalid registrations.

The EAC will be tasked with looking for illegal votes cast in the name of deceased voters or duplicate votes cast by the same person in a federal election. Any illegal votes must be referred to law enforcement for investigation and possible prosecution.

All states must make efforts to backfill missing voter registration information like missing dates of birth and Social Security numbers. A system is only as good as the data upon which it operates. It is impossible to enforce federal election laws such as "you must be alive to vote" or "you may not vote twice" when voter registration records are missing critical identifying information. One election cycle after this law has been passed, states must require voters whose registrations lack

PII or have invalid dates of birth to correct the issue before they may vote in the next election.

It is insufficient for states to rely upon election mailings marked "return to sender" to determine if a voter is ineligible to vote. After two election cycles (four years) of no voting activity, states must mark those voters as inactive in their voter rolls but must also attempt to contact those voters. After one additional voting cycle (another two years) of no voting activity and no response to any form of contact, those registrations must be removed from the voter rolls. Voters whose registrations are marked as inactive can still vote: a voter whose registration is canceled after six years of election inactivity can still show up in person and cast a vote provisionally under existing US election law.

Fair Redistricting

Partisan politics should play no role in the process of determining voting districts.

Every ten years, constitutionally mandated redistricting provides an opportunity for the party in power to tip the scales for the next decade of elections—gerrymandering. I have difficulty imagining a less democratic idea than contriving a voting district to guarantee a specific partisan outcome. The *Cook Political Report* published an April 2023 story[85] that discloses, "just 82 out of 435 [congressional] districts . . . constitute a 'swing seat.'" While gerrymandering is not wholly to blame for this lack of political competitiveness, it certainly plays a role. Competition is good in the marketplace and also in politics. Gerrymandered districts reduce political competition.

California leads the way in addressing the gerrymandering problem by implementing an independent redistricting commission.

85 David Wasserman, "Realignment, More Than Redistricting, Has Decimated Swing House Seats," *Cook Political Report*, April 5, 2023, https://www.cookpolitical.com/cook-pvi/realignment-more-redistricting-has-decimated-swing-house-seats.

Proposal

All states are required to implement independent redistricting commissions. The makeup of these commissions must be neutral—equal parts Democrat, Republican, and unaffiliated members.

High-priced consultants help make partisan-based gerrymandering possible. These consultants sometimes use detailed information about voters to suggest district lines that can provide a partisan political advantage. This activity should be made illegal, with the consultants at legal risk for engaging in an activity that is an affront to fair elections.

Drawing district lines whose primary purpose is to confer an electoral advantage to one candidate or party is anathema to fair elections and shall be deemed illegal.

Mail Ballot Harvesting and Handling

What I propose below will undoubtedly be among the most hotly debated of my suggested changes. There is no partisan slant to my suggestions—I make them because I believe they are the proper way to handle mail ballots from a technologist's perspective and the perspective of fair elections.

Many states (including my home state of Rhode Island) have strict rules about candidates, campaign staff, and political party staff interacting with voters who vote in person. Yet those same partisan individuals can literally hover over the shoulder of an individual filling out a mail ballot. Increased use of mail ballots should come with changes to the rules for handling them.

Proposal

Mail ballot applications (not the live ballots) may be handled and delivered by anyone without restriction. Those applications must be filled out by the voter for whom the application requests a mail ballot. This is the best way to ensure accurate information is placed on the application.

Mail ballot applications may only be prefilled with current data from the voter registration database (current being within two weeks of the date of the mailing). The intent of this provision is to prevent bad data from being prefilled on mail ballot application forms. In 2020, in some states, mail ballot applications were prefilled by organizations using data that differed dramatically from the voter rolls. These organizations sent multiple mail ballot applications to individuals who had died as much as a year before the election.

No mail ballot application will be accepted for voters who have not confirmed their identity to election officials as part of the voter registration process. The strongest confirmation consists of a Social Security number supplied with a voter registration application checked against the Social Security Administration's data portal. Confirmation provided by easily faked documentation like utility bills will not qualify a voter to vote by mail. The intent of this provision is to provide a check to ensure that the identity of a registered voter is not being misused in mail ballot voting.

No candidate, paid staff to a candidate, volunteer for a candidate, staff for a political party, or volunteer for a political party may handle a live mail ballot for anyone other than themselves. This restriction applies to every point in a live mail ballot's journey from mailbox to voter back to mailbox.

No organization or individual may "harvest" more than five mail ballots in an election. Anyone or any organization handling a live mail ballot, in any form, that is not their own mail ballot, is prohibited from being compensated for that work.

Employees of skilled nursing facilities, acting without partisan intent, may deliver sealed, unfilled mail ballots to individuals under their care and then collect sealed, completed mail ballots for delivery to the postal box.

Early Voting and Mail Ballot Windows

Increasingly, Americans are casting their ballots ahead of Election Day, voting early in person or by mail ballot, but the duration of time during which these votes can be cast varies significantly from state to state. There are excellent reasons to offer early voting, including making it easier for people to vote. However, large early voting windows create problems for voters and campaigns.

One problem is late-breaking news—when a candidate's campaign is ended by an adverse event after the early voting window has begun. In a recent special election primary for a congressional seat in Rhode Island, the field of a dozen Democrats was reduced by one after a well-financed candidate suffered a disqualifying issue in a media story that surfaced less than a week before the election. The candidate who ended his campaign certainly had votes cast for him by mail ballot and early voters. (Rhode Island has a three-week mail ballot window and a twenty-day early voting window.)

Another problem is a campaign issue: the most critical messaging for a campaign typically comes out when most people pay attention to the race—at the end of the campaign. With a long voting window, campaigns are challenged with how and when to push out their final messaging. The problem is worse for the presidential race, where substantial state-by-state differences in early voting windows make final messaging more problematic.

The trick is to craft a reasonable balance between an early voting window that solves most voters' voting challenges, a mail ballot window wide enough to ensure that ballots sent through the mail arrive at their destination in time, and a window no longer than is necessary so that voters and campaigns face the least impact by these windows.

I don't have the research to say with certainty where the proper balance needs to be. A ten-day early voting window seems more than sufficient to address most individuals' voting issues. Ten days would encompass two weekends before the election. I suspect a three-week window is necessary for the mail ballot window, but I would love to know if a shorter window is possible without creating Postal Service–induced chaos.

Proposal

Set a national in-person early voting window of ten days.

Commission a study to determine the appropriate mail ballot window size. Once the results are in, make that window mandatory for all states.

Voters Who Vote by Mail or Vote Early and Die before an Election

By my reckoning, this is the most surprising election problem in this book. I had no idea that states handled this situation differently from one another, with some states disallowing any vote cast early by someone who dies before the election and other states allowing the vote to be counted. It is intolerable and bizarre that a situation in one state yields a valid vote while the same situation in another yields an invalid vote.

This issue and the early voting window previously discussed are closely tied together. The longer the early voting window is, the more voters will end up casting votes and then dying before the election.

Considered without any other factor, my instinct is that an early vote cast by someone who dies before Election Day should not be counted. Before we had early voting, if someone died before Election Day, their vote could not be legally cast.

However, the reality is that it is very difficult and expensive to do a good job of determining all the early voters who died before the election within a small window of two or three weeks. This is especially true of votes cast just a few days before an election and voters who die out of state.

Proposal

A fine compromise is to be had here: Absurdly long voting windows (for me, anything beyond three weeks) set up a situation in which individuals who vote and then die before the election are voting from the grave. Keep the early voting and mail ballot windows as small as practicable while counting the ballots of all voters who died after properly casting their ballot early or by mail. The votes will count for all voters who properly vote early in person or by mail and die before the election.

Signature Matching as Identity Verification

Signature matching is challenging, especially as the art of writing by hand disappears while keyboard-induced carpal tunnel cases surge. If I sign my name twenty times in a row, it will look quite different each time I sign. Expert handwriting analysis takes a lot of training, much more training than most election workers are provided.

Better solutions exist to confirm that the sender of a mail ballot is the person who registered to vote. Unfortunately, in many circumstances, election systems may need to be changed to use those solutions. This is a worthwhile investment, as the signature solution used today was put in place many decades ago.

For the many folks who will be upset about a proposal for voter identification, signature matching *is* a form of voter identification. In fact, signature matching was the only way to verify voters were who they claimed to be until the last few decades. We have always tried to identify who was voting—now we have far better ways to do it.

This change will take years to implement across the country. Also, I do not want to be so presumptuous as to declare that I know the best way to replace signature matching. Therefore, my proposal is the funding and kick-starting of a project to identify and document how we will verify a voter's identity for our elections in the future.

While we have the national conversation about replacing signature matching, we should also consider replacing Social Security numbers as the primary identifier for our financial lives. As we have discussed, Social Security numbers are no longer secure, with hundreds of millions of stolen numbers available for purchase on the dark web.

Yes, I am proposing a monumentally large project with ramifications for computer systems in many different industries. The identifier for our financial lives—the most private piece of data we have—should not be used for voting purposes, medical purposes, or other nonfinancial purposes.

We need national identifiers for nonfinancial purposes as well. Let's take a decade and roll out a set of new identifiers. Let's make smart use of existing technology to do everything possible to secure these numbers. This will be an expensive yet necessary effort. The replacement of Social Security numbers cannot happen soon enough.

Over the last decade, several democratic countries have implemented digitized, national identification systems that include biometrics, including Spain, Portugal, Belgium, Germany, and Italy, while the vast majority of countries have implemented a digitized national identifier. The United States is an outlier relative to the rest of the world.[86]

When Social Security number version 2 (SSN2) is fully rolled out and, inevitably, some of these new numbers are stolen in a data breach, the new system should be capable of immediately canceling the stolen numbers and assigning new ones. The SSN2 number cannot be the primary identifier for an individual in the new SSN2 system. It will be the public identifier, but the SSN2 system will maintain a private identifier for everyone, making assigning new numbers straightforward. If we cancel, as quickly as possible, stolen SSN2 numbers, these numbers will have much less value to those who want to steal them.

86 Word Privacy Forum, "National IDs around the World: Interactive map," 2017, https://www.worldprivacyforum.org/2021/10/national-ids-and-biometrics.

I have danced around what I believe is the only reasonable way to conduct our elections in the modern era: move away from state-based voter registration systems and replace them with a national voter registration system. Every US citizen should be given a national voter registration number the day they are issued a Social Security number. They should not be the same number.

Citizenship means you have a right to vote. There should not be a "process" to register. A national voter registration number will take the headache of fifty states not doing enough to ensure federal election integrity and concentrate the issue in one place. Note that voters and local election officials will need a way to indicate a voter's current residence.

I know what's coming: "Not every citizen has a Social Security number." I have never seen a quantification of how many living US citizens do not have Social Security numbers, nor have I seen statistics describing how it came to be that these citizens lack a number without which it is extremely difficult to access government benefits or conduct a financial life.

How many living US citizens lack Social Security numbers? If the number is small and shrinking, let's figure out how to address the specific circumstances for this (hopefully) small population and create a better election system.

Proposal

Fund an effort to develop a new set of national identifiers, separating extremely confidential financial identifiers (currently Social Security numbers, which must be replaced) from identifiers for other purposes (such as voting).

Fully fund an effort to create an automatic, national voter registration system that issues a voter registration number when an individual is given a Social Security number. This project represents a seismic shift in how elections are conducted in America, requiring every state to modify its elections.

"No Excuse" Mail Ballot Voting

I know some folks won't like this proposal. But if my previous mail ballot proposals are implemented, the problems that worry some will be addressed. Making voting more convenient should be a goal we all share—as long as convenience does not introduce unacceptably negative consequences.

"No Excuse" mail ballot voting means anyone can vote by mail. They do not need a reason like poor health or out-of-state travel to qualify to vote by mail.

Proposal

Every state must offer no-excuse mail ballot voting.

Don't Certify Election Results without Providing Complete Election Data to Campaigns and the Public

One of the bigger surprises to me in my work for the Trump campaign was that no state provided data for votes made in person until after the election results were certified. Once election results are certified, it is too late to contest them. This strange situation is solvable with technology but will (and I know I am repeating myself) require states to upgrade their election systems.

Most states provide data on who voted early or by mail immediately after the election. Before 2000, most election systems tracked who came in to vote in person with a thick binder containing the names of everyone registered at that polling place. A sticker was placed next to the voter's name if they cast a ballot. A manual system of reconciling who voted was performed after the election; it took many days to complete the process.

Incredibly, some election jurisdictions today still use a sticker system to track who has voted in person. These jurisdictions are using an ancient technique to track who is voting in our elections—one that can be prone to error. Although Rhode Island moved to e-poll books in 2018, the state did not replace the sticker element of the election process in that election. I helped a candidate in my town run for the general assembly in 2018. After the election, I was shocked to see that the data for the election released by officials showed that the candidate's wife had not cast a ballot. I knew she voted in that election because I dropped her off at the polling place on Election Day! It turns out her sticker was placed alongside someone else's name.

E-poll books are computer tablets that contain the voter registration list. In Rhode Island, an in-person voter scans their driver's license into the e-poll book (or provides other identification to verify their identity), and the voter's information appears on the screen. An electronic signature is collected, and the voter is handed a ballot. Don't get me started on how worthless electronic signatures are—I struggle enough with pen and paper. The signature I create by sliding a stylus across a computer screen, usually at an odd angle, is an unrecognizable scrawl.

In theory, the list of every voter who cast a ballot in person should be able to be quickly collected from the e-poll books and provided to campaigns and the public. If upgrading technology does not solve the problem, or it takes years to change election systems, sufficient time should be built into the election calendar for in-person voting data to be supplied at least two weeks before election certification.

Our current situation is similar to allowing a consumer to contest a credit card transaction—but only before the transaction is posted to the consumer's account. You cannot challenge a result that you have not been able to look at.

Addressing this issue will require states to change their election calendars and processes. It is no small thing, but it is a set of long overdue changes.

Proposal

Mandate that all election jurisdictions computerize voter check-in for in-person voting. Manual reconciliation processes must be phased out within two election cycles. Provide federal funds to help pay for this effort.

Mandate that no state shall certify election results less than two weeks after final election data for every vote cast in an election is made available to campaigns and the public.

PART V

CONSEQUENCES

Chapter 31

THREE SUBPOENAS

There is never a good time to receive a call from the FBI.

For me, it happened early in the morning on February 23, 2023, while I was at home onboarding a new employee and ignoring the two times my business landline rang. (Yes, a landline.) When the third call rolled around, I decided to pick up the phone. I was ready to give the scammer at the other end of the line an earful and slam the phone back onto its cradle. (Yes, a cradle.)

When the caller identified himself as an FBI agent asking for my legal department, I felt my adrenaline rush and my stomach heave. I had fully expected this call to come, but that did not lessen the shock of its arrival. I couldn't help but laugh at the thought of having my own legal department. I run a lean business and have never had an administrative staff. Having prior experience working with federal investigators, I was comfortable starting things off with a joke.

"I am janitorial, accounts payable, and legal," I told the FBI agent. "How may I help you?"

He chuckled, and so it began.

The First Subpoena

I asked the agent to call me back on my cell phone so I could take the call in a more private place and not risk having my new employee head for the hills because the boss was receiving subpoenas from federal grand juries.

This phone call felt like a long time coming. On February 11, 2023, the *Washington Post* broke a story that the Berkeley Research Group (BRG) had been issued a subpoena to produce documents to the grand jury convened by special counsel Jack Smith in Washington, DC.[87] BRG had performed voting data work for the Trump campaign at the same time I did. They were asked to provide their findings directly to the White House (as opposed to the Trump campaign). According to news reports, Berkeley was not paid one of their invoices because voter fraud was not discovered.[88]

I read every article with a knot in my stomach, knowing it was only a matter of time before a similar story emerged about me. There was no way that BRG would receive a subpoena and I would not.

I was steeled for it. I had told my lawyer and my family (in that order) that when it happened, we should expect some press. My files were already well-organized, as my work on this book was underway.

The prosecution team was unsure if they could use my materials as evidence, worried about the issue of "privilege"—could the Trump legal team claim that my work materials were legally protected communications? I transmitted the requested documents in three files to the FBI agent. I placed a password on these files that I did not share with the agent—at his request—so that if or when the privilege issue

87 Josh Dawsey, "Trump Campaign Paid Researchers to Prove 2020 Fraud but Kept Findings Secret," *Washington Post*, February 11, 2023, https://www.washingtonpost.com/politics/2023/02/11/trump-campaign-report-electoral-fraud.

88 Josh Dawsey and Amy Gardner, "Trump-Funded Studies Disputing Election Fraud Are Focus in Two Probes," *Washington Post*, June 5, 2023, https://www.washingtonpost.com/nation/2023/06/05/trump-funded-studies-disputing-election-fraud-are-focus-two-probes.

was resolved, they could request the password and open my files. Then, I waited.

The subpoena asked for every shred of correspondence I had with a long list of names everyone knows: "Donald J. Trump for President, Inc. (also known as the 'Trump Campaign'), the Republican National Committee, the Trump Make America Great Again Committee, Make America Great Again PAC, Save America, the Save America Joint Fundraising Committee, any officer, director, employee, or agent of any of the foregoing entities, Donald J. Trump, Mark Meadows, William 'Bill' Stepien, Alex Cannon, Matthew Morgan, Justin Clark, Kurt Olsen, Mark Martin, Kenneth Chesebro, Joe DiGenova, John Eastman, Jenna Ellis, Boris Epshteyn, Rudolph Giuliani, Bernard Kerik, Bruce Marks, Cleta Mitchell, William Olson, Stefan Passantino, Sidney Powell, Victoria Toensing, James Troupis, L. Lin Wood, Jr., or Ray S. Smith, III."

I attended a conference call with two federal lawyers and the FBI agent to discuss, in general terms, the nature of my work and my thoughts about whether my work was privileged or not. No specifics were to be discussed. They wanted to know who on my team worked on the project. I did not include a lawyer mentioned by name on my contract in case a court challenge was to be made based on my data. When they asked me about the lawyer, I realized that someone at the highest levels of the Trump campaign must have provided my contract under subpoena to the Department of Justice.

I gave the FBI the password to my files on March 29, 2023, in response to this email from the agent:

> Good afternoon Ken – We are cleared to download and review your production. Could you please provide the password for the three .pst files?

I called my wife and warned her that she had limited time to tell friends and coworkers about my campaign work before they learned about it through the media.

We had kept my work for the Trump campaign close to the vest. I used to keep a running tally of how many people knew about it. Before I started working on this book and received the subpoena, only sixteen people knew that I had done the work because issues regarding voter fraud and the events of January 6 were more likely to initiate an argument than a rational conversation. I did not want to publicly fan the flames of an already hot topic. However, it was clear that our closely held secret would shortly be made known.

Almost a month later, on April 26, as I sat in a meeting on a business trip, a call came to my cell phone from the *Washington Post*. The meeting was going to have to wait. Before answering the phone, I knew my story had leaked.

On the other end of the line was a *Washington Post* reporter named Josh Dawsey. My first thought was not, *How did this get out?* but, *How did this guy get my cell number?* When I asked, Dawsey explained that he looked up my information on Lexus/Nexus and then told me my wife's cell phone number as proof of the wealth of information he had at his fingertips. For all my work with data, I am still uncomfortable with how much of mine is so readily accessible to others.

My subpoena included the following paragraph:

> Although you are not required to do so, you are requested not to disclose the existence of this subpoena or the fact of your compliance. Any such disclosure could impede the investigation being conducted and thereby interfere with the enforcement of the law. Thank you for your cooperation in this matter.

I reviewed that paragraph with attorneys, PR-savvy friends, and my family. I decided the best way to handle the media regarding this subpoena, if it leaked, would be to confirm that I had received the subpoena, that I had done work for the Trump campaign, and that I had found no voter fraud sufficient to overturn an election in any of the six swing states. I decided to protect the details of the work I had performed and the results of that work, as those results were likely part of the case being made to the grand jury.

My phone call with Dawsey brought me back to what I had learned as a candidate for office: provide careful answers and make clear statements. I knew how to answer questions and pivot away if necessary. However, Dawsey's detailed knowledge of my work took me by surprise. The grand jury process was leaking, providing reporters such as Dawsey with detailed information. I confirmed that none of the claims the Trump campaign had me investigate were true, being careful not to reveal the details. I would not be responsible for screwing with the integrity of a grand jury investigation.

Leaks from Jack Smith's grand jury, a massive investigation involving hundreds of witnesses (and likely several times as many lawyers) were inevitable. And now my name and company would imminently explode in news stories nationwide.

My story broke while I was in midair returning home from a business trip when the *Washington Post* released Dawsey's report.[89] When the wheels touched down and I turned off airplane mode, my cell phone exploded with calls from friends, local reporters, and unknown numbers. Patience for scammers be damned; I had many calls to attend to.

In my conversations with Dawsey, I told him this would be a front-page story. He chuckled and told me it might make page six in his

89 Josh Dawsey, "A Second Firm Hired by Trump Campaign Found No Evidence of Election Fraud," *Washington Post*, April 27, 2023, https://www.washingtonpost.com/nation/2023/04/27/trump-false-election-fraud-claims.

newspaper. But I didn't mean the national media; I was talking about how Rhode Island media were going to react. I expected this story to generate pretty big waves in the Ocean State. I also told Dawsey I fully expected to give at least one interview from my house, which he found incredible. Rhode Island can be driven end-to-end in about an hour. Many media members live in my small town, and reporters in the past have come to my house seeking comments on one thing or another.

The *New York Times*, *Politico*, the ABC, NBC, and CBS national desks, the *Hill*, *Boston Globe*, *Providence Journal*, *Daily Beast*, CNN, and MSNBC were all trying to reach me simultaneously, as well as many Rhode Island–based reporters. Notably, not one "conservative" media outlet reached out to me. I did sit for an interview with a local television reporter in my kitchen. The *Providence Journal* put my story above the fold on the front page, with a headline in what looked to me at the time like a D-Day font stating, "Ken Block probed election for Trump."

Most reporters who contacted me called me on my cell phone, a fact that continues to amaze me.

The *Washington Post* story quoted me as saying, "It is just not appropriate at this time for me to comment further regarding my work, which is in front of the grand jury." I thought this single sentence would head off any further questioning. I was wrong.

Every reporter asked me repeatedly for information that I would not give. I declined to go on television because it would make for boring TV, where I would have declined to provide further details repeatedly. Angering an army of federal prosecutors is not my idea of a good time. As I paced around speaking with one reporter after another, my smartwatch logged more than 20,000 steps—all made within my house and around the yard. I averaged about a mile and a quarter per interview.

Stories emerged about me and my work in media outlets that made no effort to reach out to me, which was disconcerting. Information that should have been readily verifiable, such as how much I got paid for the work, was almost comically misreported in some places. For the record, I received $755,000 over about a month, which is public information found on the federal campaign finance website. A large chunk of that money sat briefly in my bank account and then went out the door to pay vendors I had hired to perform the work I could not.

Many online comments to some of the stories wondered if I had received the money I had charged—a reference to stories that Trump sometimes stiffed contractors who worked for him.

The Second Subpoena

Are two subpoenas better than one? Hell, no. On May 4, soon after the insanity of the first round of news stories, my front doorbell rang. Out of habit, I answered the door while my dog barked—hoping against hope that whoever was there had a treat or would at least scratch her ears. The man at the door did not have a treat—he had a subpoena from Ruby Freeman's legal team.

Ruby Freeman had worked the Georgia election in Atlanta in 2020. Supporters of Donald Trump and, ultimately, members of his legal team, including Rudy Giuliani, accused Freeman and her daughter of committing acts of election fraud. Georgia election officials have determined that these claims of wrongdoing are false. However, the claims caused massive disruption to Freeman's family's lives. They even abandoned their home under threats of violence.

I assume that after seeing the news stories about the subpoena I received from Jack Smith, Freeman's legal team decided to see if any of my work could help their case claiming Giuliani had defamed their clients. The subpoena asked for all my work performed for the Trump campaign and any communications I had with Giuliani—with whom I had none. My campaign communications were almost exclusively made to just one person, campaign lawyer Alex Cannon.

Why on earth would a Georgia election worker's defamation case need my work? I asked Mark Freel, my longtime lawyer, to reach out to Freeman's legal team to see if we could narrow down the scope of the documents they had requested.

As I mentioned earlier, I was introduced to Mark by the Rhode Island ACLU, who put the two of us together when I asked them to help me overturn a bad Rhode Island law that made it impossible to start a new political party. I am sure that I frustrate Mark with my layman's legal knowledge (I like to call myself a junior attorney) and the things I ask him to pursue that might skirt the edge of mainstream legal thought.

Mark clearly and repeatedly stated his opinion that Freeman's legal team would probably not voluntarily agree to narrow the scope of their request to just Georgia-specific fraud claims. Our back-and-forth conversation on this went on for quite a long time. I figured the less material I had to provide to yet another court case, set of lawyers, and group of witnesses, the less material would ultimately leak. We went around and around, and Mark made the request, which Freeman's legal team accepted. I quickly complied with a modified subpoena and earned my wings as an experienced subpoena recipient.

As of this writing, October 23, 2023, that subpoena's existence has not been reported by any media outlet—a remarkable thing in my experience with newsworthy subpoenas.

The Third Subpoena

My third subpoena was delivered on July 17, 2023, although many national news outlets reported that I had received it much earlier.

The district attorney in Fulton County, Georgia, is named Fani Willis. She is investigating potential crimes committed by the Trump campaign regarding, among other things, Trump's infamous call to Georgia secretary of state Brad Raffensperger, during which Trump asked him to "find" 11,780 votes.

One of Willis's investigators called me in May 2023 to explore what information I had in preparation for serving me with a subpoena. As

I described the types of information I had, the investigator expressed concern over privilege and asked if I would meet with some lawyers to discuss the privilege issue further. During that meeting, the lawyers determined that I should not be asked for any information until they had worked through the privilege issues. It took them a long time to work through those issues and produce my subpoena.

The *Washington Post* broke another Josh Dawsey story on June 2, 2023, saying that the two firms that had done research on voter fraud for the Trump campaign (Berkeley Research Group and my company) had both been contacted by Fulton County investigators and one of them had been issued a subpoena.[90] When Dawsey asked me if I had received a subpoena in his lead-up to writing the story, I told him no.

While the *Post* story did not claim that I had received a subpoena from Fulton County, many follow-up stories by other media outlets did. A second round of national media stories and a half dozen media inquiries from Atlanta-based news organizations ensued. I spent another full day fielding media contacts and not answering questions.

Fulton County indicted nineteen individuals, including former president Trump, with multiple crimes related to their activities protesting the results of the 2020 election.

90 Amy Gardner and Josh Dawsey, "Georgia Probe of Trump Broadens to Activities in Other States," *Washington Post*, June 2, 2023, https://www.washingtonpost.com/nation/2023/06/02/trump-georgia-election-investigation-fulton-county.

CONCLUSION

Impact

The court case that will impact me the least will be the Freeman defamation lawsuit against Rudy Giuliani. I have never had a conversation with Giuliani, nor have I communicated with him in any way. A search of my emails does not turn up his name, except in those containing subpoenas I have been served. None of the election fraud claims I researched for the campaign had anything to do with the claims of fraud made against Freeman and her daughter.

The fraud claims I looked into were based on data analytics or claims that could be evaluated using data analytics. The false fraud claims against Freeman were accusations of wrongdoing based on a video of her simply doing her job.

Notably, Giuliani has admitted that he lied about Freeman's allegedly illegal activities.[91]

The Fulton County and federal indictments have the most significant potential to impact me in the short and medium terms. My involvement in these matters will continue until these cases end, as the work I performed for the Trump campaign showed that no substantial fraud was found and that fraud claims made by others were false. It is not inconceivable that I could be called to testify in either of these legal actions.

91 Kate Brumback, "Giuliani Concedes He Made Public Comments Falsely Claiming Georgia Election Workers Committed Fraud," AP News, July 26, 2023, https://apnews.com/article/giuliani-georgia-election-workers-lawsuit-false-statements-afc64a565ee778c6914a1a69dc756064.

I was prepared to defend my work in court on behalf of the Trump campaign had I found voter fraud sufficient to impact the outcome of an election. It never occurred to me that my work could provide an essential set of facts on which the fate of a former president might rest. If I am called to testify in court, I anticipate an extraordinary impact on me and my family.

Final Argument

My work stands out from most of the other discussions of voter fraud because my work was wholly based on facts in the form of data. There is nothing theoretical about what I did—I produced empirical results.

Most of the voter fraud claims made in the aftermath of the 2020 election had no basis in fact. Most of them were hearsay or outright lies. "Johnny saw someone doing something bad." "Many people placed ballots in a drop box." "Ruby Freeman accessed a box of ballots and committed fraud with it." "Dead people are voting." "Mail ballots are corrupt." And on and on.

There was a manic search in November and December 2020 for anything that could cast doubt on the election's outcome or be twisted into a claim of fraud. Unfortunately, there are more than enough weaknesses in our current election system to feed the fires of mania that overtook parts of the country after Trump's loss. I was aware of that mania and took great care to carefully document my work so that there was no way my results could be misinterpreted. We'll see how that plays out.

An unsubstantiated claim of fraud is not a credible claim of fraud. A potential weakness in how an election is conducted is not proof that the election was invalid—but it is proof that we need to rethink the way we conduct our national elections.

I cannot understand what would compel prominent, successful individuals to risk their careers, reputations, and perhaps freedom in a bid to overturn an election by any means possible. To me, politicians have never been role models or people to venerate. They are temporary public servants in my eyes. I caused a mini uproar within my 2014 gubernatorial campaign when I was asked during a debate what politician I most admired. My honest answer was none.

Even with overwhelming evidence to the contrary, millions of people will continue to believe that the 2020 election was stolen from Trump by massive voter fraud. The only way to push back against this false narrative is to present facts produced by honest analysis.

Elections in our country need to be fair. As I have demonstrated in this book, they are not in many ways—but not because they are fraudulent.

Is there a way out from where we are at this moment in time? Is our democracy doomed to destruction? Our system of government is not doomed. We are in a mess of our own making. We have allowed partisan elected officials to slowly but effectively make our elections uncompetitive. As a result, partisanship and extremism—on both ends of the political spectrum—have increased.

Our elections are in fact rigged and unfair. Not because of voter fraud—massive voter fraud as the cause of Trump's loss in 2020 has been thoroughly disproven. Our elections are rigged because the playing field on which our elections are conducted is not level for all. I believe that most voters (except for the political extremes) are not looking for revolution from their elected officials. Voters in the middle simply want the government to make the trains run on time and govern in a way that is fair to as many people as possible.

The fate of our democracy rests on the ability to educate the majority of voters about what is happening to our elections and motivate them to take action. Our country was founded when its citizens revolted against despotic governance. Incumbent politicians working to tilt our elections to their advantage is a form of despotic governance, and it is having serious consequences.

Our public servants must step up, set aside partisan pressures, and fix some of the worst problems that plague our elections.

I am an optimist.

ACKNOWLEDGMENTS

I have taken on several intensely difficult endeavors, but none was more challenging than authoring and bringing this book to market. Many people and organizations helped me to get to this point.

I thank my late parents, who sacrificed much, pushed me to excel, and provided the support and love necessary to become who I am today.

To my wife, Jennifer, who has been the most patient and loving partner, I cannot thank you enough for your support and help with everything I have done, from my businesses to political campaigns to writing this book. Your perspectives have been invaluable in every endeavor I have undertaken.

My children, Sam and Anna, grew up watching me advocate for change and conduct two gubernatorial campaigns. Their support, encouragement, and understanding as I did these very time-consuming things meant everything to me. How many grammar school kids can recite the reasons why the master lever had to be eliminated or whose candidacies for student government shamelessly copied my campaign slogans? Anna helped me find my narrative voice, for which I cannot thank her enough. She gets full credit for the language in my dedication.

My sister, Talia Shuffett, was my main sounding board for every word in this book. Her edits and encouragement were vital to making it to this point.

The support and editing help provided by my family have been extraordinary. My brother, Steve, Nanna and Papa, and Phyllis A.'s efforts helped me as I figured out how to write actual book chapters instead of 650-word opinion pieces.

Friends who reviewed and commented on chapters provided the encouragement and direction I needed to communicate complicated material. Many thanks to Dave Paratore, Sham Ganglani, Scott Douglas, Rob Cote, Kent Zehner, and Neil Fradin.

Mark Freel, my friend and lawyer, has played a critical role in my professional and political lives for over a decade. His advice and perspectives have proven invaluable time and again.

Arlene Violet, my partner in crime who helped me launch a new political party and my political career, provided essential advice as I embarked on this book project. If only all politicians were as courageous as Arlene.

I would be politically nowhere without the Rhode Island chapter of the American Civil Liberties Union, who took on my case challenging Rhode Island's outrageous ballot access laws, introduced me to Mark Freel, and helped me get some bad laws declared unconstitutional.

The employees of my company deserve special recognition as they dealt with the disruptions my political activities have brought to the office over the years. They have had ringside seats to the collection of 35,000 signatures, multiple political campaigns, countless press conferences, and the mayhem that accompanied each. Businesses are only as good as their employees—our business is very good! Special thanks to Peter for his contributions to our data work.

Special thanks must be given to the paid and volunteer staff who ran my gubernatorial campaigns. I give my most heartfelt thanks to Chris, Jeff, the hundreds of folks who helped make my campaigns happen, and my donors.

Thank you to the Public Interest Legal Foundation for entrusting me with its data analytics needs. I understand that working with nerds can be difficult for non-nerds—and I appreciate your patience and willingness to hear me out.

Attorney General William Barr provided early assistance as I explored publishing this book. I thank him for that help and his kind words of endorsement.

I am most appreciative of Georgia Secretary of State Brad Raffensperger's foreword for this book. It is crucial for those who know the truth to make sure everyone learns of it. Secretary Raffensperger's truth-telling is brave and exemplary.

The team at Forefront Books has been outstanding. Getting a book to market is challenging. Doing it in a compressed timeframe is harder. Add in working with a new author, and I am sure you have a recipe for a severe headache. Thank you for your professionalism and the excellence of your team members who made this book possible.

As I write this, the publicity team at the Meryl Morris Media Group is engaged in the tough task of gently but persistently pressing me for time and work as we launch our multimonth publicity campaign. We have an ambitious plan, and I am eager to experience the results of their labor when the book launches.

And finally, I thank the professional staff of the Donald J. Trump for President Campaign for their efforts to learn more than they ever wanted to know about data analytics, voter data, and the truth about the role of voter fraud in the 2020 election. You enabled a straight-up assessment of voter fraud to be conducted, and you communicated the findings of no fraud to the top of our nation's government. This is one of the more remarkable things I reveal in this book, and you deserve credit for your actions.

APPENDIX

Swing State Data

Arizona county-level data

County	DEM 2016 Votes	GOP 2016 Votes	Total 2016 Votes	DEM 2020 Votes	GOP 2020 Votes	
APACHE	17,083	8,240	27,661	23,293	11,442	
COCHISE	17,450	28,092	50,015	23,732	35,557	
COCONINO	32,404	21,108	59,784	44,698	27,052	
GILA	7,003	14,182	22,312	8,943	18,377	
GRAHAM	3,301	8,025	12,134	4,034	10,749	
GREENLEE	1,092	1,892	3,270	1,182	2,433	
LA PAZ	1,575	4,003	5,951	2,236	5,129	
MARICOPA	702,907	747,361	1,567,834	1,040,774	995,665	
MOHAVE	17,455	58,282	79,943	24,831	78,535	
NAVAJO	16,459	20,577	40,294	23,383	27,657	
PIMA	224,661	167,428	421,640	304,981	207,758	
PINAL	47,892	72,819	129,546	75,106	107,077	
SANTA CRUZ	11,690	3,897	16,433	13,138	6,194	
YAVAPAI	35,590	71,330	114,450	49,602	91,527	
YUMA	24,605	25,165	53,010	32,210	36,534	

Georgia county-level data

County	DEM 2016 Votes	GOP 2016 Votes	Total 2016 Votes	DEM 2020 Votes	GOP 2020 Votes	
APPLING	1,434	5,494	7,012	1,779	6,526	
ATKINSON	697	1,878	2,610	825	2,300	
BACON	608	3,364	4,020	625	4,018	
BAKER	650	775	1,440	652	897	
BALDWIN	7,970	7,697	16,116	9,140	8,903	

	Total 2020 Votes	DEM 2016 % of Vote	GOP 2016 % of Vote	DEM 2020 % of Vote	GOP 2020 % of Vote	GOP Margin Diff 2020 - 2016	Vote Diff
	35,172	61.76%	29.79%	66.23%	32.53%	-1.73%	-607
	60,442	34.89%	56.17%	39.26%	58.83%	-1.71%	-1,036
	73,272	54.20%	35.31%	61.00%	36.92%	-5.19%	-3,801
	27,662	31.39%	63.56%	32.33%	66.43%	1.93%	534
	14,995	27.20%	66.14%	26.90%	71.68%	5.85%	877
	3,685	33.39%	57.86%	32.08%	66.02%	9.48%	349
	7,458	26.47%	67.27%	29.98%	68.77%	-2.01%	-150
	2,068,144	44.83%	47.67%	50.32%	48.14%	-5.02%	-103,749
	104,668	21.83%	72.90%	23.72%	75.03%	0.24%	250
	51,767	40.85%	51.07%	45.17%	53.43%	-1.96%	-1,017
	520,397	53.28%	39.71%	58.61%	39.92%	-5.11%	-26,585
	184,974	36.97%	56.21%	40.60%	57.89%	-1.96%	-3,621
	19,556	71.14%	23.71%	67.18%	31.67%	11.91%	2,330
	143,221	31.10%	62.32%	34.63%	63.91%	-1.95%	-2,799
	69,881	46.42%	47.47%	46.09%	52.28%	5.13%	3,586

	Total 2020 Votes	DEM 2016 % of Vote	GOP 2016 % of Vote	DEM 2020 % of Vote	GOP 2020 % of Vote	GOP Margin Diff 2020 - 2016	Vote Diff
	8,341	20.45%	78.35%	21.33%	78.24%	-0.99%	-83
	3,155	26.70%	71.95%	26.15%	72.90%	1.50%	47
	4,668	15.12%	83.68%	13.39%	86.08%	4.13%	193
	1,555	45.14%	53.82%	41.93%	57.68%	7.08%	110
	18,251	49.45%	47.76%	50.08%	48.78%	0.40%	72

County	DEM 2016 Votes	GOP 2016 Votes	Total 2016 Votes	DEM 2020 Votes	GOP 2020 Votes	
BANKS	684	6,134	6,975	932	7,795	
BARROW	6,580	21,108	29,060	10,453	26,804	
BARTOW	8,212	29,911	39,550	12,092	37,674	
BEN HILL	2,101	3,739	5,936	2,392	4,110	
BERRIEN	1,047	5,422	6,590	1,269	6,419	
BIBB	36,787	24,043	62,596	43,468	26,585	
BLECKLEY	1,101	3,719	4,974	1,311	4,328	
BRANTLEY	619	5,567	6,301	699	6,991	
BROOKS	2,528	3,701	6,336	2,790	4,260	
BRYAN	4,014	10,529	15,173	6,739	14,244	
BULLOCH	9,261	15,097	25,316	11,243	18,386	
BURKE	4,731	4,491	9,351	5,209	5,400	
BUTTS	2,566	6,717	9,514	3,274	8,406	
CALHOUN	1,179	830	2,025	1,260	923	
CAMDEN	5,930	12,310	18,901	7,967	15,251	
CANDLER	1,026	2,664	3,763	1,269	3,133	
CARROLL	12,464	30,029	44,121	16,238	37,476	
CATOOSA	4,771	20,876	26,757	6,932	25,167	
CHARLTON	1,004	2,951	4,016	1,103	3,419	
CHATHAM	62,290	45,688	112,142	78,254	53,237	
CHATTAHOOCHEE	594	751	1,390	667	880	
CHATTOOGA	1,613	6,462	8,252	1,854	8,064	
CHEROKEE	25,231	80,649	112,043	42,794	99,587	
CLARKE	29,603	12,717	44,976	36,048	14,446	
CLAY	697	566	1,273	790	637	
CLAYTON	78,220	12,645	92,859	95,476	15,813	
CLINCH	686	1,727	2,455	747	2,105	
COBB	160,121	152,912	330,819	221,846	165,459	
COFFEE	4,094	9,588	13,915	4,511	10,578	
COLQUITT	3,463	9,898	13,624	4,187	11,777	
COLUMBIA	18,887	43,085	64,743	29,236	50,013	
COOK	1,753	4,176	6,057	2,059	4,900	
COWETA	16,583	42,533	61,745	24,210	51,501	
CRAWFORD	1,421	3,635	5,176	1,615	4,428	
CRISP	2,837	4,549	7,512	2,986	4,987	
DADE	965	5,051	6,242	1,261	6,066	
DAWSON	1,448	9,900	11,765	2,486	13,398	
DECATUR	4,124	6,020	10,286	4,780	6,758	
DEKALB	251,370	51,468	314,757	308,227	58,373	
DODGE	1,839	5,021	7,009	2,171	5,843	
DOOLY	1,872	1,951	3,859	1,911	2,159	
DOUGHERTY	23,311	10,232	34,087	24,577	10,454	
DOUGLAS	31,005	24,817	57,738	42,809	25,451	
EARLY	2,168	2,552	4,785	2,437	2,722	
ECHOLS	156	1,007	1,182	167	1,256	
EFFINGHAM	4,853	17,874	23,458	7,720	23,358	

	Total 2020 Votes	DEM 2016 % of Vote	GOP 2016 % of Vote	DEM 2020 % of Vote	GOP 2020 % of Vote	GOP Margin Diff 2020 - 2016	Vote Diff
	8,801	9.81%	87.94%	10.59%	88.57%	-0.16%	-14
	37,921	22.64%	72.64%	27.57%	70.68%	-6.87%	-2,607
	50,467	20.76%	75.63%	23.96%	74.65%	-4.17%	-2,107
	6,560	35.39%	62.99%	36.46%	62.65%	-1.41%	-92
	7,743	15.89%	82.28%	16.39%	82.90%	0.12%	10
	70,802	58.77%	38.41%	61.39%	37.55%	-3.49%	-2,468
	5,706	22.14%	74.77%	22.98%	75.85%	0.24%	14
	7,746	9.82%	88.35%	9.02%	90.25%	2.70%	209
	7,100	39.90%	58.41%	39.30%	60.00%	2.19%	156
	21,340	26.45%	69.39%	31.58%	66.75%	-7.77%	-1,658
	30,084	36.58%	59.63%	37.37%	61.12%	0.69%	208
	10,684	50.59%	48.03%	48.76%	50.54%	4.35%	465
	11,771	26.97%	70.60%	27.81%	71.41%	-0.03%	-4
	2,194	58.22%	40.99%	57.43%	42.07%	1.87%	41
	23,688	31.37%	65.13%	33.63%	64.38%	-3.01%	-712
	4,431	27.27%	70.79%	28.64%	70.71%	-1.46%	-65
	54,474	28.25%	68.06%	29.81%	68.80%	-0.82%	-449
	32,593	17.83%	78.02%	21.27%	77.22%	-4.24%	-1,383
	4,566	25.00%	73.48%	24.16%	74.88%	2.24%	102
	133,420	55.55%	40.74%	58.65%	39.90%	-3.95%	-5,265
	1,582	42.73%	54.03%	42.16%	55.63%	2.17%	34
	10,050	19.55%	78.31%	18.45%	80.24%	3.03%	304
	144,830	22.52%	71.98%	29.55%	68.76%	-10.25%	-14,842
	51,333	65.82%	28.28%	70.22%	28.14%	-4.54%	-2,329
	1,434	54.75%	44.46%	55.09%	44.42%	-0.38%	-5
	112,344	84.24%	13.62%	84.99%	14.08%	-0.29%	-328
	2,864	27.94%	70.35%	26.08%	73.50%	5.01%	144
	393,746	48.40%	46.22%	56.34%	42.02%	-12.14%	-47,807
	15,214	29.42%	68.90%	29.65%	69.53%	0.40%	60
	16,083	25.42%	72.65%	26.03%	73.23%	-0.04%	-6
	80,579	29.17%	66.55%	36.28%	62.07%	-11.59%	-9,340
	7,035	28.94%	68.95%	29.27%	69.65%	0.38%	27
	76,799	26.86%	68.88%	31.52%	67.06%	-6.49%	-4,986
	6,102	27.45%	70.23%	26.47%	72.57%	3.33%	203
	8,039	37.77%	60.56%	37.14%	62.04%	2.10%	169
	7,434	15.46%	80.92%	16.96%	81.60%	-0.82%	-61
	16,081	12.31%	84.15%	15.46%	83.32%	-3.98%	-641
	11,627	40.09%	58.53%	41.11%	58.12%	-1.42%	-165
	370,804	79.86%	16.35%	83.12%	15.74%	-3.87%	-14,357
	8,070	26.24%	71.64%	26.90%	72.40%	0.10%	8
	4,105	48.51%	50.56%	46.55%	52.59%	3.99%	164
	35,311	68.39%	30.02%	69.60%	29.61%	-1.63%	-574
	69,097	53.70%	42.98%	61.95%	36.83%	-14.40%	-9,953
	5,187	45.31%	53.33%	46.98%	52.48%	-2.53%	-131
	1,441	13.20%	85.19%	11.59%	87.16%	3.58%	52
	31,570	20.69%	76.20%	24.45%	73.99%	-5.97%	-1,886

County	DEM 2016 Votes	GOP 2016 Votes	Total 2016 Votes	DEM 2020 Votes	GOP 2020 Votes	
ELBERT	2,539	5,292	7,987	2,879	6,226	
EMANUEL	2,435	5,335	7,860	2,884	6,551	
EVANS	1,130	2,404	3,613	1,324	2,888	
FANNIN	1,923	9,632	11,812	2,571	12,169	
FAYETTE	23,284	35,048	60,913	33,065	37,952	
FLOYD	9,159	24,114	34,608	12,008	29,123	
FORSYTH	23,462	69,851	98,221	42,203	85,122	
FRANKLIN	1,243	7,054	8,502	1,593	9,069	
FULTON	297,051	117,783	431,391	381,144	137,240	
GILMER	1,965	10,477	12,773	2,932	13,429	
GLASCOCK	138	1,235	1,390	155	1,403	
GLYNN	11,775	21,512	34,263	15,879	25,616	
GORDON	3,181	15,191	18,959	4,384	19,405	
GRADY	3,013	6,053	9,213	3,619	7,034	
GREENE	3,199	5,490	8,852	4,088	7,068	
GWINNETT	166,153	146,989	328,331	241,827	166,413	
HABERSHAM	2,483	13,190	16,243	3,563	16,637	
HALL	16,180	51,733	70,694	25,031	64,170	
HANCOCK	2,701	843	3,580	2,985	1,159	
HARALSON	1,475	9,585	11,357	1,792	12,331	
HARRIS	4,086	11,936	16,502	5,457	14,319	
HART	2,585	7,286	10,117	3,157	9,464	
HEARD	743	3,370	4,223	824	4,516	
HENRY	50,057	45,724	98,766	73,276	48,187	
HOUSTON	22,553	35,430	60,079	32,232	41,534	
IRWIN	891	2,716	3,670	1,008	3,134	
JACKSON	4,491	21,784	27,190	7,642	29,497	
JASPER	1,544	4,360	6,045	1,761	5,822	
JEFF DAVIS	901	4,104	5,096	1,028	4,695	
JEFFERSON	3,821	3,063	6,968	4,061	3,537	
JENKINS	1,123	1,895	3,056	1,266	2,161	
JOHNSON	1,136	2,519	3,686	1,222	2,850	
JONES	3,961	8,305	12,551	4,888	9,965	
LAMAR	2,270	5,190	7,612	2,615	6,330	
LANIER	806	1,984	2,871	1,019	2,509	
LAURENS	6,752	12,411	19,530	8,073	14,493	
LEE	3,170	10,646	14,143	4,558	12,007	
LIBERTY	9,556	6,134	16,143	13,099	7,959	
LINCOLN	1,273	2,759	4,102	1,435	3,179	
LONG	1,360	2,626	4,117	2,033	3,528	
LOWNDES	15,064	21,635	37,805	20,117	25,691	
LUMPKIN	2,220	9,619	12,425	3,126	12,163	
MACON	2,705	1,540	4,287	2,857	1,783	
MADISON	2,425	9,201	11,998	3,411	11,326	
MARION	1,213	1,921	3,190	1,311	2,275	
MCDUFFIE	3,699	5,432	9,268	4,168	6,169	

	Total 2020 Votes	DEM 2016 % of Vote	GOP 2016 % of Vote	DEM 2020 % of Vote	GOP 2020 % of Vote	GOP Margin Diff 2020 - 2016	Vote Diff
	9,171	31.79%	66.26%	31.39%	67.89%	2.03%	186
	9,501	30.98%	67.88%	30.35%	68.95%	1.70%	162
	4,247	31.28%	66.54%	31.17%	68.00%	1.56%	66
	14,850	16.28%	81.54%	17.31%	81.95%	-0.63%	-94
	71,993	38.23%	57.54%	45.93%	52.72%	-12.52%	-9,017
	41,648	26.46%	69.68%	28.83%	69.93%	-2.12%	-882
	129,305	23.89%	71.12%	32.64%	65.83%	-14.04%	-18,151
	10,765	14.62%	82.97%	14.80%	84.25%	1.10%	118
	524,659	68.86%	27.30%	72.65%	26.16%	-4.93%	-25,878
	16,525	15.38%	82.02%	17.74%	81.26%	-3.12%	-515
	1,566	9.93%	88.85%	9.90%	89.59%	0.77%	12
	41,984	34.37%	62.78%	37.82%	61.01%	-5.23%	-2,194
	24,033	16.78%	80.13%	18.24%	80.74%	-0.85%	-203
	10,707	32.70%	65.70%	33.80%	65.70%	-1.10%	-118
	11,247	36.14%	62.02%	36.35%	62.84%	0.61%	69
	413,865	50.61%	44.77%	58.43%	40.21%	-12.39%	-51,258
	20,432	15.29%	81.20%	17.44%	81.43%	-1.93%	-394
	90,523	22.89%	73.18%	27.65%	70.89%	-7.05%	-6,386
	4,165	75.45%	23.55%	71.67%	27.83%	8.06%	336
	14,248	12.99%	84.40%	12.58%	86.55%	2.56%	365
	19,991	24.76%	72.33%	27.30%	71.63%	-3.24%	-648
	12,727	25.55%	72.02%	24.81%	74.36%	3.09%	393
	5,391	17.59%	79.80%	15.28%	83.77%	6.28%	338
	122,742	50.68%	46.30%	59.70%	39.26%	-16.05%	-19,704
	74,823	37.54%	58.97%	43.08%	55.51%	-9.00%	-6,735
	4,168	24.28%	74.01%	24.18%	75.19%	1.28%	53
	37,670	16.52%	80.12%	20.29%	78.30%	-5.58%	-2,103
	7,644	25.54%	72.13%	23.04%	76.16%	6.54%	500
	5,771	17.68%	80.53%	17.81%	81.36%	0.69%	40
	7,642	54.84%	43.96%	53.14%	46.28%	4.02%	307
	3,455	36.75%	62.01%	36.64%	62.55%	0.64%	22
	4,100	30.82%	68.34%	29.80%	69.51%	2.19%	90
	14,966	31.56%	66.17%	32.66%	66.58%	-0.69%	-103
	9,039	29.82%	68.18%	28.93%	70.03%	2.74%	248
	3,576	28.07%	69.10%	28.50%	70.16%	0.64%	23
	22,729	34.57%	63.55%	35.52%	63.76%	-0.73%	-166
	16,714	22.41%	75.27%	27.27%	71.84%	-8.29%	-1,386
	21,389	59.20%	38.00%	61.24%	37.21%	-2.83%	-606
	4,650	31.03%	67.26%	30.86%	68.37%	1.28%	59
	5,656	33.03%	63.78%	35.94%	62.38%	-4.32%	-244
	46,355	39.85%	57.23%	43.40%	55.42%	-5.36%	-2,483
	15,531	17.87%	77.42%	20.13%	78.31%	-1.36%	-212
	4,662	63.10%	35.92%	61.28%	38.25%	4.14%	193
	14,937	20.21%	76.69%	22.84%	75.83%	-3.49%	-521
	3,624	38.03%	60.22%	36.18%	62.78%	4.41%	160
	10,455	39.91%	58.61%	39.87%	59.01%	0.44%	46

County	DEM 2016 Votes	GOP 2016 Votes	Total 2016 Votes	DEM 2020 Votes	GOP 2020 Votes	
MCINTOSH	2,303	3,487	5,903	2,612	4,016	
MERIWETHER	3,804	5,222	9,217	4,287	6,524	
MILLER	623	1,891	2,544	749	2,066	
MITCHELL	3,493	4,279	7,880	3,995	4,935	
MONROE	3,571	8,832	12,687	4,384	11,060	
MONTGOMERY	847	2,670	3,576	979	2,960	
MORGAN	2,663	6,559	9,475	3,355	8,230	
MURRAY	1,800	10,341	12,458	2,302	12,943	
MUSCOGEE	39,851	26,976	69,032	49,529	30,049	
NEWTON	21,943	20,913	43,987	29,794	23,869	
OCONEE	5,581	13,425	20,149	8,162	16,595	
OGLETHORPE	1,831	4,625	6,674	2,436	5,593	
PAULDING	18,025	44,662	64,890	29,704	54,525	
PEACH	5,100	5,413	10,752	5,920	6,502	
PICKENS	1,979	11,651	14,038	2,808	14,075	
PIERCE	903	6,302	7,311	1,100	7,899	
PIKE	1,240	7,278	8,725	1,505	9,127	
POLK	2,867	11,014	14,215	3,658	13,589	
PULASKI	1,104	2,437	3,605	1,217	2,805	
PUTNAM	2,758	6,544	9,488	3,448	8,291	
QUITMAN	461	575	1,044	497	604	
RABUN	1,444	6,287	7,992	1,984	7,474	
RANDOLPH	1,598	1,271	2,899	1,671	1,391	
RICHMOND	48,814	24,461	75,515	59,124	26,781	
ROCKDALE	23,255	13,478	37,869	31,244	13,012	
SCHLEY	401	1,472	1,909	462	1,800	
SCREVEN	2,300	3,305	5,715	2,661	3,916	
SEMINOLE	1,189	2,345	3,588	1,254	2,611	
SPALDING	9,357	15,646	25,704	11,784	18,057	
STEPHENS	1,837	7,686	9,815	2,385	9,368	
STEWART	1,222	805	2,058	1,182	801	
SUMTER	5,520	5,276	10,974	6,318	5,732	
TALBOT	2,002	1,196	3,246	2,114	1,392	
TALIAFERRO	545	349	897	561	360	
TATTNALL	1,681	5,096	6,903	2,061	6,053	
TAYLOR	1,296	2,064	3,408	1,387	2,418	
TELFAIR	1,313	2,450	3,796	1,487	2,825	
TERRELL	2,267	1,874	4,189	2,376	2,004	
THOMAS	7,142	11,228	18,802	8,708	12,954	
TIFT	4,347	9,584	14,219	5,322	10,784	
TOOMBS	2,338	6,615	9,138	2,939	7,872	
TOWNS	1,210	5,383	6,764	1,550	6,384	
TREUTLEN	862	1,809	2,703	952	2,101	
TROUP	9,713	15,750	26,111	11,578	18,143	
TURNER	1,246	2,095	3,398	1,410	2,349	
TWIGGS	1,971	2,035	4,059	2,044	2,370	

	Total 2020 Votes	DEM 2016 % of Vote	GOP 2016 % of Vote	DEM 2020 % of Vote	GOP 2020 % of Vote	GOP Margin Diff 2020 - 2016	Vote Diff
	6,696	39.01%	59.07%	39.01%	59.98%	0.91%	61
	10,877	41.27%	56.66%	39.41%	59.98%	5.18%	564
	2,835	24.49%	74.33%	26.42%	72.87%	-3.39%	-96
	8,963	44.33%	54.30%	44.57%	55.06%	0.51%	46
	15,592	28.15%	69.61%	28.12%	70.93%	1.35%	210
	3,966	23.69%	74.66%	24.68%	74.63%	-1.03%	-41
	11,707	28.11%	69.22%	28.66%	70.30%	0.52%	61
	15,389	14.45%	83.01%	14.96%	84.11%	0.59%	91
	80,543	57.73%	39.08%	61.49%	37.31%	-5.54%	-4,458
	54,239	49.89%	47.54%	54.93%	44.01%	-8.58%	-4,655
	25,168	27.70%	66.63%	32.43%	65.94%	-5.42%	-1,365
	8,131	27.43%	69.30%	29.96%	68.79%	-3.04%	-247
	85,385	27.78%	68.83%	34.79%	63.86%	-11.98%	-10,229
	12,545	47.43%	50.34%	47.19%	51.83%	1.73%	217
	17,116	14.10%	83.00%	16.41%	82.23%	-3.07%	-526
	9,048	12.35%	86.20%	12.16%	87.30%	1.30%	117
	10,720	14.21%	83.42%	14.04%	85.14%	1.90%	203
	17,399	20.17%	77.48%	21.02%	78.10%	-0.23%	-41
	4,059	30.62%	67.60%	29.98%	69.11%	2.15%	87
	11,855	29.07%	68.97%	29.08%	69.94%	0.95%	112
	1,106	44.16%	55.08%	44.94%	54.61%	-1.25%	-14
	9,568	18.07%	78.67%	20.74%	78.11%	-3.22%	-308
	3,074	55.12%	43.84%	54.36%	45.25%	2.17%	67
	87,016	64.64%	32.39%	67.95%	30.78%	-4.92%	-4,281
	44,686	61.41%	35.59%	69.92%	29.12%	-14.98%	-6,695
	2,275	21.01%	77.11%	20.31%	79.12%	2.71%	62
	6,628	40.24%	57.83%	40.15%	59.08%	1.35%	89
	3,884	33.14%	65.36%	32.29%	67.22%	2.72%	106
	30,116	36.40%	60.87%	39.13%	59.96%	-3.64%	-1,095
	11,885	18.72%	78.31%	20.07%	78.82%	-0.84%	-100
	1,990	59.38%	39.12%	59.40%	40.25%	1.12%	22
	12,150	50.30%	48.08%	52.00%	47.18%	-2.60%	-316
	3,522	61.68%	36.85%	60.02%	39.52%	4.33%	153
	928	60.76%	38.91%	60.45%	38.79%	0.19%	2
	8,183	24.35%	73.82%	25.19%	73.97%	-0.69%	-56
	3,839	38.03%	60.56%	36.13%	62.99%	4.32%	166
	4,333	34.59%	64.54%	34.32%	65.20%	0.93%	40
	4,416	54.12%	44.74%	53.80%	45.38%	0.96%	42
	21,853	37.99%	59.72%	39.85%	59.28%	-2.30%	-503
	16,283	30.57%	67.40%	32.68%	66.23%	-3.29%	-535
	10,914	25.59%	72.39%	26.93%	72.13%	-1.61%	-175
	7,979	17.89%	79.58%	19.43%	80.01%	-1.11%	-89
	3,077	31.89%	66.93%	30.94%	68.28%	2.31%	71
	30,049	37.20%	60.32%	38.53%	60.38%	-1.27%	-382
	3,792	36.67%	61.65%	37.18%	61.95%	-0.22%	-8
	4,444	48.56%	50.14%	45.99%	53.33%	5.76%	256

County	DEM 2016 Votes	GOP 2016 Votes	Total 2016 Votes	DEM 2020 Votes	GOP 2020 Votes	
UNION	1,963	9,852	12,063	2,801	12,651	
UPSON	3,475	7,292	10,934	4,201	8,608	
WALKER	4,215	18,950	23,956	5,769	23,174	
WALTON	8,292	31,125	40,698	12,682	37,842	
WARE	3,440	8,513	12,184	4,211	9,865	
WARREN	1,314	991	2,334	1,469	1,166	
WASHINGTON	4,200	4,149	8,461	4,730	4,663	
WAYNE	2,041	8,153	10,413	2,687	9,987	
WEBSTER	473	630	1,116	639	748	
WHEELER	646	1,421	2,102	689	1,583	
WHITE	1,674	9,761	11,823	2,411	12,222	
WHITFIELD	7,937	21,537	30,658	10,670	25,636	
WILCOX	852	2,096	2,976	862	2,403	
WILKES	1,848	2,572	4,486	2,160	2,823	
WILKINSON	1,894	2,333	4,287	2,075	2,664	
WORTH	2,020	6,152	8,295	2,395	6,830	

Michigan county-level data

County	DEM 2016 Votes	GOP 2016 Votes	Total 2016 Votes	DEM 2020 Votes	GOP 2020 Votes	
ALCONA	1,732	4,201	6,198	2,142	4,848	
ALGER	1,663	2,585	4,518	2,053	3,014	
ALLEGAN	18,050	34,183	55,786	24,449	41,392	
ALPENA	4,877	9,090	14,698	6,000	10,686	
ANTRIM	4,448	8,469	13,582	5,960	9,748	
ARENAC	2,384	4,950	7,696	2,774	5,928	
BARAGA	1,156	2,158	3,490	1,478	2,512	
BARRY	9,114	19,202	30,329	11,797	23,471	
BAY	21,642	28,328	52,977	26,151	33,125	
BENZIE	4,108	5,539	10,228	5,480	6,601	
BERRIEN	29,495	38,647	72,031	37,438	43,519	
BRANCH	5,061	11,786	17,663	6,159	14,064	
CALHOUN	24,157	31,494	58,902	28,877	36,221	
CASS	7,270	14,243	22,595	9,130	16,699	
CHARLEVOIX	5,137	8,674	14,589	6,939	9,841	
CHEBOYGAN	4,302	8,683	13,672	5,437	10,186	
CHIPPEWA	5,379	9,122	15,456	6,648	10,681	
CLARE	4,249	8,505	13,389	5,199	10,861	
CLINTON	16,492	21,636	40,655	21,968	25,098	
CRAWFORD	2,110	4,354	6,844	2,672	5,087	
DELTA	6,436	11,121	18,492	7,606	13,207	
DICKINSON	3,923	8,580	13,165	4,744	9,617	

	Total 2020 Votes	DEM 2016 % of Vote	GOP 2016 % of Vote	DEM 2020 % of Vote	GOP 2020 % of Vote	GOP Margin Diff 2020 - 2016	Vote Diff
	15,560	16.27%	81.67%	18.00%	81.30%	-2.09%	-326
	12,905	31.78%	66.69%	32.55%	66.70%	-0.76%	-98
	29,354	17.59%	79.10%	19.65%	78.95%	-2.22%	-650
	51,095	20.37%	76.48%	24.82%	74.06%	-6.86%	-3,506
	14,192	28.23%	69.87%	29.67%	69.51%	-1.80%	-255
	2,651	56.30%	42.46%	55.41%	43.96%	2.41%	64
	9,459	49.64%	49.04%	50.01%	49.30%	-0.11%	-10
	12,778	19.60%	78.30%	21.03%	78.16%	-1.57%	-200
	1,390	42.38%	56.45%	45.97%	53.81%	-6.23%	-87
	2,285	30.73%	67.60%	30.15%	69.28%	2.26%	52
	14,816	14.16%	82.56%	16.27%	82.49%	-2.18%	-323
	36,746	25.89%	70.25%	29.04%	69.77%	-3.63%	-1,335
	3,281	28.63%	70.43%	26.27%	73.24%	5.17%	170
	5,029	41.19%	57.33%	42.95%	56.13%	-2.96%	-149
	4,770	44.18%	54.42%	43.50%	55.85%	2.11%	101
	9,285	24.35%	74.17%	25.79%	73.56%	-2.05%	-190

	Total 2020 Votes	DEM 2016 % of Vote	GOP 2016 % of Vote	DEM 2020 % of Vote	GOP 2020 % of Vote	GOP Margin Diff 2020 - 2016	Vote Diff
	7,064	27.94%	67.78%	30.32%	68.63%	-1.53%	-108
	5,128	36.81%	57.22%	40.04%	58.78%	-1.67%	-85
	67,094	32.36%	61.28%	36.44%	61.69%	-3.67%	-2,460
	16,969	33.18%	61.85%	35.36%	62.97%	-1.05%	-178
	15,949	32.75%	62.35%	37.37%	61.12%	-5.85%	-934
	8,831	30.98%	64.32%	31.41%	67.13%	2.37%	210
	4,038	33.12%	61.83%	36.60%	62.21%	-3.10%	-125
	35,905	30.05%	63.31%	32.86%	65.37%	-0.75%	-269
	60,255	40.85%	53.47%	43.40%	54.97%	-1.05%	-631
	12,262	40.16%	54.16%	44.69%	53.83%	-4.85%	-595
	82,391	40.95%	53.65%	45.44%	52.82%	-5.32%	-4,387
	20,536	28.65%	66.73%	29.99%	68.48%	0.42%	86
	66,281	41.01%	53.47%	43.57%	54.65%	-1.38%	-912
	26,216	32.18%	63.04%	34.83%	63.70%	-1.99%	-521
	17,000	35.21%	59.46%	40.82%	57.89%	-7.17%	-1,220
	15,868	31.47%	63.51%	34.26%	64.19%	-2.12%	-336
	17,642	34.80%	59.02%	37.68%	60.54%	-1.36%	-239
	16,281	31.74%	63.52%	31.93%	66.71%	2.99%	487
	47,927	40.57%	53.22%	45.84%	52.37%	-6.12%	-2,934
	7,861	30.83%	63.62%	33.99%	64.71%	-2.07%	-162
	21,151	34.80%	60.14%	35.96%	62.44%	1.15%	242
	14,589	29.80%	65.17%	32.52%	65.92%	-1.97%	-288

County	DEM 2016 Votes	GOP 2016 Votes	Total 2016 Votes	DEM 2020 Votes	GOP 2020 Votes	
EATON	24,938	27,609	56,221	31,299	31,798	
EMMET	6,972	10,616	18,802	9,662	12,135	
GENESEE	102,751	84,175	196,296	119,390	98,714	
GLADWIN	3,794	8,124	12,472	4,524	9,893	
GOGEBIC	2,925	4,018	7,329	3,570	4,600	
GRAND TRAVERSE	20,965	27,413	51,589	28,683	30,502	
GRATIOT	5,666	9,880	16,465	6,693	12,102	
HILLSDALE	4,799	14,095	19,940	5,883	17,037	
HOUGHTON	6,018	8,475	15,624	7,750	10,378	
HURON	4,579	10,692	15,917	5,490	12,731	
INGHAM	79,110	43,868	131,138	94,212	47,639	
IONIA	8,352	16,635	26,854	10,901	20,657	
IOSCO	4,345	8,345	13,361	5,373	9,759	
IRON	2,004	3,675	5,910	2,493	4,216	
ISABELLA	11,404	12,338	25,392	14,072	14,815	
JACKSON	25,795	39,793	69,677	31,995	47,372	
KALAMAZOO	67,148	51,034	126,299	83,686	56,823	
KALKASKA	2,280	6,116	8,833	3,002	7,436	
KENT	138,683	148,180	308,184	187,915	165,741	
KEWEENAW	527	814	1,434	672	862	
LAKE	1,939	3,159	5,328	2,288	3,946	
LAPEER	12,734	30,037	45,183	16,367	35,482	
LEELANAU	6,774	7,239	14,757	8,795	7,916	
LENAWEE	16,750	26,430	45,939	20,918	31,541	
LIVINGSTON	34,384	65,680	105,866	48,220	76,982	
LUCE	681	1,756	2,579	842	2,109	
MACKINAC	2,085	3,744	6,097	2,632	4,304	
MACOMB	176,317	224,665	419,312	223,952	263,863	
MANISTEE	4,979	6,915	12,599	6,107	8,321	
MARQUETTE	16,042	14,646	32,976	20,465	16,286	
MASON	5,281	8,505	14,685	6,802	10,207	
MECOSTA	5,827	10,305	17,168	7,375	13,267	
MENOMINEE	3,539	6,702	10,768	4,316	8,117	
MIDLAND	15,635	23,846	42,506	20,493	27,675	
MISSAUKEE	1,565	5,386	7,317	1,967	6,648	
MONROE	26,863	43,261	74,218	32,975	52,710	
MONTCALM	7,874	16,907	26,609	9,703	21,815	
MONTMORENCY	1,287	3,498	5,009	1,628	4,171	
MUSKEGON	37,304	36,127	78,088	45,643	45,133	
NEWAYGO	6,212	15,173	22,640	7,873	18,857	
OAKLAND	343,070	289,203	664,614	434,148	325,971	
OCEANA	3,973	7,228	11,930	4,944	8,892	
OGEMAW	3,030	6,827	10,387	3,475	8,253	
ONTONAGON	1,176	2,066	3,426	1,391	2,358	
OSCEOLA	2,705	7,336	10,609	3,214	8,928	
OSCODA	1,044	2,843	4,073	1,342	3,466	

	Total 2020 Votes	DEM 2016 % of Vote	GOP 2016 % of Vote	DEM 2020 % of Vote	GOP 2020 % of Vote	GOP Margin Diff 2020 - 2016	Vote Diff
	64,327	44.36%	49.11%	48.66%	49.43%	-3.98%	-2,557
	22,177	37.08%	56.46%	43.57%	54.72%	-8.23%	-1,825
	221,360	52.34%	42.88%	53.93%	44.59%	0.12%	272
	14,603	30.42%	65.14%	30.98%	67.75%	2.05%	299
	8,266	39.91%	54.82%	43.19%	55.65%	-2.45%	-203
	60,236	40.64%	53.14%	47.62%	50.64%	-9.48%	-5,710
	19,127	34.41%	60.01%	34.99%	63.27%	2.69%	514
	23,302	24.07%	70.69%	25.25%	73.11%	1.25%	291
	18,501	38.52%	54.24%	41.89%	56.09%	-1.52%	-281
	18,437	28.77%	67.17%	29.78%	69.05%	0.87%	160
	144,550	60.33%	33.45%	65.18%	32.96%	-5.35%	-7,727
	32,209	31.10%	61.95%	33.84%	64.13%	-0.55%	-179
	15,363	32.52%	62.46%	34.97%	63.52%	-1.39%	-213
	6,789	33.91%	62.18%	36.72%	62.10%	-2.89%	-197
	29,421	44.91%	48.59%	47.83%	50.36%	-1.15%	-339
	80,861	37.02%	57.11%	39.57%	58.58%	-1.07%	-868
	143,414	53.17%	40.41%	58.35%	39.62%	-5.97%	-8,565
	10,631	25.81%	69.24%	28.24%	69.95%	-1.72%	-183
	361,048	45.00%	48.08%	52.05%	45.91%	-9.22%	-33,300
	1,557	36.75%	56.76%	43.16%	55.36%	-7.81%	-122
	6,323	36.39%	59.29%	36.19%	62.41%	3.32%	210
	52,650	28.18%	66.48%	31.09%	67.39%	-1.99%	-1,048
	16,900	45.90%	49.05%	52.04%	46.84%	-8.35%	-1,412
	53,375	36.46%	57.53%	39.19%	59.09%	-1.17%	-624
	127,197	32.48%	62.04%	37.91%	60.52%	-6.95%	-8,840
	3,001	26.41%	68.09%	28.06%	70.28%	0.54%	16
	7,015	34.20%	61.41%	37.52%	61.35%	-3.38%	-237
	494,256	42.05%	53.58%	45.31%	53.39%	-3.46%	-17,078
	14,655	39.52%	54.89%	41.67%	56.78%	-0.26%	-38
	37,462	48.65%	44.41%	54.63%	43.47%	-6.92%	-2,593
	17,254	35.96%	57.92%	39.42%	59.16%	-2.22%	-383
	21,049	33.94%	60.02%	35.04%	63.03%	1.91%	402
	12,607	32.87%	62.24%	34.23%	64.38%	0.78%	98
	49,088	36.78%	56.10%	41.75%	56.38%	-4.69%	-2,300
	8,755	21.39%	73.61%	22.47%	75.93%	1.25%	109
	87,148	36.19%	58.29%	37.84%	60.48%	0.55%	480
	32,100	29.59%	63.54%	30.23%	67.96%	3.78%	1,215
	5,859	25.69%	69.83%	27.79%	71.19%	-0.74%	-43
	92,444	47.77%	46.26%	49.37%	48.82%	0.96%	883
	27,161	27.44%	67.02%	28.99%	69.43%	0.86%	234
	770,351	51.62%	43.51%	56.36%	42.31%	-5.94%	-45,740
	14,062	33.30%	60.59%	35.16%	63.23%	0.79%	111
	11,907	29.17%	65.73%	29.18%	69.31%	3.57%	425
	3,804	34.33%	60.30%	36.57%	61.99%	-0.56%	-21
	12,329	25.50%	69.15%	26.07%	72.41%	2.69%	332
	4,874	25.63%	69.80%	27.53%	71.11%	-0.59%	-29

County	DEM 2016 Votes	GOP 2016 Votes	Total 2016 Votes	DEM 2020 Votes	GOP 2020 Votes	
OTSEGO	3,556	8,266	12,538	4,743	9,779	
OTTAWA	44,973	88,467	142,734	64,705	100,913	
PRESQUE ISLE	2,400	4,488	7,218	2,911	5,342	
ROSCOMMON	4,287	8,141	13,041	5,166	9,670	
SAGINAW	44,396	45,469	94,320	51,088	50,785	
SANILAC	4,873	13,446	19,249	5,966	16,194	
SCHOOLCRAFT	1,369	2,556	4,154	1,589	3,090	
SHIAWASSEE	12,546	19,230	34,111	15,347	23,149	
ST. CLAIR	24,553	49,051	78,003	31,363	59,185	
ST. JOSEPH	7,526	14,884	23,757	9,262	18,127	
TUSCOLA	7,429	17,102	25,796	8,712	20,297	
VAN BUREN	13,258	17,890	33,274	16,803	21,591	
WASHTENAW	128,483	50,631	188,578	157,136	56,241	
WAYNE	519,444	228,993	777,838	597,170	264,553	
WEXFORD	4,436	10,000	15,298	5,838	12,102	

Nevada county-level data

County	DEM 2016 Votes	GOP 2016 Votes	Total 2016 Votes	DEM 2020 Votes	GOP 2020 Votes	
CARSON CITY	9,610	13,125	25,016	12,735	16,113	
CHURCHILL	2,210	7,830	10,938	3,048	9,367	
CLARK	402,227	320,057	767,156	521,777	430,809	
DOUGLAS	8,454	17,415	27,885	11,570	21,623	
ELKO	3,401	13,551	18,559	4,555	16,734	
ESMERALDA	65	329	423	72	395	
EUREKA	74	723	854	104	887	
HUMBOLDT	1,386	4,521	6,433	1,689	5,877	
LANDER	403	1,828	2,413	496	2,198	
LINCOLN	285	1,671	2,132	330	2,067	
LYON	6,146	16,005	23,762	8,472	20,906	
MINERAL	637	1,179	1,997	824	1,420	
NYE	5,094	13,324	19,595	7,287	17,527	
PERSHING	430	1,403	1,982	547	1,731	
STOREY	752	1,616	2,558	900	1,901	
WASHOE	97,379	94,758	209,909	128,052	116,653	
WHITE PINE	707	2,723	3,773	856	3,400	

	Total 2020 Votes	DEM 2016 % of Vote	GOP 2016 % of Vote	DEM 2020 % of Vote	GOP 2020 % of Vote	GOP Margin Diff 2020 - 2016	Vote Diff
	14,757	28.36%	65.93%	32.14%	66.27%	-3.44%	-508
	168,713	31.51%	61.98%	38.35%	59.81%	-9.01%	-15,202
	8,344	33.25%	62.18%	34.89%	64.02%	0.21%	17
	15,018	32.87%	62.43%	34.40%	64.39%	0.44%	66
	103,349	47.07%	48.21%	49.43%	49.14%	-1.43%	-1,479
	22,446	25.32%	69.85%	26.58%	72.15%	1.03%	231
	4,745	32.96%	61.53%	33.49%	65.12%	3.06%	145
	39,224	36.78%	56.37%	39.13%	59.02%	0.30%	116
	92,064	31.48%	62.88%	34.07%	64.29%	-1.19%	-1,092
	27,936	31.68%	62.65%	33.15%	64.89%	0.76%	213
	29,445	28.80%	66.30%	29.59%	68.93%	1.85%	544
	39,066	39.84%	53.77%	43.01%	55.27%	-1.66%	-650
	216,418	68.13%	26.85%	72.61%	25.99%	-5.34%	-11,550
	872,469	66.78%	29.44%	68.45%	30.32%	-0.78%	-6,830
	18,265	29.00%	65.37%	31.96%	66.26%	-2.08%	-379

	Total 2020 Votes	DEM 2016 % of Vote	GOP 2016 % of Vote	DEM 2020 % of Vote	GOP 2020 % of Vote	GOP Margin Diff 2020 - 2016	Vote Diff
	29,739	38.42%	52.47%	42.82%	54.18%	-2.69%	-801
	12,881	20.20%	71.59%	23.66%	72.72%	-2.32%	-299
	972,308	52.43%	41.72%	53.66%	44.31%	1.36%	13,176
	34,117	30.32%	62.45%	33.91%	63.38%	-2.67%	-911
	21,957	18.33%	73.02%	20.75%	76.21%	0.78%	171
	480	15.37%	77.78%	15.00%	82.29%	4.88%	23
	1,008	8.67%	84.66%	10.32%	88.00%	1.68%	17
	7,771	21.55%	70.28%	21.73%	75.63%	5.16%	401
	2,765	16.70%	75.76%	17.94%	79.49%	2.50%	69
	2,446	13.37%	78.38%	13.49%	84.51%	6.00%	147
	30,229	25.86%	67.36%	28.03%	69.16%	-0.36%	-108
	2,327	31.90%	59.04%	35.41%	61.02%	-1.53%	-36
	25,376	26.00%	68.00%	28.72%	69.07%	-1.65%	-418
	2,320	21.70%	70.79%	23.58%	74.61%	1.94%	45
	2,868	29.40%	63.17%	31.38%	66.28%	1.13%	32
	251,956	46.39%	45.14%	50.82%	46.30%	-3.28%	-8,253
	4,363	18.74%	72.17%	19.62%	77.93%	4.88%	213

Pennsylvania county-level data

County	DEM 2016 Votes	GOP 2016 Votes	Total 2016 Votes	DEM 2020 Votes	GOP 2020 Votes	
ADAMS	14,219	31,423	47,489	18,207	37,523	
ALLEGHENY	367,617	259,480	650,114	429,065	282,324	
ARMSTRONG	7,178	23,484	31,618	8,457	27,489	
BEAVER	32,531	48,167	83,571	38,122	54,759	
BEDFORD	3,645	19,552	23,637	4,367	23,025	
BERKS	78,437	96,626	183,065	92,895	109,736	
BLAIR	13,958	39,135	54,909	17,636	45,306	
BRADFORD	6,369	18,141	25,708	8,046	21,600	
BUCKS	167,060	164,361	344,297	204,712	187,367	
BUTLER	28,584	64,428	97,071	37,508	74,359	
CAMBRIA	18,867	42,258	63,072	21,730	48,085	
CAMERON	531	1,589	2,186	634	1,771	
CARBON	8,936	18,743	28,776	11,212	21,984	
CENTRE	37,088	35,274	76,148	40,055	36,372	
CHESTER	141,682	116,114	268,800	182,372	128,565	
CLARION	4,273	12,576	17,535	4,678	14,578	
CLEARFIELD	8,200	24,932	34,271	9,673	29,203	
CLINTON	4,744	10,022	15,394	5,502	11,902	
COLUMBIA	8,934	18,004	28,228	10,532	20,098	
CRAWFORD	10,971	24,987	37,492	12,924	28,559	
CUMBERLAND	47,085	69,076	121,617	62,245	77,212	
DAUPHIN	64,706	60,863	130,872	78,983	66,408	
DELAWARE	177,402	110,667	297,634	206,423	118,532	
ELK	3,853	10,025	14,426	4,522	12,140	
ERIE	58,112	60,069	123,679	68,286	66,869	
FAYETTE	17,946	34,590	53,767	20,444	41,227	
FOREST	626	1,683	2,401	728	1,882	
FRANKLIN	17,465	49,768	69,731	22,422	57,245	
FULTON	912	5,694	6,771	1,085	6,824	
GREENE	4,482	10,849	15,764	4,911	12,579	
HUNTINGDON	4,539	14,494	19,706	5,445	17,061	
INDIANA	11,528	24,888	37,770	12,634	28,089	
JEFFERSON	3,650	15,192	19,478	4,527	17,960	
JUNIATA	1,821	8,273	10,454	2,253	9,649	
LACKAWANNA	51,983	48,384	103,456	61,991	52,334	
LANCASTER	91,093	137,914	241,112	115,847	160,209	
LAWRENCE	14,009	25,428	40,753	15,978	29,597	
LEBANON	18,953	40,525	61,845	23,932	46,731	
LEHIGH	81,324	73,690	160,993	98,288	84,259	
LUZERNE	52,451	78,688	134,983	64,873	86,929	
LYCOMING	13,020	35,627	50,565	16,971	41,462	
MCKEAN	4,025	11,635	16,296	5,098	14,083	
MERCER	18,733	31,544	52,309	21,067	36,143	

	Total 2020 Votes	DEM 2016 % of Vote	GOP 2016 % of Vote	DEM 2020 % of Vote	GOP 2020 % of Vote	GOP Margin Diff 2020 - 2016	Vote Diff
	56,540	29.94%	66.17%	32.20%	66.37%	-2.06%	-1,167
	719,733	56.55%	39.91%	59.61%	39.23%	-3.75%	-27,024
	36,370	22.70%	74.27%	23.25%	75.58%	0.76%	275
	94,122	38.93%	57.64%	40.50%	58.18%	-1.03%	-973
	27,574	15.42%	82.72%	15.84%	83.50%	0.37%	102
	205,540	42.85%	52.78%	45.20%	53.39%	-1.74%	-3,581
	63,595	25.42%	71.27%	27.73%	71.24%	-2.34%	-1,490
	30,159	24.77%	70.57%	26.68%	71.62%	-0.85%	-256
	396,234	48.52%	47.74%	51.66%	47.29%	-3.59%	-14,239
	113,305	29.45%	66.37%	33.10%	65.63%	-4.40%	-4,987
	70,574	29.91%	67.00%	30.79%	68.13%	0.26%	182
	2,434	24.29%	72.69%	26.05%	72.76%	-1.69%	-41
	33,629	31.05%	65.13%	33.34%	65.37%	-2.05%	-689
	77,493	48.71%	46.32%	51.69%	46.94%	-2.37%	-1,837
	314,502	52.71%	43.20%	57.99%	40.88%	-7.60%	-23,892
	19,493	24.37%	71.72%	24.00%	74.79%	3.44%	670
	39,422	23.93%	72.75%	24.54%	74.08%	0.72%	283
	17,625	30.82%	65.10%	31.22%	67.53%	2.03%	357
	31,171	31.65%	63.78%	33.79%	64.48%	-1.44%	-450
	42,004	29.26%	66.65%	30.77%	67.99%	-0.16%	-68
	141,595	38.72%	56.80%	43.96%	54.53%	-7.51%	-10,636
	147,368	49.44%	46.51%	53.60%	45.06%	-5.60%	-8,248
	327,931	59.60%	37.18%	62.95%	36.15%	-4.38%	-14,363
	16,906	26.71%	69.49%	26.75%	71.81%	2.28%	385
	137,083	46.99%	48.57%	49.81%	48.78%	-2.62%	-3,586
	62,139	33.38%	64.33%	32.90%	66.35%	2.49%	1,547
	2,646	26.07%	70.10%	27.51%	71.13%	-0.41%	-11
	80,783	25.05%	71.37%	27.76%	70.86%	-3.22%	-2,600
	7,977	13.47%	84.09%	13.60%	85.55%	1.32%	105
	17,669	28.43%	68.82%	27.79%	71.19%	3.01%	532
	22,792	23.03%	73.55%	23.89%	74.86%	0.45%	102
	41,198	30.52%	65.89%	30.67%	68.18%	2.14%	882
	22,824	18.74%	78.00%	19.83%	78.69%	-0.40%	-92
	12,043	17.42%	79.14%	18.71%	80.12%	-0.30%	-37
	115,410	50.25%	46.77%	53.71%	45.35%	-4.89%	-5,642
	280,239	37.78%	57.20%	41.34%	57.17%	-3.59%	-10,057
	46,076	34.38%	62.40%	34.68%	64.24%	1.54%	708
	71,652	30.65%	65.53%	33.40%	65.22%	-3.06%	-2,194
	184,713	50.51%	45.77%	53.21%	45.62%	-2.85%	-5,270
	153,321	38.86%	58.29%	42.31%	56.70%	-5.05%	-7,745
	59,254	25.75%	70.46%	28.64%	69.97%	-3.38%	-2,001
	19,466	24.70%	71.40%	26.19%	72.35%	-0.54%	-105
	57,954	35.81%	60.30%	36.35%	62.36%	1.52%	882

County	DEM 2016 Votes	GOP 2016 Votes	Total 2016 Votes	DEM 2020 Votes	GOP 2020 Votes	
MIFFLIN	3,877	14,094	18,601	4,603	16,670	
MONROE	33,918	33,386	69,752	44,060	38,726	
MONTGOMERY	256,082	162,731	434,687	319,511	185,460	
MONTOUR	2,857	5,288	8,556	3,771	5,844	
NORTHAMPTON	66,272	71,736	143,519	85,087	83,854	
NORTHUMBERLAND	9,788	25,427	36,622	12,677	28,952	
PERRY	4,632	15,616	21,158	5,950	18,293	
PHILADELPHIA	584,025	108,748	707,631	603,790	132,740	
PIKE	9,256	16,056	26,101	13,019	19,213	
POTTER	1,302	6,251	7,784	1,726	7,239	
SCHUYLKILL	16,770	44,001	62,869	20,727	48,871	
SNYDER	4,002	11,725	16,363	4,910	13,983	
SOMERSET	7,376	27,379	35,773	8,654	31,466	
SULLIVAN	750	2,291	3,136	921	2,619	
SUSQUEHANNA	5,123	12,891	18,863	6,236	15,207	
TIOGA	3,901	13,614	18,325	4,955	15,742	
UNION	6,180	10,622	17,468	7,475	12,356	
VENANGO	6,309	16,021	23,348	7,585	18,569	
WARREN	5,145	12,477	18,434	6,066	14,237	
WASHINGTON	36,322	61,386	101,450	45,088	72,080	
WAYNE	7,008	16,244	24,018	9,191	18,637	
WESTMORELAND	59,669	116,522	182,051	72,129	130,218	
WYOMING	3,811	8,837	13,144	4,704	9,936	
YORK	68,524	128,528	205,986	88,114	146,733	

Wisconsin county-level data

County	DEM 2016 Votes	GOP 2016 Votes	Total 2016 Votes	DEM 2020 Votes	GOP 2020 Votes	
ADAMS	3,770	5,983	10,164	4,329	7,362	
ASHLAND	4,228	3,302	8,029	4,801	3,841	
BARRON	7,879	13,606	22,643	9,194	15,803	
BAYFIELD	4,954	4,125	9,529	6,147	4,617	
BROWN	53,364	67,199	128,979	65,511	75,871	
BUFFALO	2,531	4,049	6,988	2,860	4,834	
BURNETT	2,948	5,412	8,743	3,569	6,462	
CALUMET	9,646	15,348	26,650	12,116	18,156	
CHIPPEWA	11,886	17,909	31,561	13,983	21,317	
CLARK	4,227	8,646	13,596	4,524	10,002	
COLUMBIA	13,526	14,160	29,771	16,410	16,927	
CRAWFORD	3,425	3,844	7,744	3,953	4,620	
DANE	217,526	71,279	310,017	260,185	78,800	
DODGE	13,968	26,643	43,065	16,356	31,355	

	Total 2020 Votes	DEM 2016 % of Vote	GOP 2016 % of Vote	DEM 2020 % of Vote	GOP 2020 % of Vote	GOP Margin Diff 2020 - 2016	Vote Diff
	21,502	20.84%	75.77%	21.41%	77.53%	1.19%	257
	83,829	48.63%	47.86%	52.56%	46.20%	-5.60%	-4,695
	510,157	58.91%	37.44%	62.63%	36.35%	-4.80%	-24,492
	9,771	33.39%	61.80%	38.59%	59.81%	-7.20%	-703
	170,942	46.18%	49.98%	49.78%	49.05%	-4.53%	-7,741
	42,283	26.73%	69.43%	29.98%	68.47%	-4.21%	-1,781
	24,652	21.89%	73.81%	24.14%	74.20%	-1.85%	-455
	741,377	82.53%	15.37%	81.44%	17.90%	3.63%	26,892
	32,554	35.46%	61.51%	39.99%	59.02%	-7.03%	-2,287
	9,064	16.73%	80.31%	19.04%	79.87%	-2.76%	-250
	70,603	26.67%	69.99%	29.36%	69.22%	-3.45%	-2,437
	19,140	24.46%	71.66%	25.65%	73.06%	0.21%	39
	40,543	20.62%	76.54%	21.35%	77.61%	0.35%	142
	3,595	23.92%	73.05%	25.62%	72.85%	-1.91%	-69
	21,752	27.16%	68.34%	28.67%	69.91%	0.06%	13
	21,075	21.29%	74.29%	23.51%	74.70%	-1.82%	-384
	20,115	35.38%	60.81%	37.16%	61.43%	-1.16%	-234
	26,528	27.02%	68.62%	28.59%	70.00%	-0.19%	-51
	20,650	27.91%	67.68%	29.38%	68.94%	-0.21%	-42
	118,478	35.80%	60.51%	38.06%	60.84%	-1.92%	-2,279
	28,089	29.18%	67.63%	32.72%	66.35%	-4.83%	-1,355
	204,697	32.78%	64.01%	35.24%	63.62%	-2.85%	-5,836
	14,858	28.99%	67.23%	31.66%	66.87%	-3.02%	-449
	238,471	33.27%	62.40%	36.95%	61.53%	-4.55%	-10,848

	Total 2020 Votes	DEM 2016 % of Vote	GOP 2016 % of Vote	DEM 2020 % of Vote	GOP 2020 % of Vote	GOP Margin Diff 2020 - 2016	Vote Diff
	11,818	37.09%	58.86%	36.63%	62.29%	3.89%	460
	8,757	52.66%	41.13%	54.82%	43.86%	0.57%	50
	25,346	34.80%	60.09%	36.27%	62.35%	0.78%	198
	10,880	51.99%	43.29%	56.50%	42.44%	-5.36%	-583
	144,017	41.37%	52.10%	45.49%	52.68%	-3.53%	-5,088
	7,816	36.22%	57.94%	36.59%	61.85%	3.53%	276
	10,141	33.72%	61.90%	35.19%	63.72%	0.35%	35
	30,774	36.20%	57.59%	39.37%	59.00%	-1.77%	-544
	35,938	37.66%	56.74%	38.91%	59.32%	1.32%	476
	14,898	31.09%	63.59%	30.37%	67.14%	4.27%	636
	33,869	45.43%	47.56%	48.45%	49.98%	-0.60%	-204
	8,695	44.23%	49.64%	45.46%	53.13%	2.26%	197
	344,791	70.17%	22.99%	75.46%	22.85%	-5.43%	-18,734
	48,436	32.43%	61.87%	33.77%	64.73%	1.53%	743

County	DEM 2016 Votes	GOP 2016 Votes	Total 2016 Votes	DEM 2020 Votes	GOP 2020 Votes	
DOOR	8,026	8,584	17,608	10,044	9,752	
DOUGLAS	11,345	9,659	22,511	13,218	10,923	
DUNN	9,026	11,488	22,091	9,897	13,173	
EAU CLAIRE	27,294	23,311	54,885	31,620	25,341	
FLORENCE	666	1,897	2,657	781	2,133	
FOND DU LAC	17,391	31,044	51,327	20,588	35,754	
FOREST	1,584	2,788	4,540	1,721	3,285	
GRANT	10,046	12,349	24,321	10,998	14,142	
GREEN	9,122	8,693	18,985	10,851	10,169	
GREEN LAKE	2,701	6,213	9,388	3,344	7,168	
IOWA	6,669	4,809	12,260	7,828	5,909	
IRON	1,273	2,090	3,497	1,533	2,438	
JACKSON	3,821	4,907	9,272	4,256	5,791	
JEFFERSON	16,561	23,410	43,146	19,904	27,208	
JUNEAU	4,073	7,123	11,732	4,746	8,749	
KENOSHA	35,771	36,025	77,076	42,193	44,972	
KEWAUNEE	3,623	6,616	10,758	3,976	7,927	
LA CROSSE	32,406	26,389	62,968	37,846	28,684	
LAFAYETTE	3,288	3,977	7,662	3,647	4,821	
LANGLADE	3,260	6,436	10,132	3,704	7,330	
LINCOLN	5,370	8,400	14,706	6,261	10,017	
MANITOWOC	14,506	23,193	40,346	16,818	27,218	
MARATHON	26,477	39,013	69,515	30,808	44,624	
MARINETTE	6,243	12,995	20,046	7,366	15,304	
MARQUETTE	2,809	4,714	7,893	3,239	5,719	
MENOMINEE	1,003	269	1,279	1,303	278	
MILWAUKEE	288,797	125,846	440,247	317,270	134,357	
MONROE	7,048	11,352	19,670	8,433	13,775	
OCONTO	5,884	13,253	19,978	6,715	16,226	
ONEIDA	8,104	12,117	21,473	10,105	13,671	
OUTAGAMIE	38,087	49,884	93,868	47,667	58,385	
OZAUKEE	20,168	30,430	54,523	26,517	33,912	
PEPIN	1,345	2,206	3,739	1,489	2,584	
PIERCE	8,382	11,258	21,189	9,796	12,815	
POLK	7,570	13,815	22,749	9,370	16,611	
PORTAGE	18,521	17,306	38,496	20,428	19,299	
PRICE	2,669	4,562	7,577	3,032	5,394	
RACINE	42,512	46,611	94,133	50,159	54,479	
RICHLAND	3,577	4,023	8,055	3,995	4,871	
ROCK	39,343	31,488	76,068	46,658	37,138	
RUSK	2,171	4,564	7,087	2,517	5,257	
SAUK	14,692	14,791	31,318	18,108	17,493	
SAWYER	3,504	5,185	9,121	4,498	5,909	
SHAWANO	6,056	12,742	19,751	7,131	15,173	
SHEBOYGAN	22,956	32,458	59,655	27,101	37,609	
ST. CROIX	17,486	26,220	47,508	23,190	32,199	

	Total 2020 Votes	DEM 2016 % of Vote	GOP 2016 % of Vote	DEM 2020 % of Vote	GOP 2020 % of Vote	GOP Margin Diff 2020 - 2016	Vote Diff
	20,117	45.58%	48.75%	49.93%	48.48%	-4.62%	-930
	24,677	50.40%	42.91%	53.56%	44.26%	-1.81%	-447
	23,524	40.86%	52.00%	42.07%	56.00%	2.78%	654
	58,275	49.73%	42.47%	54.26%	43.49%	-3.52%	-2,050
	2,940	25.07%	71.40%	26.56%	72.55%	-0.34%	-10
	57,251	33.88%	60.48%	35.96%	62.45%	-0.11%	-63
	5,053	34.89%	61.41%	34.06%	65.01%	4.43%	224
	25,608	41.31%	50.78%	42.95%	55.22%	2.81%	719
	21,406	48.05%	45.79%	50.69%	47.51%	-0.93%	-198
	10,671	28.77%	66.18%	31.34%	67.17%	-1.57%	-168
	13,992	54.40%	39.23%	55.95%	42.23%	1.46%	204
	4,010	36.40%	59.77%	38.23%	60.80%	-0.79%	-32
	10,184	41.21%	52.92%	41.79%	56.86%	3.36%	342
	47,979	38.38%	54.26%	41.48%	56.71%	-0.65%	-312
	13,709	34.72%	60.71%	34.62%	63.82%	3.20%	439
	88,738	46.41%	46.74%	47.55%	50.68%	2.80%	2,487
	12,095	33.68%	61.50%	32.87%	65.54%	4.85%	586
	67,884	51.46%	41.91%	55.75%	42.25%	-3.94%	-2,675
	8,555	42.91%	51.91%	42.63%	56.35%	4.73%	405
	11,165	32.18%	63.52%	33.18%	65.65%	1.13%	126
	16,497	36.52%	57.12%	37.95%	60.72%	2.16%	357
	44,829	35.95%	57.49%	37.52%	60.72%	1.67%	748
	76,751	38.09%	56.12%	40.14%	58.14%	-0.03%	-25
	22,979	31.14%	64.83%	32.06%	66.60%	0.86%	198
	9,065	35.59%	59.72%	35.73%	63.09%	3.22%	292
	1,590	78.42%	21.03%	81.95%	17.48%	-7.08%	-113
	458,971	65.60%	28.59%	69.13%	29.27%	-2.84%	-13,032
	22,611	35.83%	57.71%	37.30%	60.92%	1.74%	394
	23,215	29.45%	66.34%	28.93%	69.89%	4.08%	948
	24,159	37.74%	56.43%	41.83%	56.59%	-3.93%	-949
	108,022	40.58%	53.14%	44.13%	54.05%	-2.65%	-2,858
	61,486	36.99%	55.81%	43.13%	55.15%	-6.79%	-4,178
	4,144	35.97%	59.00%	35.93%	62.36%	3.40%	141
	23,317	39.56%	53.13%	42.01%	54.96%	-0.63%	-146
	26,371	33.28%	60.73%	35.53%	62.99%	0.01%	2
	40,603	48.11%	44.96%	50.31%	47.53%	0.38%	153
	8,546	35.23%	60.21%	35.48%	63.12%	2.66%	227
	106,451	45.16%	49.52%	47.12%	51.18%	-0.30%	-315
	9,014	44.41%	49.94%	44.32%	54.04%	4.18%	377
	85,360	51.72%	41.39%	54.66%	43.51%	-0.83%	-705
	7,886	30.63%	64.40%	31.92%	66.66%	0.98%	77
	36,203	46.91%	47.23%	50.02%	48.32%	-2.01%	-729
	10,510	38.42%	56.85%	42.80%	56.22%	-5.00%	-526
	22,615	30.66%	64.51%	31.53%	67.09%	1.71%	386
	66,011	38.48%	54.41%	41.06%	56.97%	-0.01%	-6
	56,707	36.81%	55.19%	40.89%	56.78%	-2.50%	-1,416

County	DEM 2016 Votes	GOP 2016 Votes	Total 2016 Votes	DEM 2020 Votes	GOP 2020 Votes	
TAYLOR	2,398	6,589	9,484	2,693	7,657	
TREMPEALEAU	5,636	7,364	13,675	6,285	8,833	
VERNON	6,352	6,996	14,213	7,457	8,218	
VILAS	4,770	8,169	13,612	5,903	9,261	
WALWORTH	18,706	28,851	51,324	22,789	33,851	
WASHBURN	3,284	5,404	9,148	3,867	6,334	
WASHINGTON	20,855	51,729	78,003	26,650	60,237	
WAUKESHA	79,200	142,521	239,042	103,906	159,649	
WAUPACA	8,440	16,189	26,024	9,703	18,952	
WAUSHARA	3,792	7,669	11,999	4,388	9,016	
WINNEBAGO	37,054	43,448	87,144	44,060	47,796	
WOOD	14,232	21,503	37,800	16,365	24,308	

	Total 2020 Votes	DEM 2016 % of Vote	GOP 2016 % of Vote	DEM 2020 % of Vote	GOP 2020 % of Vote	GOP Margin Diff 2020 - 2016	Vote Diff
	10,686	25.28%	69.47%	25.20%	71.65%	2.26%	242
	15,380	41.21%	53.85%	40.86%	57.43%	3.93%	605
	15,923	44.69%	49.22%	46.83%	51.61%	0.25%	40
	15,369	35.04%	60.01%	38.41%	60.26%	-3.12%	-480
	57,600	36.45%	56.21%	39.56%	58.77%	-0.56%	-324
	10,378	35.90%	59.07%	37.26%	61.03%	0.60%	62
	88,070	26.74%	66.32%	30.26%	68.40%	-1.44%	-1,272
	267,996	33.13%	59.62%	38.77%	59.57%	-5.69%	-15,248
	29,130	32.43%	62.21%	33.31%	65.06%	1.97%	575
	13,568	31.60%	63.91%	32.34%	66.45%	1.80%	244
	94,032	42.52%	49.86%	46.86%	50.83%	-3.36%	-3,163
	41,298	37.65%	56.89%	39.63%	58.86%	0.00%	-1